M000032223

VICTORIO

THE OKLAHOMA WESTERN BIOGRAPHIES
RICHARD W. ETULAIN, GENERAL EDITOR

VICTORIO

Apache Warrior and Chief

By Kathleen P. Chamberlain

UNIVERSITY OF OKLAHOMA PRESS : NORMAN

Also by Kathleen P. Chamberlain
Under Sacred Ground: A History of Navajo Oil, 1922–1982
   (Albuquerque, 2000)

Library of Congress Cataloging-in-Publication Data

Chamberlain, Kathleen (Kathleen P.)
   Victorio : Apache warrior and chief / by Kathleen P. Chamberlain.
      p.   cm — (Oklahoma western biographies ; v. 21)
   Includes bibliographical references and index.
   ISBN 978-0-8061-3843-5 (hardcover : alk. paper)   1. Victorio,
Apache Chief, d. 1881.   2. Warm Spring Apache Indians — Kings and
rulers — Biography.   3. Warm Spring Apache Indians — Wars.
I. Title.
   E99.W36V533 2007
   979.004'972560092 — dc22
[B]   2006102641

Victorio: Apache Warrior and Chief is Volume 22 in The Oklahoma
Western Biographies series.

The paper in this book meets the guidelines for permanence and
durability of the Committee on Production Guidelines for Book
Longevity of the Council on Library Resources, Inc. ∞

1 2 3 4 5 6 7 8 9 10

To my parents, Ada Mae and James Egan,
who have always loved and supported me

Contents

Illustrations

Figures

Maps

Series Editor's Preface

STORIES of heroes and heroines have intrigued many generations of listeners and readers. Americans, like people everywhere, have been captivated by the lives of military, political, and religious figures and intrepid explorers, pioneers, and rebels. The Oklahoma Western Biographies endeavor to build on this fascination with biography and to link it with two other abiding interests of Americans: the frontier and the American West. Although volumes in the series carry no notes, they are prepared by leading scholars, are soundly researched, and include a list of sources used. Each volume is a lively synthesis based on thorough examination of pertinent primary and secondary sources.

Above all, The Oklahoma Western Biographies aim at two goals: to provide readable life stories of significant westerners and to show how their lives illuminate a notable topic, an influential movement, or a series of important events in the history and cultures of the American West.

Kathleen P. Chamberlain achieves all the major aims for a volume in this series. Most of all, she provides a sprightly written story of Victorio, an important westerner and a notable Apache warrior and chief. She also illuminates the wider contexts of Native American contacts, conflicts, and compromises with other cultures in the Southwest in the decades during and immediately after the American Civil War. In this series, we ask writers to prepare life stories that will have a broad appeal to a wide variety of readers. Professor Chamberlain does exactly that.

The author utilizes an appealing variety of sources in her study of Victorio. Drawing thoroughly on the books and essays published about this Apache leader, Chamberlain also delves into several major manuscript collections. Of special note is the writer's adroit use of ethnographic sources to clarify the sociocultural contexts surrounding and shaping Victorio's life and career. In addition, Chamberlain's expansive bibliographical essay cites and helpfully evaluates the most important primary and secondary sources, published and manuscript, for her discussion of Victorio and Apache culture.

This book supplies what we have not had before: a well-written, compact, but thorough life of Victorio. Previous biographers of this Apache leader emphasize his military career; Chamberlain does that and much more. She moves beyond earlier monographs and biographies of other Apache leaders in her skillful employment of ethnographic materials. Moreover, the author extensively—and judiciously—sorts through oral histories of Apaches (some recorded later, in the early twentieth century) and adds much from these controversial but nonetheless essential sources.

In short, this is an appealing and valuable book. It is lively and well written, deals with an intriguing subject in broad sociocultural contexts, and will attract many readers. Kathleen Chamberlain has produced a valuable biography of Victorio, precisely the kind of volume we aim for in the Oklahoma Western Biographies series.

Richard W. Etulain
Professor Emeritus of History
University of New Mexico

Preface

IN researching and writing this book, I came to respect Victorio tremendously. I found him an introspective, quiet, and complex chief, unlike too many leaders today who pontificate the moment the camera rolls but seem to possess few real convictions. Victorio believed in his people and his culture. Above all, he was a man who valued peace, but whose patience with incompetence and deception had its limits. Most of what we know about this Warm Springs Apache leader comes from Department of War records, and the majority of these focus on his final year of life, the series of close calls and skirmishes commonly called the Victorio Campaign or War. The events of 1879–80 have largely defined Victorio. An earlier biographer, Dan L. Thrapp, called him a brilliant military strategist who died only after his luck and ammunition finally ran out. A contemporary of Victorio, Jason Betzinez, rated him "head and shoulders" above even Cochise. There is no doubt that Victorio was a formidable warrior.

Still, these analyses and the records upon which they depend fall short and leave the picture extremely one-sided. Interior Department archives, for example, were written by Indian agents, superintendents, and commissioners, and thus reveal *their* concerns and priorities. We discover, for example, that in 1853 Victorio signed a provisional compact, a sort of peace treaty. This mark on a piece of paper was his first appearance in the historical record. Still, it sheds no light on Victorio himself or his role at this negotiation. In another instance, General O. O. Howard initially described Victorio as so aloof that he seemed hostile. Fortunately Howard later revealed his second impression: that the chief possessed great strength of character. Agent John Clum, who at first barely noticed Victorio, was subsequently so impressed with his leadership abilities that he made the chief a member of the San Carlos Indian court immediately. Although Clum liked to give nicknames to all of the Apache leaders in his charge, it is telling that he dared not come up with one for Victorio. Nevertheless, these sources are highly selective in what they reveal.

From the available oral histories, we discover that Victorio was a beloved husband, father, and grandfather and that his people thought him trustworthy. We see evidence that Victorio skillfully utilized diplomacy. He made promises to whites—sometimes kept and sometimes not—and he alternated between accommodation and violence to achieve his ends. Families whose names we will never know chose to follow him. Warriors who favored waging war against the Americans tended to gravitate toward other Apache chiefs. Victorio even cooperated with the Indian agents, at times, to banish those off-reservation Apaches who used his Warm Springs region as the hub of their raiding operations. We know that his primary goal was to keep his people on their sacred Warm Springs land permanently, but few, if any, whites realized the depth of his attachment to the land. They merely thought him stubborn. But an examination of Apache beliefs reveals that Victorio was persistent because he absolutely believed Ussen, the Creator, had made Warm Springs specifically for his people. It was their source of power and their place of origin. They were responsible for its safekeeping, but to carry out the sacred trust they must remain.

Today a drive south on Interstate 25 toward Truth or Consequences, New Mexico, takes one right through the Cañada Alamosa on former Warm Springs land. The area is still sparsely populated. If one takes the exit and roams the back roads, it is easy to drive for miles without meeting a single person. There are a few farms, of course, and a couple of tiny, isolated villages. Monticello, where Victorio once traded, is evidently being recreated as an artist community. But it is difficult to understand why the Indian Office so vehemently refused to allow Victorio's Warm Springs people to remain here.

Victorio made one thing quite clear. He refused to live at San Carlos, a denuded, rattlesnake-ridden stretch of desert in Arizona, approximately ninety miles due east of present-day Phoenix, that the military dubbed "Hell's Forty Acres." In the end, the Interior Department excluded all other options. The Victorio Campaign was neither a last stand nor a suicide mission. Rather, it was an attempt to renegotiate a satisfactory middle ground with the Indian Office. Federal authorities rejected such a middle ground, destroyed any hope of compromise, and this ultimately led to Victorio's death at Tres Castillos in October 1880.

This study reconsiders previous assumptions regarding Victorio. At times, he was a war leader and a chief, but he was a sensitive man as well. He was both pragmatic and profoundly spiritual. Americans favored the more gregarious Cochise. Neither has Victorio generally appealed to Hollywood filmmakers, who consistently see Geronimo as making the better story. This work also uses Victorio's life to examine the absurdities of post–Civil War Indian policy, especially the reforms sometimes known as the Peace Policy. Most distasteful was the disconnect between what reformers in the East envisioned and how their imposed measures in reality affected Indians. What looked good on paper sometimes caused extreme physical and psychological distress when put into practice. Sadly, a capricious Indian policy was not peculiar to the United States. This study also shines a spotlight on Mexico, whose absence of unified leadership from Mexico City resulted in savage scalp-bounty policies in the states of Chihuahua, Sonora, and Durango.

Finally, Victorio exemplifies what Edward Said labeled "orientalizing" or "othering," which continues in literature and Hollywood films. As Ward Churchill accurately observes, if one were to watch too many western movies, it would seem that Apaches made up the largest tribe in North America, that they scalped indiscriminately and tortured every passing white man. In his essay titled "Fantasies of the Master Race: The Cinematic Colonization of American Indians," Churchill notes that, "although the empty desert was/is filled with a host of peoples, anyone taking their ethnographic cues from the movies would be led rapidly to the conclusion that there was but one: the Apaches." Moreover, they warred to the exclusion of nearly everything else.

Such pseudohistory is not innocent fun, but has far-reaching consequences. Stereotypes, says English professor Joyce Kilpatrick in her book *Celluloid Indians: Native Americans and Film*, create deep social, ideological, and political predicaments for Indian peoples. At the very least, they suggest to an uninformed public that Indians—and Apaches, in particular—are cruel, sadistic people who lack mental prowess and any sort of "real" religion. This, in turn, has had tremendous implications for government policy and social interactions. As we explore Victorio's late-nineteenth-century world, we see the origins of this Hollywood history. Looking more closely, we discover that warfare and occasional torture were usually the Apaches' reactions to post-1835 scalp-bounty policies, massacres, or the wanton invasion of their land, wildlife, and water sources. But the problem is that mainstream society has seldom looked more closely. "Othering" made it impossible for Victorio to remain in New Mexico in 1880, and the myths still affect Apaches today.

This book is an ethnohistorical account of Victorio's life. Every attempt has been made to analyze Victorio within the context of his culture and his time. In some instances, oral narrative and archival histories support each other; at other times there are major discrepancies. These have often been noted, with oral history favored in most instances. Readers should also know that, except in a few places, this book makes no attempt to follow day-by-day military accounts, as previous studies have done. My purpose was to put Victorio, not the U.S. federal government or any other non-Native individual or institution, at the center of the story.

I alternate terms such as Chihenne, Warm Springs, and occasionally Mimbres and Chiricahua Apaches, to designate Victorio's people. Most of the oral histories use the first two terms. Warm Springs is called Ojo Caliente, and the agency there was also called the Cañada Alamosa agency. Similarly, "Native," "indigenous," and "American Indian" are used interchangeably to provide variety and enliven the narrative. I indicate Apache names where appropriate, but in most instances call individuals by their commonly known Spanish or Anglicized names. Victorio was nearly always written as "Victoria" in archival sources, but for the sake of uniformity and convenience, I use "Victorio"—or, occasionally, his Apache name "Bi-duye."

This is not a definitive biography of Victorio; nor is such a study ever likely to be written. During his lifetime, Victorio made no speeches, wrote no letters, and generated no documents for historians to use. Nevertheless, although necessarily sketchy at times, this book attempts to present a more well-rounded picture of Victorio than previously seen. He was indeed an eminent warrior and military leader. At the same time, he was an honest, skilled chief who successfully negotiated an ever-changing and shrinking middle ground. I would like to think that this study helps us to correct stereotypes, come to grips with our nation's shameful treatment of its Indigenous peoples, and realize that sometimes the term "terrorism" is relative.

Acknowledgments

RESEARCH and writing seem such solitary endeavors that it is always amazing to come to the end of a project and discover how many people were actually involved. First, it is only through the assistance and persistence of my mentor and friend Richard Etulain that this book was written. He invited me to write a biography in this series and encouraged me at various steps along the way. Once I began my research into Victorio's life, Margaret Connell Szasz, who ushered me through my dissertation and first book, was again a positive influence, especially when frustration set in, and that was often. As the project progressed, two of my former graduate student colleagues from the University of New Mexico came to Michigan to teach Latin American history. Both understood the Mexican side of the issues with which Victorio dealt and that I was struggling to put into context. Bruce Erickson and Susan Richards provided insights into Mexican history and kept me connected with New Mexico.

I also turned to one of Lincoln County's foremost historians and writers, Nora Henn, who was secretary and assistant to Eve Ball. During several summer visits and over many glasses of wine on her deck, Nora shared with me her valuable thoughts regarding Victorio's impact on southern New Mexico. So, too, did Karen Mills of the Lincoln County Courthouse in Carrizozo and Drew Gomber of the Lincoln Heritage Trust open their archives and friendship to me in my quest. I want to thank those staffing the Mescalero Apache Cultural Center for answering various and sundry questions during the course of my research. Similarly, the staff at the Geronimo Springs Museum in Truth or Consequences, New Mexico, provided assistance.

My visit to the University of New Mexico's Center for Southwest Research was most fruitful. Mary Alice Tsosie and Nancy

Brown-Martinez, in particular, were eager to help me find collections, and in a couple of instances they allowed me to read the paper copies rather than the microfilm versions. Although new technology has gone a long way in preserving archives and making collections more widely available, historians do love to touch the real thing from time to time. The archivists at the New Mexico State Records and Archives deserve much credit for helping me wade through the reams of territorial and governor papers as well.

Living so far from the site of my research sometimes created headaches, and I could not have accessed the primary material that I did without my local college and university libraries. I started this research at Castleton State College in Vermont, where Sandy Duling worked at locating some of my odder requests. Without balking, she nearly always found them. Similarly, I thank Linda Shirato and other members of the Halle Library at Eastern Michigan University for their suggestions and assistance. I hope that the donation of my footnoted manuscript and my research will expand that library's archives and assist students interested in doing research into American Indian history.

A couple of years ago, I handed one of my students, Brittany Ford, a jumble of notes, Xeroxed photos, and a few telephone numbers and asked her to help me locate photos for this book. She spent weeks tracking down names, numbers, e-mails, and specific information. Considering the confusing and impersonal electronic path to photos these days, she will never know how helpful I found her efforts when it came time to locate images. My colleague Michael Homel in the Department of History and Philosophy, in particular, offered encouragement at steps along the way. From time to time, I gave lectures to my history students based on my research and sought feedback. I want my students to know that many of the questions they asked helped me to hone my writing and rethink, at times, my conclusions.

I thank Eastern Michigan University for its financial support. When I first arrived here in 2001, I immediately applied for funding in order to do the archival research. The New Faculty Research Grant and the Spring/Summer Research Grant proved invaluable to my completion of this project.

Finally, I want to apologize to all of my colleagues, friends, and relatives who did not get letters, e-mails, and/or visits from me during the past several years and for the meetings that I missed. I sincerely hope that publication of this biography of Victorio will help students and general readers understand the Apache peoples of the nineteenth century and the complexity of interactions between Indians, Mexicans, Anglos, and African American buffalo soldiers during this period. I especially want them to realize that what is in the past cannot be changed, but the future always offers new possibilities.

VICTORIO

CHAPTER I

In the Beginning

ON the last morning of his life, October 10, 1880, Victorio watched the night sky change color ever so slightly. With dawn perhaps an hour away, the all-embracing ebony became a canopy of deep charcoal and then gradually grew lighter until threads of pale gray appeared to announce the impending sunrise. At any moment, Victorio knew that gunfire would explode around him and destroy the serenity of the desert. General Joaquin Terrazas's Mexican militia surrounded him and his people, and therefore Victorio dared not stand up or in any way relinquish his meager, rocky hiding place in order to face east and pray, as was customary for an Apache man. He nevertheless dipped into a tiny buckskin pouch that hung around his neck, removed a pinch of *hádndín* or sacred pollen, and held it between his fingers. Then Victorio lifted his hand in the direction of the slowly rising sun to thank Ussen for his many blessings.

Two hours later, Terrazas's soldiers overwhelmed the craggy hiding place, killed Victorio and most of his band, and took the remaining women and children prisoner. Victorio had undoubtedly anticipated the worst. For one thing, his people were exhausted and dangerously low on ammunition. So, as he greeted that final morning on the desert plains of northern Mexico, Victorio also must have wondered why Ussen and the deities had withdrawn power previously bestowed upon the Apaches. Had Killer of Enemies, along with his white men and guns, finally beaten Child of the Water? Perhaps monsters again walked the land, or maybe it was because his Chihenne people could no longer live on or care for their sacred land. What had he and his people done wrong? His thoughts must have turned,

3

albeit briefly, to the stories that had always sustained the Apache people and supplied all of the answers.

Thus, the story of Victorio's life begins with earlier stories. Indeed, to better understand Victorio—a man who left no written records and few oral accounts—we must go all the way back to the Apache Creation story because it explains his connection to the land, his values, and in fact, what Victorio and his people believed it meant to be Apache. On that October morning in 1880, Victorio knew very well that this story explained his peoples' situation and perhaps had even predicted it. The Creation story gave meaning to the universe and thus embodied the past, present, and future. It opens a window into his essential character, and so we will begin Victorio's story there.

The Apache Creation Story

Victorio never questioned that before there were Apaches, the Creator, Ussen, had made the Apache world, including his beloved home at Warm Springs. Ussen had created the earth and everything on it. He created the vast treeless plains teeming with caribou in the north, where the ancestral Apaches began their American journey, and He made the seemingly unlimited buffalo herds on the great prairies to the south, where Victorio's relatives, the plains Apaches, now lived.

Ussen had fashioned the thick, jade-colored forests and the rugged, nearly impenetrable mountains of southwestern New Mexico, which would one day provide sanctuary for Victorio and his Warm Springs Apache children. Ussen made the cool, glassy springs and streams that bubbled out of the mountains, as well as the sacred hot springs of the Cañada Alamosa region. The white-tailed deer, the stately elk and antelope, the mischievous rabbits and squirrels, even the lowly field mice were all part of Ussen's design, as were the bear, mountain lion, and rattlesnake. Because these were spiritual manifestations, Victorio and his men would one day learn to hunt, in large part, by following specific rituals and prayers and observing well-understood taboos, which honored the Creator and the spirits of the animals. The Creator had also devised the piñon pines, wild strawberries, yucca, and mescal to grow in exactly the right places. He had scattered all of the healing plants and stones for his people to find when they needed these items. Victorio had understood from an early age that Ussen's gifts were blessings and with them came the intrinsic responsibility to care for the land. If for any reason Victorio's people neglected this duty, an imbalance would result. They would endure misfortunes, chaos, and might even cease to exist as a people.

The Creator also placed White Painted Woman and her brother, Killer of Enemies, onto this beautiful and abundant earth. According to the Apache stories, monsters also found their way onto Ussen's domain. Hence, it was a good world, but it was not perfect because the monsters terrorized every living thing. Neither White Painted Woman nor Killer of Enemies dared to come out of hiding for fear of encountering these monsters. The few human beings who lived on the earth at the time could not enjoy the fresh woodlands or bathe in the clear rivers for constant fear of attack. The Warm Springs *di-yins* or medicine men realized, of course, that "monsters" were both literal and metaphoric. Thus, White Painted Woman and Killer of Enemies feared hideous, savage beasts, but evil came in many packages, including smallpox, drought, and even Mexican soldiers.

The ominous presence of these first monsters filled White Painted Woman with such dread that she hid her younger brother in a dark and isolated cave. Even so, out of sheer desperation, Killer of Enemies periodically armed himself with bow and a quiver of arrows and went in search of deer or elk to eat. Usually, the moment Killer of Enemies brought down his game, the monsters lurking nearby leaped out and stole it. They found great sport in taking the fresh venison or elk and laughing when Killer of Enemies cried. White Painted Woman and her brother faced certain starvation and death at the hands of the monsters. She finally asked Ussen for help in much the same way as Victorio would pray from his hiding place at Tres Castillos. In the case of White Painted Woman, Ussen answered her prayers for help in such a way that all who followed might benefit.

The Apaches, or Indeh as they refer to themselves, tell many versions of this story and of how Water subsequently impregnated White Painted Woman. Victorio undoubtedly had his favorite and over the span of his lifetime had retold it many times. Possibly in his version, she stretched out at the foot of a great waterfall and allowed Water to glide between her legs. Or maybe Victorio preferred the version that said, she begged Ussen to end a withering drought on earth and offered to surrender her own life in exchange for the badly needed rain. Ussen took pity upon her. He summoned Water, who nourished earth and at the same time fathered White Painted Woman's son. In all versions of the story, she named the boy Child of the Water. Besides Ussen the Creator, Child of the Water and White Painted Woman were the most sacred deities to the Apache people. The monsters remained on the prowl, however, and so White Painted Woman felt compelled to conceal her infant inside the secret cave just as she had hidden Killer of Enemies. She knew the monsters would especially delight in feasting upon her child's tender flesh if they detected his presence.

Much to her dismay, one day White Painted Woman found Child of the Water standing bravely outside of the cave asking Lightning for power. "Go back inside," White Painted Woman pleaded. "You are just a boy, and you are taking on a man's task." But Lightning agreed to test the boy. "Face east," Lightning commanded, and suddenly a powerful streak of black lightning lashed at Child of the Water. He barely flinched. "Now face south," Lightning ordered. Blue lightning struck with full force. Again, Child of the Water stood his ground. From the west, streaks of yellow ignited the sky, and lastly, from the north came white lightning. Lightning was impressed. "Your son possesses great stamina and courage," he told White Painted Woman. "I want you to fashion for him four arrows. Make one each of black, blue, yellow, and white." White Painted Woman carried out her task as Lightning commanded. When she finished, she handed the four arrows to her son. From that time on, Victorio's people would honor each of the four cardinal directions as associated with color, holy people, natural phenomenon, and life cycles.

Child of the Water took the arrows and left the cave. He traveled across the earth and stalked each of the monsters individually. He first challenged Owl-Man Giant, who taunted the child and, after laughing, pounced on him with every intention of killing him. Suddenly, Child of the Water reached into his quiver for the black arrow and destroyed Owl-Man with a single shot. Next, Child of the Water pursued Buffalo Monster and slew him with the blue arrow. With the yellow arrow, he killed the Eagle monsters, and finally, he tracked down and used his white arrow to kill Antelope Monster. Now, Child of the Water had vanquished all of the monsters. It was safe for White Painted Woman, Killer of Enemies, and all the human beings to come forward and live happily upon Ussen's beautiful earth. At this point, however, there were still no Apaches. Victorio's people had not yet arrived.

So Ussen placed two weapons—the gun and the bow and arrow—before Killer of Enemies and Child of the Water. Since he was older, Killer of Enemies was allowed to select first. Killer of Enemies picked up the gun. "You are now the chief of the white men," Ussen told him. "Go and find your people." Then, armed with bow and arrows, Child of the Water became the first Apache. Many years would pass before Killer of Enemies and Child of the Water's people would meet again in the American Southwest. In the meantime, Ussen called White Painted Woman and Child of the Water to join him in the Sky Land. But before they did so, the Creator asked them to instruct the Indeh regarding everything—the rituals, songs, prayers, and taboos—necessary for their survival.

Each generation thereafter would pass on these teachings. Like every Apache male, Victorio would learn the Creation and other stories, and these would form his view of the world around him and shape his behavior. One day he would receive Child of the Water's most sacred messages when he made the transition from boy to adult warrior. Similarly, his sisters would hear White Painted Woman's words and seek her blessings during their four-day puberty ceremonies, the most sacred of all Apache rituals. This was White Painted Woman's and Child of the Water's gift to Victorio's ancestors. These stories told them how to care for their land and how to live peacefully. Finally, Ussen assigned new homes to his Apache people. On these lands, he placed game, wild fruits and vegetables, healing plants, and wood for their shelters and their weapons. The climate on Victorio's future homeland was warm and pleasant. Water flowed abundantly. All Indeh received everything they needed to lead happy lives. It was up to them, however, to find their specially chosen, sacred places.

White Painted Woman and Child of the Water feared that, despite all of Ussen's blessings and their sacred instructions, Victorio's people might still need further assistance one day. Therefore, before they traveled to their new home in Sky Land, mother and son asked Ussen to send the Mountain Spirits or the Gááns to finish teaching the ceremonies. After they completed their task, the Gááns drew pictures of themselves upon rocks throughout the Apache landscape and vowed that, whenever needed, they would return to bestow further lessons or assistance. It was the Mountain Spirits' gift to the Apache people. The knowledge that the Gááns lived in a cave deep within the Guadalupe Mountains tied Victorio's Warm Springs people, and indeed all Apaches, even more closely to their assigned homes in the American Southwest. When once asked why the Chiricahua Apaches lived in the sun-baked expanses of the Arizona desert, the great chief Cochise replied without hesitation, "God told them to do so." Therefore, on the last day of his life, when Victorio held his sacred hádndín in his fingers and thanked Ussen, he undoubtedly did so with a sense of remorse for having somehow lost the land over which his people were responsible. He perhaps also wondered which instruction or lesson they had violated. Or had Killer of Enemies returned and a new cycle of fighting monsters begun?

What the Scholars Say

Ussen had selected lands for each of his Apache peoples. He did not, however, automatically place them there. It was up to the people to find their designated place. The first Apaches began their search for the desert and rugged mountain ranges, the well-watered valleys, even the stretches of lava-pocked badlands of southern New Mexico and northern Mexico, at least a thousand years before Victorio was born. In fact, the monsters, caves, and emphasis on direction found in the Apache stories may recall a long-ago and lengthy migration. Although scholars have painstakingly tried to reconstruct this migration, scientific evidence remains scanty.

Cultural anthropologists linguistically classify the Indeh as an Athapascan-speaking people. Shared grammatical features and words link the Apache distantly to such bands still residing in western Canada as the Dogrib and Hare, to the Sarci of southern Alberta, and to the Blackfoot of present-day Montana. Thus, the journey probably began in the Subarctic region of western Canada or eastern Alaska. Some of these early Athapascan speakers undoubtedly trailed the vast caribou herds, which once covered the northern interior, and they lived almost exclusively on a diet of meat. Other Athapascans fished the icy glacial waters of the Great Bear and Great Slave lakes or harvested salmon from the fast-flowing Mackenzie River in today's Northwest Territory.

According to one version of the scholarly story, Victorio's distant ancestors followed the caribou south as the migrating herds tried to escape the coming cycle of global cooling commonly called an Ice Age. Afterward, when the climate finally began to warm again, the caribou shifted back to the north, but not all of the Athapascan people followed them. Some, indeed, trailed the caribou herds north, but others continued traveling southward. Thus, never a united group to begin with, the Athapascans splintered even further.

Another story, however, suggests an entirely different triggering event. In about A.D. 700, a volcano erupted unexpectedly in the St. Elias mountain range along the Alaska and Yukon border with such intensity that massive quantities of volcanic ash spewed across the Yukon and as far east as Northwest Territory. The ash obscured the sunlight for weeks, maybe months. It choked off waterways and suffocated huge numbers of fish. It painted a thick blanket of grit across normally brown and relatively fertile earth. According to this scenario, the eruption and devastating aftermath forced many indigenous peoples to flee. Still other Athapascans began moving south between A.D. 950 and 1000, when a series of cataclysmic earthquakes rocked the Pacific Coast. Large numbers of them settled in the Great Lakes region and eventually became known as the Chippewa groups. Other bands stopped their migration in southern Alberta or Saskatchewan, Montana, or the Dakotas. These became the Sarci, Blackfoot, and Cree. However, those who came to be called the Lipan and Kiowa Apaches continued traveling. Somewhere around present-day Montana or Wyoming, they encountered buffalo herds and followed these animals onto the Great Plains.

Victorio's immediate ancestors progressed slowly down the spine of the Rockies, taking hundreds of years to arrive in the Southwest. Those who eventually became the Mescalero and Jicarilla Apaches probably remained east of the Continental Divide. The future Chiricahuas, Western Apaches, and Navajos perhaps followed a route that kept them west of the Divide. It is noteworthy that Victorio's people would always prefer mountains to flat regions, a trait that survived the long migration. They camped in high valleys whenever they could. They fled to the most isolated, rugged mountain ranges they could find when pursued, and they fought their enemies with a canyon wall or cliff at their backs whenever possible.

The final split between eastern and western Apaches probably occurred no earlier than about A.D. 1300. This would explain the large number of shared cultural characteristics. In many respects, therefore, Victorio's ancestors—the Chiricahuas, or more specifically, the Chihennes—were very much a people in-between because they found their sacred land midway between the Mescalero and the Western Apaches.

The Chiricahua Bands Separate

According to their stories, the Chiricahuas all originated at Warm Springs. More accurately, perhaps, this is where they became

Apaches. The mystical, perpetually 110-degree mineral springs offered them great healing powers, and the surrounding canyons protected the people from outsiders. At these springs, they say, White Painted Woman and Child of the Water first handed down their lessons to the Indeh. Here they gave each band its own supernatural gifts of power. Indeed, it was at Warm Springs—which the Spanish called Ojo Caliente—where the people truly became Chiricahua. They never saw themselves as members of a larger or far-reaching nation or tribe, although they acknowledged a degree of kinship. They traded, intermarried, and occasionally—albeit rarely—fought among themselves. Having received their powers and instructions from White Painted Woman and Child of the Water, the various bands had simply departed for the land Ussen assigned them. All traveled to their own rugged yet beautiful environments. Each region was biologically diverse and teeming with delicious wild foods. In most areas, the river bottoms offered women, elders, and children the opportunity to grow corn, beans, pumpkins, and squash. Most important, the Guadalupe Mountains, where the Mountain Spirits resided, were central to all of the Chiricahua people.

Spanish and American records reflect a recurring inability to identify accurately the various groups, and for that reason, a brief explanation seems appropriate. Victorio's people—the Chihenne or Red Paint People—remained at Warm Springs. They were the largest of the Chiricahua groups, and they saw Warm Springs as their spiritual center. Some students of Apache history claim they were not Chiricahuas at all, but a distinctly separate people. Other interpretations say that the term "Chiricahua" generally referred to those who lived between the Mescaleros and the Western Apache bands. Because of the uncertainty and the close association between the Warm Springs and other Chiricahua bands, this book accepts the second interpretation.

The Chihennes came to control a vast region in extreme western New Mexico that lay west of the Rio Grande and all the way to the Gila River. It was a place recently abandoned. Victorio's ancestors came to know the enigmatic Mogollon people who had previously lived there from the broken black-and-white ceramic

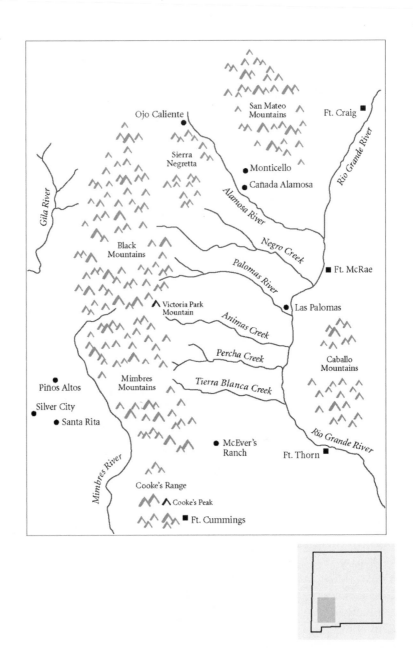

Warm Springs country, New Mexico

12

pottery shards strewn about the riverbanks. It is possible that the Mogollons were still living in the region when the earliest Apaches arrived and that they merged with the Pueblos after the newcomers moved in. But once these ancient ones had moved away, long before Victorio's time, they left a geographical vacuum to fill. It encompassed what are today the Mimbres, Black, Sierra Negretta, and San Mateo mountain ranges and valleys—the Chihenne homeland where Victorio would one day live. If historians have found it difficult to pinpoint the Chihennes, it is because their numerous bands remained small, fluid, and extremely mobile. They never traveled as a single unit, but in many extended family groups dubbed *rancherias*. This made them even more difficult for European-Americans to categorize. The Spanish, Mexicans, and Americans referred to them as the Warm Springs, Copper Mines, or Mimbres Apaches, depending on where they resided, or simply lumped them together as Gilas or Gileños. One of the first Chihenne leaders of historical record was Ojos Coloradas, whose heyday roughly spanned the 1780s and '90s. Victorio was the last primary chief of the Chihenne people.

There were three other Chiricahua bands, and during his lifetime Victorio would interact with them all. The Chokonens— sometimes called the Central Chiricahua—lived in the Chiricahua and Dragoon Mountains of southern Arizona. Cochise, or Goci for his prominent nose, was the last great Chokonen chief. Victorio considered Cochise a friend, and after the great chief's death on June 8, 1874, many of his followers made Victorio their leader. The Bedonkohes, the smallest Chiricahua band, lived northwest of the Chihennes along the Gila River and into the Mogollon and Tularosa mountain ranges. Geronimo was the most famous of the Bedonkohes. Occasionally, Victorio and Geronimo came together to war or raid, but their interactions were few. There is some evidence, in fact, that Victorio did not entirely trust Geronimo and even considered him a troublemaker.

Finally, the Nednhis lived in roughly the same region as the Chihennes until some time in the early nineteenth century. They eventually migrated to the rugged and forbidding Sierra Madres of northern Mexico, which they called the Blue Mountains. Juh (pronounced Whoa) was the last great chief of the Nednhis. For years, no white man crossed the Blue Mountains without Chief Juh's permission. In October 1880, Victorio and his band were fleeing to Juh's stronghold when Joaquin Terrazas's soldiers caught up with them. As late as 1927, a small group of supposed Apaches killed a Mexican woman and kidnapped her young son on a lonely road winding through the Sierra Madres. This event sent anthropologists such as Western Apache scholar Grenville Goodwin into action. For several years, they searched diligently for so-called wild Apaches still camped in those mountain recesses. They discovered some old camps, but no inhabitants. Goodwin, for one, guessed that these represented the last of Juh's Nednhis—with perhaps some of Geronimo's Bedonkohes who had managed to elude the U.S. Army's roundup in 1886—but, of course, he would never know for certain.

The Spanish Story Begins

By most scholarly accounts, Victorio's ancestors arrived in their new homeland no later than 1550. If this is accurate—and there are few historians who dispute this—it means that Victorio's ancestors and the Spanish conquistadors set foot in the American Southwest at about the same time, and both were newcomers. In 1519, Hernán Cortés encountered the vast and powerful Aztec Empire. He led his soldiers into the Aztec capital of Tenochtitlán, a wealthy trade center where farmers sold corn and traders brought brilliant macaw feathers and exotic leopard skins from the jungles to tempt the rich. The Aztecs had expanded their political and economic stranglehold outward until only the tribes far to the north escaped their crushing military and penchant for captives.

In August 1521, aided by shattering epidemics of smallpox and pneumonia, Cortés defeated the Aztec Empire. The Spanish had come to the New World in search of gold or other wealth. Within a few years, aggressive Spanish slave traders headed north, and they encountered a region in flux. At this time, Mesoamerica was suffering from a cycle of extreme drought that lasted throughout the sixteenth century and into seventeenth.

Once dependable rivers became dry beds; ponds and seasonal streams frequently saw no water at all for years. Corn, squash, chilies, and melons withered in the fields. This was an already fragile environment, and these Indians lived always on the edge, so to speak. As a result, in northern Mexico, the sedentary and agricultural Opata Indians, for example, were pushing others such as the Yaquis and Lower Pimas in Sonora southward down the Rio Yaqui, probably in a search for more and better land.

Farther east, at the confluence of the Rio Grande and Rio Conchos, a large group of Indian peoples, whom the Spanish loosely dubbed Jumanos, also vied for land. The nomadic Sumas, Jovas, and Mansos were in the process of adjusting their territories when the Tepehuans and "wild" Tarahumaras—sometimes called Raramuri—moved in. The result was a sort of no-man's-land of unsettled borders and extreme fluidity. And as the Spanish explored Gran Chichimeca—that vast cactus-strapped desert hundreds of miles north of Tenochtitlán—and moved into what would one day be the Mexican state of Chihuahua, Victorio's ancestors were settling onto lands just north of there. To understand the situation in which Victorio's people found themselves, it is imperative to examine, albeit briefly, the changes taking place and the instability that resulted.

Spanish slavers carried smallpox, typhus, dysentery, and pneumonia to many of the Native peoples of New Spain's northern frontier. Then in 1534, a new plague called measles hit the region. More Natives died. The survivors experienced tremendous shock and remained weak from prolonged illness. Some became permanently disfigured. Apaches, however, were not yet directly affected. But they would not escape for long. Slave raiders also brought horses, swine, cattle, and chickens to the region, and the Indians came to value the additional food sources, even though these new animals drove off indigenous wildlife and trampled gardens. With the Spanish arrival, many sedentary tribes deserted their irrigated fields to avoid enslavement and disease. Prospective ranchers and Spaniards seeking new deposits of gold and silver to exploit saw this flight as an invitation to move into the abandoned villages.

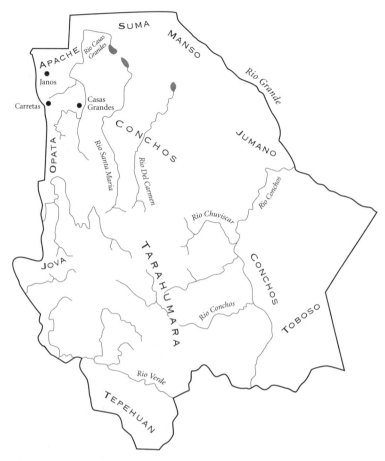

Principal Indian groups in Chihuahua, Mexico

Although in 1542, King Carlos V of Spain issued the New
Laws, reinforcing an earlier ban on Indian slavery, Indian captives remained lucrative trade items. Even in Victorio's lifetime,
slavery was rampant. Moreover, with slavery technically deemed
illegal, the practice of *encomienda* simply increased. Encomienda
allowed a few privileged upper-class citizens to demand tribute
in the form of goods or labor from Indian peoples. A feudal in-

stitution that predated 1492, the *encomendero* was obliged to protect and provide religious instruction for his Indian workers. Abuses were rampant. When in 1548 explorers discovered three immense and astonishingly pure veins of silver in Zacatecas, miners swarmed in, and with the increased demand for Indian labor, slavers penetrated Gran Chichimeca with newfound vigor.

Indians, in turn, ambushed Spanish slave caravans and bullion-filled wagon trains. They especially liked to hide atop tall outcroppings of volcanic rocks called *mixtons,* which rose oddly from the flat llano or plain below. From this vantage point, Indians could see for miles in every direction. Victorio would one day in the future discover that strategic advantage. Once Natives spotted a wagon train weighted down with silver ore and plodding towards their hiding place, they might watch it for hours. When the heavy wagons were directly below the mixton, warriors hurled boulders or spears.

Called the Chichimeca War, this conflict dominated Gran Chichimeca until about 1580. The Spanish so feared the Chichimecas—a loose confederation of many indigenous peoples of the region—that they initiated the practice of beheading captured Indian males over twelve years of age. The government paid bounties for these grisly souvenirs, thus establishing a dangerous and lasting tradition that would later plague Victorio and his Chihenne people.

Once the Chichimeca War ended, the Spanish again ventured north. The conflict had probably given Apaches time to gain somewhat of a foothold in the Southwest, however. This time Franciscan and Jesuit friars accompanied the soldiers and explorers. War, cycles of disease, and continuing slave raids made the Indians of Chihuahua, especially the sedentary Indians, fair game for slave raids or the alternative, Christianity. In 1590 the Tepehuans converted. The Tarahumaras fled. So, too, did the Opatas, who lived north of the Tarahumaras and had met their first Spaniards in 1540 with the arrival of explorer Francisco Vasquéz de Coronado. Coronado had constructed a hasty camp on the upper Sonora River, which he named Corazones, while he readied his men and supplies to explore Nuevo Mexico. He coerced the Opatas to perform heavy labor for his men, and when he departed Coronado handed Corazones over to the men who remained behind. They overworked the Opatas and raped their women. Enraged, the Opatas had killed the Spanish intruders and burned Corazones to the ground. Despite their hatred of the Spanish, some fifty years later, the Opatas, war-exhausted and weak from disease, surrendered their freedom, moved into the missions, and converted to Christianity. Their population declined rapidly after 1700. By the nineteenth century they were so dependent that Victorio's people came to see them as Spanish lackeys.

The prosperous, agricultural Jumanos were next. In 1580, the Jumanos lived in the Rio Grande Valley; they probably numbered about twenty thousand to thirty thousand and represented not one but many different people united through trade, intermarriage, and anti-Spanish sentiment. Although the Jumanos used trade to hold off the Spanish for a while, many of them eventually fled, entered the mission system, or allied with the newly arrived Apaches in order to survive.

In 1598, a Basque explorer named Juan de Oñate established the first permanent Spanish settlement north of the Rio Grande near present-day Santa Fe. His small colony failed by 1610, but the Spanish Crown agreed to finance a Franciscan mission colony in its stead. As friars saved souls and civilian governors worked to enrich themselves, the Pueblos grew increasingly disenchanted and restless under the Spanish thumb. Demands for Indian labor intensified even as disease, drought, and famine robbed them of their livelihoods and sapped their energy. The Pueblos rebelled in 1680.

The great Pueblo Revolt, as it was called, inspired other rebellions, which raked across northern Mexico and caught the missionaries, in particular, by surprise. The Opatas rebelled in 1681. The Sumas and Mansos rose up in 1683, agreed to a peace in late 1684, but rebelled again in 1686. In Sonora, the Lower Pimas staged a revolt in 1687, and the Upper Pimas followed eight years later. The Tarahumaras and Conchos attacked Spanish settlers and missions in 1690, and in 1696 the Tarahumaras rebelled again. By 1689 rebellions forced the closure of nearly all missions in Nuevo León and Nueva Vizcaya. In response, the Spanish built presidios, or frontier garrisons, at Janos (1685) and Fronteras (1690) to put down rebellions and police the northern frontier. They also created mobile cavalry units to take war to the Indians. Although the Apaches in southwestern New Mexico played little if any role in these rebellions, they undoubtedly watched with great interest. Their lack of agriculture made them hunters and gatherers. Their mobility made them ideal traders. Moreover, in the tense peace that followed, Victorio's ancestors were drawn more and more frequently into the Spanish sphere. By the time of Victorio's birth around 1825, the Indeh and the Spanish had established intricate relationships based upon intermarriage, warfare, slavery, and especially trade. But building trade networks took time.

Apaches Create a Raid-and-Trade Economy

In 1693, the Spanish, including the Franciscan friars, returned to New Mexico. This time they were somewhat more tolerant toward the Pueblos and their religious practices. After their return, Spanish records seldom mention bands such as the Sumas, Mansos, and Jumanos, suggesting perhaps that these had merged with other tribes. The Spanish worried considerably about the Apaches, who were now firmly established in the region. The Apaches living west of the Rio Grande existed in small autonomous units, which the Spanish dubbed rancherías, independent of each other and extremely mobile. This was one reason why the Spanish found it so difficult to tell them apart or classify them.

In addition, the Apaches shunned Spanish missions. For one thing, Catholic beliefs ran counter to traditional Apache spirituality and beliefs. According to the Indeh, Ussen had made them caretakers of the land, but He had not given them dominion over it. Victorio's ancestors clearly thought themselves superior to the Spanish, but knew that no human ruled Ussen's natural world. Oddly, the Europeans acted as if they were superior to all else.

Also, the friars set aside the Sabbath as a day of worship and no work, while Victorio's people saw prayer and work as interconnected. Finally, the friars insisted upon isolating Christianized Indians and sealing them away in missions where they grew dependent upon garden vegetables and handouts of meat and clothing. Apaches revered freedom above all else.

Still, during times of severe drought, the Chiricahuas occasionally sought out the missions for survival purposes. Ironically, even as Spanish friars defined the Gileños as savages, they welcomed them into the missions, suggesting a more complex relationship than history has often led us to believe. If, at times, Apaches broke Christian crosses, bells, and statues of saints, their actions probably indicated a reaffirmation of their own power or perhaps an attempt to ward off witchcraft rather than overt animosity towards the friars, according to historian H. Henrietta Stockel.

Moreover, as Victorio's Chihenne ancestors established themselves in the Southwest, they sought ways to subsist that would support their autonomy and independence. The sedentary nature of tribes like the Pueblos and Opatas made them primary targets. Their livestock were easily spirited away and their corn readily confiscated. Isolated Spanish farmers were also ideal suppliers. Since Indians and Spanish alike were avid traders, Apaches became an important cog in the trade network. At first, much of the exchange was in blankets, tallow, hides, and meat. The Spanish traded tools, metal pots and pans, knives, and guns. Horses and mules became big business, and slaves always brought a profit. Liquor was always in great demand. Over time, the Chiricahuas developed what is probably best described as a raid-and-trade economy and lifestyle. Spanish literature overflows with tales of what Spaniards considered Apache thievery. Victorio's people undeniably took not only slaves but also myriad horses, oxen, cattle, and literally tons of Spanish- and Indian-grown corn. Some, of course, was for their own sustenance. Beef augmented venison and elk; corn added to a diet of wild fruits, vegetables, and nuts. Much of this, however, was filtered into the vast trade network. So, too, were Spanish and Indian captives taken and sold into slavery. It is important to note that as the raid-and-trade economy developed, Spanish and other Indians frequently invaded Apache villages as well. Moreover, Spanish and French accounts—and later those of the Americans—often conveniently neglect to mention their roles as consumers.

Raiding intensified across the Southwest after 1700, and it made Apaches a vital cog in the regional economy. The Rio Grande Jumanos and Mescaleros, for example, cooperated to move stolen livestock to points of exchange where nobody would question their identity. They took slaves to large trade fairs or gatherings and sold them or sometimes bartered them back to their own people. Plains Apaches such as the Lipans and Kiowa Apaches established trade networks that reached north into Comanche and Sioux country and beyond that into French America. Historian Gary Clayton Anderson has referred to these activities as "aggressively enterprising," and they could not have thrived without the active participation of other indigenous peoples and Europeans.

Thousands of captured Indians ended up in Spanish communities. Between 1700 and 1760, priests baptized approximately eight hundred Apache captives under the age of eighteen in their churches and missions across Chihuahua and Sonora. Historian James Brooks recorded nine hundred Apache converts alone over the course of the century and argued that the Spanish, Pimas, and Opatas sought Apache labor for their mines and in the fields. As the slave trade mushroomed, raiders herded their human cargoes north to feed a growing French and Indian trade east of the Mississippi River and into Canada. In turn, Apaches and Comanches took French-allied Indian captives for trade south. A search of records in New Mexico also reveals baptismal and burial records of people identified as Pawnee, an Indian tribe closely associated with French trade. Sometimes, too, Indians and Europeans alike took young children to raise. In fact, some accounts say, Victorio was taken captive as a child and raised as an Apache. Women and older children might serve as slaves, and Victorio reportedly had one or more Mexican slaves working for him at any given time. Many of these slaves were eventually adopted.

Raids often led to retaliatory warfare that helped fuel the Apache reputation for cruelty. Yet, in this moneyless frontier society where economic survival depended on the movement of goods, the Apaches were no more brutal than any other group.

The Spanish Expand Their Influence

When Spanish authorities discovered French-made rosaries and weapons among the trade items, they began to fret over what they perceived as French threats to New Spain. Indians played no role in these colonial intrigues, although they frequently found themselves pulled into European in-fighting. Apaches, for example, had no idea that, in 1719, France, England, Holland, and Austria aligned themselves against Spain in a conflict known as the War of the Quadruple Alliance. They did notice, however, new presidios constructed at Terrenate in Chihuahua (1741) and Tubac (1752) and Tucson (1769) in Sonora. They were naturally unaware that in 1763 the Spanish crowned a Bourbon king, who had strong ties to the French ruling family. On the other hand, with the French threat gone, Indians quickly realized that Spain had turned new attention to the northern frontier of New Spain and its Native peoples. Whenever this happened, the delicately balanced relationship between Apache and Spaniard was altered in some way.

The series of changes that followed were collectively known as the Bourbon Reforms. In 1764, the indefatigable Marqués de Rubí embarked upon a two-year inspection of Spain's frontier defenses. His stated goal was to find out why the Indians "are so audacious" and Spanish soldiers "of so little use." It is possible that Victorio's direct ancestor, Chihenne chief Ojos Coloradas, watched Rubí as he entered Apache country. In all, Rubí surveyed twenty-three of the twenty-four presidios between eastern Texas and the Gulf of California and concluded that, above all else, corruption undermined Spain's military efforts on the northern frontier. He found sixty-one soldiers manning one Texas garrison and only two serviceable muskets and twenty-five functional horses between them. Why, he asked? It turned out that the presidio's commanding officer customarily traded the best supplies and lined his own pockets. Sometimes he sold goods to the very Indians whom the Spanish were seeking to subdue, undermining his government's efforts and contributing to the Apache raid-and-trade network. While Apaches and Comanches possessed Spanish-made firearms, Spanish soldiers rode into battle in shirtsleeves instead of the regulation *cuera*, or heavy layered leather jacket, and with bows and arrows. Soldiers had to purchase equipment from their commanders, who marked up prices and sometimes withheld pay, thereby reducing the typical frontier soldier to debt servitude. His family usually lived in substandard housing. Horses pastured outside of the presidio walls fell prey to Indian raids. Therefore, it was nearly impossible to recruit soldiers, and only the most desperate or deficient would agree to serve. The mobile cavalry units were as poorly mounted and badly armed, Rubí concluded, and almost entirely ineffective.

The Marqués de Rubí recommended a line of evenly spaced, solidly built presidios about one hundred miles apart and stretching from Altar (Sonora) to LaBahia (Texas). He advocated well-defined policies regarding frontier defense. He sanctioned an immediate alliance with the Comanches in Texas to war against the Apaches. The Regulations of 1772 put much of Rubí's plan in place, but corruption ran deep. When, in 1773, several decaying Louisiana presidios were scheduled for abandonment, settlers living nearby screamed their protests and the viceroy in Mexico City allowed them to stay. As a result, contraband firearms flowed freely through the region. Thus, Indian trade was lucrative, and locals wholeheartedly supported it.

Victorio's ancestors watched while the Spanish consolidated the administration of the northern frontier and implemented a new peace plan. As revolution broke out in the English colonies in 1776, the Spanish began to distribute corn, wheat, and liquor to Apaches who agreed to settle and farm near the presidios. Any who refused felt the force of Spanish military. By spring 1780, the Spanish and Comanches forced the Lipans to make peace. In 1786, the Spanish in New Mexico allied with Navajos and attacked the Gila Apaches, who in turn agreed to move onto the newly formed peace settlements or *establecimientos de paz* surrounding the presidios. They received food, liberal quantities of liquor, and weak-barreled rifles, which frequently misfired and required constant Spanish-provided maintenance. All of this, of course, reinforced dependency.

On the other hand, a Chihenne leader named Ojos Coloradas—Red Eyes—taught the Spanish something about the Apaches. In May 1787, and without warning, Ojos Coloradas bolted from presidio life and therein revealed an Apache idiosyncrasy that would forever frustrate European Americans. He spent nearly two years terrorizing the region, as the Spanish would have described it, and then in 1789, just as abruptly returned and negotiated a peace. The Spanish, as would the Americans after them, interpreted such actions as hostile, but Ojos Coloradas obviously saw Janos as a sort of headquarters and not a prison. When he had business elsewhere, his people simply moved away and might later return. They found the all-or-nothing mentality of the Spanish difficult to comprehend.

By 1795 some 850 Apaches, many of them Victorio's immediate ancestors, lived at Janos. Ojos Coloradas remained there until 1796, and his conversations with Spanish commanders should have taught them much about the Chihennes. For one thing, the stereotype of the anti-social Apache was rendered false. Peace between the Apaches and Spanish during this time reinforced established trade networks and opened new ones. Moreover, it is from Ojos Coloradas that the Spanish learned much about the Apaches who lived west of the Rio Grande. For instance, he informed them that the Chihennes were the largest of the Chiricahua bands, but at the time, they also included the Nednhis. Afterward, Spanish commanders often found it easier to identify the various Apache bands.

In all, the Spanish government in Mexico spent 23,000 pesos annually for food and supplies throughout the 1790s. Because of this effort, the Apache wars halted, and frontier defense became routine. Mines reopened, especially the Santa Rita del Cobre copper mines, which operated on and off after 1804. *Hacienderos* breathed more easily. Explorers discovered new salt deposits in New Mexico in 1816. Soldiers in the Interior Provinces were urged to learn the Apache language and some of the customs. The Royal Corps of Engineers praised the "courageous" Apaches and expressed belief in a sustained peace. Many undoubtedly became convinced that a new chapter in Apache and Spanish relations had begun.

Unfortunately, when funds ran out in 1796, the Apaches drifted away from the presidios. Hostilities began anew, Spain's problems in Europe also increased. By 1810, revolution broke out in Spain just as the newly created United States began to take control of the Ohio and Mississippi River valleys. The Napoleonic wars generated political upheaval in Spain and in the United States. By the time Napoleon's armies left Spain, the Americans had defeated the British in the War of 1812 and firmly controlled the western Great Lakes. In 1812, the first threats of rebellion gripped Mexico. Years of Spanish neglect had taken their toll. Unable to hold her colonies, Mexico and others began to slip away.

In a final effort to maintain control, Mexico City diverted funds from the northern frontier. Presidios deteriorated. Corruption returned. Finally, on April 11, 1821, an aging Spanish-born governor of Mexico pulled down the Spanish flag flying over the plaza in Monterey one last time, and the new Mexican flag replaced it. Thus, the Spanish era came to an end. Mexico took charge. Americans arrived almost immediately. That fall ambitious, enterprising William Becknell opened the Santa Fe Trail from Missouri to New Mexico previously forbidden to Americans. His wagon train rattled into New Mexico's capital piled high with American-manufactured tools, pots and pans, steel knives, eating utensils, food, bolts of calico, woolen, and cotton, and many other goods. Becknell sold out and returned to Missouri for more. Others streamed into New Mexico and, when they saturated that market, took their goods into merchandise-starved Chihuahua.

In August 1825, Governor Antonio Narbona of New Mexico handed out the very first permits to American fur traders, allowing them to enter newly independent Nuevo Mexico and to hunt, trap, and trade. The only stipulation was that they agree to convert to Catholicism, become Mexican citizens, and take an oath of loyalty to Mexico. The influx of American fur trappers and traders would soon have profound consequences for the Chihennes and other Apache peoples across New Mexico. Moreover, between William Becknell's first journey to Santa Fe and Narbona's invitation to traders, Victorio was born. And this is where his story begins.

CHAPTER 2

The Warrior's Path

VICTORIO was born between 1820 and 1825. A genealogy of the Warm Springs Apaches estimates his birth year as 1820, and those who knew him claimed that he was about fifty-five years old at the time of his death in 1880. Because Victorio was a Chihenne, his life undoubtedly began somewhere near the sacred warm springs located a few miles northwest of present-day Truth or Consequences, New Mexico. By the time Victorio reached adulthood, he had scaled every foot of the San Mateo, Black, and Mimbres mountain ranges. He recognized each threadlike river and could estimate with amazing accuracy when their beds would swell with seasonal rains and when they would dry up again. He could ride directly to their sources or to the exact place where these humble streams slid peacefully into the Rio Grande or the Gila. So well did Victorio know this land that as an Apache warrior he would one day elude and outwit every cavalry unit and civilian militia that dared to follow him into this place.

Some Mexicans claimed that Victorio was, in fact, not Apache at all, but rather a child stolen from the Hacienda del Carmen in Chihuahua. El Carmen was at the time a walled and heavily fortified ranch on the lonely fringe of Mexico's northern frontier. It was so isolated that only the low rumble of wind or mournful howl of a coyote broke an otherwise pervading silence. All alone, the various haciendores and their vaqueros and servants fought off Apaches and Comanches over the years and lost more than a few children to raiders. One captive named Rufino Padilla apparently swore to Chihuahua authorities that Chief Victorio bore an uncanny resemblance to the father of

27

the missing El Carmen child. Another theory said Victorio was, in reality, Francisco Cedrillo, Jr., and his name came from his Aunt Victoria.

No Apache oral histories support these rumors, and when Eve Ball interviewed more than sixty Mescaleros in the 1950s, she found none who believed them. Apaches indeed took captives to sustain their numbers, but a man or woman's background was

Portrait of Victorio, ca. 1877. Courtesy of National Anthropological Archives (negative #75-8239).

Victorio, Apache chief. Drawing by Clarence Batchelor. The artist probably intentionally altered Victorio's features to make him appear less Apache and more Mexican. Courtesy of Palace of the Governors (MNM/DCA) (negative #2109).

hardly kept secret. Nor did a Mexican birth carry any stigma or impediment to leadership. Another child whom the Apaches took from El Carmen circa 1825 and renamed Costáles rose to a position of subchief among the Indeh. The Mescaleros told Ball that if Victorio were born Mexican, their own stories would contain some support for that. Nevertheless, the inability to substantiate conclusively or refute the rumor clearly indicates that little is known regarding Victorio's early life. What we surmise about his childhood and youth comes down to us from oral stories and anthropological accounts of how pre-reservation Apaches were raised and lived within their family groups.

We do know that the period between 1820 and 1825 was a busy five years in the history of the Southwest. Newly independent Mexico struggled to establish a coherent and workable central government while the northern frontier fell into disarray. Presidios crumbled. Soldiers struggled with dwindling food stores and ever-deteriorating weapons. Corruption was rampant. Ordinary citizens scrambled to arm themselves even as they traded with the Indians they feared, and regional authorities turned to brutal policies of extermination. As this occurred, Americans trickled in. So, although Victorio grew up in the traditional Apache lifestyle, he belonged to perhaps the last generation of Chihennes for whom that was possible. By the time he was an adult, parents taught their children lessons while on the run, and rituals were frequently abbreviated. And although Victorio grew up a greatly loved and treasured member by his people, his larger world contained an increasing number of outsiders who hated the very word "Apache" and wanted them exterminated. Thus, Victorio's life very much represents a crossroads between old and new.

A Chihenne Childhood

Although it is impossible to detail Victorio's own life as a child, we can make some broad assumptions concerning his culture and the Apache world into which he was born. Almost certainly, from the moment Victorio's mother discovered that her regular menstrual periods had stopped, she began to alter her lifestyle to accommodate the new life inside of her. It was not the Apache way to announce such things or to discuss the intricacies of pregnancy with either the father or with other women, so at first his mother quietly changed her activities. For one thing, she stopped riding horses. She also avoided eating fat meats or any foods that

Apaches deemed unfit for an unborn child. Over time others noticed her condition and without a word started to carry the heavy bundles of firewood to her wickiup. Women increasingly took over the more arduous tasks and frequently reminded her to rest.

Like all Apache mothers-to-be, Victorio's worked especially hard to protect her child spiritually. She argued with no one because such negative interactions might harm the child emotionally. Both prospective parents took special pains to avoid any man or woman who might use special powers for witchcraft. The Indeh greatly feared witches. Chief Loco once said, "Witches do all sorts of bad things . . . especially to children," a sentiment that all Apaches shared. The expectant mother also refrained from watching any ceremony in which the Mountain Spirits with their black-shrouded faces and flashing magical wands might appear. Despite their benevolent nature and their considerable healing abilities, the Gááns could inadvertently frighten the unborn, who could not, of course, understand their significance or the blessings they bestowed.

We do not know the name of Victorio's mother. According to the many stories handed down to descendants, she was one of the women who in 1878 fled the San Carlos Reservation in Arizona with her son. She allegedly was living at Warm Springs in 1879 when Victorio went to the Mescalero Reservation in eastern New Mexico to secure a permanent home for his band. He returned to Warm Springs to find that soldiers had attacked and destroyed the camp and killed many of the women living there, including his mother and his first wife. The death of these two women, according to his eldest daughter Dilth-cleyhen, was the final straw that sent him on his last rampage through New Mexico, Texas, and Chihuahua between October 1879 and October 1880.

As soon as Victorio's mother experienced the first labor pains, her own mother and sisters surrounded her in preparation for the impending birth. Victorio's father, whose name is also lost to history, stayed away. Like all Apache men, he found childbirth—indeed all things related to sexuality—highly embarrassing. Men were ashamed to be seen naked even by other men.

Also, he dared not encounter his mother-in-law face to face. After marriage, Apache husbands usually moved in with the wife's band and built their new lives among her male relatives. Avoiding the mother-in-law made family peace more probable. Rather than speak to the man directly, the mother-in-law handed down praise, requests, or criticisms through her daughter.

Traditional Apache men continued to observe this custom into the twentieth century. Sometimes a family strung a blanket between the front and back seat of a car, for example, when it became necessary for mother-in-law and son-in-law to travel in an automobile together. However, during Victorio's time, if the husband's family held a higher heredity status—or if the woman was a second or third wife—she might move into her husband's rancheria. This explains in large part why later wives were frequently sisters of the first. In 1879, the *Prescott Arizonian* called Victorio "a hereditary chief of the Apaches, directly descended on his father's side from a long line of royal ancestors," but it is doubtful that the author possessed any factual evidence to support his statement.

After his birth, Victorio's grandmother bathed him in tepid water. His aunts rubbed in a mixture of animal fat and red ochre from head to feet in order to feed his limbs. They wrapped him in prayers and a blanket and offered a pinch of sacred cattail pollen called hádndín to East, South, West, and North to guarantee a long and moral life. A specially chosen di-yin— called Cradlemaker—carved the *tsoch* or wooden cradleboard. This di-yin prayed and sang of Ussen and Child of the Water continuously as he cut wood, stripped the heavy bark, and bound back, sides, and canopy together with deer sinew. Cradlemaker attached the laces—from the left for a boy—and painted sacred symbols. From the canopy, he dangled sacred amulets to amuse the child and to convey strength. Because Victorio was male, the di-yin hung a turkey wattle as one of these amulets to guarantee that the boy would never fear lightning. Before noon on the fourth day of his life, amid the prayers of a special cradling ceremony, Victorio's grandmother laced her grandson snugly into the cradleboard, where he would live until he was about two

Apache baby in a *tsoch* or cradleboard, ca. 1883. Courtesy of Palace of the Governors (MNM/DCA) (negative #15918).

years of age, or until he walked. Then came his putting-on-moccasins ceremony to celebrate his first steps and the following spring his hair-cutting ceremony, which marked the passage from infancy to childhood. During his infancy, Victorio's ears were probably pierced and white beads or turquoise inserted.

A respected family member gave Victorio his first name, which did not survive past childhood. As an adult, his Indian name was Beduiat, or Bi-duye. Victorio was merely a name of convenience when dealing with Mexicans and Americans, neither of which bothered to learn or pronounce Indian words. Moreover, taking on a Spanish or English name proved advantageous to Apaches. Names, they believed, contained great power. When a person died, for instance, nobody dared speak his name again for fear of summoning his spirit back from the Happy Place. That was the power which a name held. Family members might dare refer to the deceased as "He Who Is Gone," but would go no further. Moreover, some Apaches even changed their own names if the deceased had bestowed it upon them. Thus, it is possible that no white man ever uttered Victorio's Apache name, and that fact would undoubtedly have pleased him.

Victorio Learns Important Lessons

As with all Chihenne babies, when the umbilical cord dried and fell off after a couple of weeks, Victorio's mother carefully wrapped it and chose a healthy fruit tree somewhere near their camp beneath which to bury the umbilical cord. Victorio knew this location intimately and would always consider it sacred. Like all Chihennes, he would return to this place periodically to roll in the dirt around the tree and thus revive his physical and his spiritual strength. This ritual provided yet another physical and sacred link between the Chihenne people and the Warm Springs region.

As young Victorio grew and moved away from his cradleboard, he would have discovered that a complex spiritual world awaited him. Indeed, there was no aspect of Apache life removed from the spiritual realm, and one found the religious lessons enmeshed in their many stories. Even as a young child, he heard the stories. Victorio laughed with everyone else at Coyote's misadventures, but gained moral insights from Coyote's antics. These stories operated at many philosophical levels. Victorio learned that one never killed a bear unless in defense because criminals or witches sometimes reincarnated as bears and contact might cause madness, seizures, or debilitating disease. At other times, a long-dead relative might return as a bear with a mission to protect the living. One never knew for sure.

Similarly, if he ever encountered a dead bear, he must not under any circumstances disturb the meat or skin. Coyote once killed a bear, ate its flesh, and then foolishly used the hide to sew a quiver. The quiver came back to life and chased Coyote mercilessly. In desperation, Coyote went so far as to ask Badger to hide the quiver in his mouth. But Bear found out. Coyote was forced to keep running, probably for eternity, Victorio learned. The stories entertained, but at the same time taught valuable lessons. According to Lakota scholar Vine Deloria in *Red Earth, White Lies*, tribal members understood the philosophical overview of the stories although not always the details.

> Indians came to understand that all things were related, and while many tribes understood this knowledge in terms of religious rituals, it was also a methodology/guideline which instructed them in making observations of the behavior of other forms of life. Attuned to their environment, Indians could find food, locate trails, protect themselves from inclement weather, and anticipate coming events by their understanding of how entities related to each other.

In another story, Victorio discovered that darkness had once dominated Ussen's beautiful world. The birds hated the darkness and sought perpetual light; the beasts preferred the constant darkness. The argument between them grew so venomous that they agreed to settle the matter with a great battle to the death. No one on either side survived the battle, and finally Ussen stepped in and divided the world into both light and dark.

Thus, the child learned the importance of both sunlight and nighttime and the folly of greed. Moreover, Victorio discovered why every winter the Indeh played something called the moccasin game. It recreated this epic battle. But instead of a life-or-death struggle, the moccasin game required strategy and a bit of luck. Whereas the birds and beasts had bet their lives, Chihennes wagered horses, knives, and other valued items on their team's ability to locate a bone hidden in one of many moccasins. A night of social dancing always followed this important game. It was no secret that as an adult Victorio loved to gamble. His granddaughter once reported that he especially enjoyed traveling north to gamble with the Navajos.

The elders also would have talked to him repeatedly of the Creation and of White Painted Woman and Child of the Water. Victorio learned that the solutions to many of the problems plaguing humans, such as disease and starvation, were found in these instructions. While still a young boy Victorio undoubtedly accompanied his grandfather and uncles to the Guadalupe Mountains, located far to the east, where he stared in awe at the petroglyphs decorating the area. The images of the Mountain Spirits, he learned, were etched right into these very rocks. In fact, the Gááns still lived somewhere in a deep cave up there on those forbidding slopes. Only one had ever dared to search for that cave.

The Mountain Spirits occasionally adorned themselves in deerhide kilts and intricately painted headdresses, covered their faces in black, and descended from the mountains to dance and bestow blessings upon the Chihennes. When he first saw them, Victorio realized immediately that he was in the midst of a deeply spiritual experience. He also watched the Crown Dancers or clowns, who frequently danced along with the Gááns and at times caricatured their movements to relieve the intensity of the ceremony. If as a boy he giggled at their antics, his father told him emphatically that these were respected intermediaries between the Gááns and the people and not to be taken lightly. Apache mothers sometimes went so far as to warn their children: "That Clown, the 'Gray One,' he will grab you and put you in a

basket and he will take you off somewhere!" Later, Victorio realized that the dancers were really men of his own band imper-
sonating the Mountain Spirits, and it was through these men
that the deities conveyed blessings. This belief differed from that
of their Pueblo neighbors, who assumed that once men donned
the masks of the Kachinas, they became those spirits.

During his childhood, Victorio undoubtedly asked his mother
why the men and women of his band seemed to talk to themselves as they stripped bark for weapons, ground corn, or even
as they bathed. He observed the lips of the elders moving while
they planted corn, melons, and squash along the river bottom in
early spring. Warm Springs Chihennes, in fact, practiced some
farming long before whites arrived. The men dug holes, sprin-
kled a pinch of hádndín, the sacred cattail and seed, into each
hole, and spoke silently to themselves the entire time. Medicine
men followed along behind them, burying prayer sticks at intervals for rain and spiritual nourishment and also with lips
moving. "Everything is spiritual," she reminded her son. "You,
too, must learn to follow every ritual, observe every taboo, and
pray or sing while you do these things." The men and women,
she explained, were praying.

Prayer was indeed an absolute necessity for a hunting and
gathering society. So-called modern civilizations generally
dismiss hunting and gathering as primitive and, therefore, sim-
plistic. Nevertheless, success depended upon an intricate knowledge of the land and the elements and upon perfect timing.
Because the world was imbued with spiritual powers, the appropriate prayers and practices were required. After planting
time—usually in late spring—the band broke camp and headed
to cooler, higher summer grounds. There Ussen provided deer,
elk, and antelope for them to hunt. Thus, replacement of the
deer occurred on a supernatural, mystical level, as did success or
failure of crops. Ussen also supplied porcupines for quills, birds
for their feathers, and small game for practice and emergency rations. High in the mountains Victorio watched trout dart unmolested in and out of the slippery rocks in the cold streams, but
never thought to eat, or even touch them. Apaches considered

fish repulsive. So, too, were turkeys because they touched and occasionally even ate snakes.

Victorio had four sisters and apparently no brothers. One sister married the Chihenne chief Kas-tziden—meaning "Make It Come Alive"—better known to history as Nana. Another married the scout Kayitah, who in 1886 was instrumental in Geronimo's surrender. Gouyen married the son of Chief Sanchez and later the warrior Kaytennae. The youngest sister was Lozen, about twenty years younger than Victorio and thus they did not share a childhood. One day he would come to depend on Lozen's abilities almost as much as he did any man's. As a small child, Victorio accompanied his mother and older sisters. Together they gathered yucca leaves and sweet yucca flowers in the spring and watched the women dry and string them. The flowers, in particular, provided a way to sweeten other foods. The children helped their mother and the other women when they moved into Arizona to harvest the ripe agave in summer. The women dug out large earthen pits and roasted the heart of the plant until it turned into thick, gooey mescal syrup. Then they spread it on the ground and dried it. Once dried, mescal preserved well, and although the Chihennes, unlike the Mescaleros, never enjoyed eating it, the concoction often meant the difference between food and going hungry in the worst winter months. Summer also brought wild onions and a host of wild vegetables, berries of all sorts, potatoes, greens, grapes, and currants. Early autumn produced the piñons and sunflower seeds. In fact, wild foods grew in surprising abundance in an otherwise stingy desert if one knew where to look and moved about frequently to take advantage.

Each time his people moved camp, Victorio helped his mother and sisters gather new saplings to bend taut into the dome-shaped wickiups that served as the family shelter. Over the framework they spread several thick layers of fresh beargrass and enough scrub brush to keep out the harsh sun and the occasional rain or snow. Every so often one of the women would spot a beehive lodged among the high rocks. The older boys eagerly practiced shooting their arrows at the hive until it eventually broke

loose and toppled onto the ground. Then everyone licked the
sticky sweetness from their fingers as they worked the wax into
buckskin bags for later use. It was one of the few real sweeten-
ing agents that Apaches had.

About the time that the stately aspens shimmered gold each
autumn, the bands returned to the river bottoms. The medicine
men blessed the fields once more, and the elders harvested their
ripe corn crop. Again, Victorio watched, and from this learned
a little farming, knowledge that would stay with him into adulthood. By the time he entered his teens, Victorio was intricately
familiar with the natural cycles of the land and the seasons. In addition, his mother had shown him every available waterhole and
hidden spring, and she taught him to seek water in the rocky
basin of a dry waterfall in an emergency. Like all Chihenne children, Victorio quickly memorized the life-and-death lessons
and never dismissed the supernatural aspects of his world.

Victorio Begins His Warrior Training

One day when young Victorio became rambunctious, a male relative probably sent him on an errand. "Run up that hill!" his father or uncle commanded. The irritating behavior halted; the
discipline began. At first, Victorio ran up small hills. Over time
his uncles pointed to steeper inclines, and then they told him to
carry rocks or some small load as he ran. The ultimate goal, of
course, was strong arm and leg muscles and increased lung ca-
pacity. Furthermore, running was a critical skill because Apaches
did not always have horses available. They did not breed or herd
them as did other tribal groups. Moreover, being on horseback
was not always advantageous. Warriors must often slip past an
enemy silently—on foot. Runners carried messages to other
bands, and might sprint great distances in short periods of time.

Soon, Victorio's father added yet another command: "Fill your
mouth with this water. Run up that hill, and then spit out the water when you return!" At first this proved a difficult task. "You
must breathe through your nose as you run," the men told him.
This was sound advice; the arid Southwest desert dehydrated

anyone who inhaled through his mouth. Such lessons would later mean the difference between survival and death, especially when having to escape American soldiers.

As a child, Victorio was ordered to bathe regularly in a nearby river or stream, even though Chihenne men and women frequently washed themselves in the 110-degree warm springs nearby. "Break the ice and go in!" his grandfather said the first time young Victorio hesitated, peering down at the layer of frost that had iced over the water overnight. "Never mind the pain. Just go in!" The ritual kept the child clean and impervious to cold. It eventually made his limbs rock hard. As an adult, Victorio would sometimes wonder why white men prided themselves so ardently on their weekly Saturday-night bath and yet had the nerve to call Apaches—who washed every day—dirty.

Every morning Victorio's father arose, stood in front of the wickiup at first light, and raised his arms to the East. "When the sun rises we cast a pinch of hoddentin [*sic*] toward him, and we do the same thing to the moon" and then we say "Gun-ju-le, chigo-na-ay, si-chi-zi, gun-ju-le, inzayu, injanale," or "Be good, O Sun, be good. Dawn, [a] long time let me live … and at night, 'Be good, O Night … do not let me die." Victorio's father was adamant: "One always thanks Ussen for the glorious sun and its life-giving warmth," he told Victorio many times. An Indeh might ask for personal courage. Otherwise, "one asks Ussen for little," he learned. Apaches knew that their Creator was intelligent enough to devise and run the world, and thus needed no direction from them. "Ussen does not care for the petty quarrels of men," Victorio's father told him often. Instead, Apaches gave thanks and prayed for health, strength, protection, and wisdom. They did not ask for victory over another person.

Victorio learned that he must always give to those in need. Only witches allowed elders, for example, to go hungry. He also understood that as an adult he would owe absolute loyalty to family and band. One day he, too, would earn his own personal power. Without it, no Apache warrior could lead another into battle and no di-yin could heal. But he must first prove himself worthy. He had to earn his role as a hunter and warrior.

Already as a young boy, he had begun. Victorio had used willow branches to craft crude bows, then watched his uncles carefully search for hard woods such as mulberry or oak for their own. He tried to place his small robin feathers onto arrows and fervently hoped that he, like his father, would one day learn to perfectly align eagle feathers so that each arrow flew straight to its targets and never turned in flight and missed. Naturally, there were Mexican rifles around, and a few precious American-made guns filtered in after about 1830. The Mexican weapons given to Apaches were inferior ones and required extensive maintenance. American firearms were far superior and well worth the effort to obtain, but rarely available. Every Apache boy worked for proficiency with bow and arrows. These weapons were used to hunt deer, and they were required in war when the bullets ran out or the gun barrels jammed.

Victorio Becomes a Dihoke

For Apache males, the final stages of training began at about twelve or thirteen years old. Years of running and bathing in ice water had initiated the process. Wrestling and games with other boys his age had prepared him for combat. By his early teens, Victorio could fire off an arrow or shoot a rifle while riding a horse bareback at full gallop, even though his people preferred to ambush the enemy from behind rocks or atop a cliff. In fact, Apaches were known to release their horses altogether when taking to the mountains to fight. Victorio knew how to care for horses, even though Apaches did not raise them. He could handle a knife and wield a spear if necessary. He crafted durable weapons and the tools needed for hunting parties, raiding, and all-out war.

Now began the novice or *dihoke* stage when Victorio's training turned formal and ritualized. He was often called "Child of the Waters" during this period of his life, revealing its deeply spiritual nature. Indeed, the dihoke stage represented a boy's entry into an ancient and sacred knowledge. The rituals he underwent reached into and renewed the very Creation story itself. Just as

Child of the Water had subdued the enemies of the Apache people, so Victorio needed to prove that he could do the same when called upon.

Victorio memorized Child of the Water's instructions. Similarly, his sisters celebrated their entry into adulthood—specifically, their first menstrual periods—with the lessons of White Painted Woman. In the case of Victorio, his father or grandfather sought a di-yin who specialized in warrior training. For his sisters, Victorio's mother also sought a di-yin or asked the grandmother to instruct her daughters. In both instances, it was absolutely imperative that, in addition to giving instruction, the di-yin scrutinize the young person's every behavior, searching for signs that might suggest future dishonesty, gluttony, fear, or cowardice.

During their puberty ceremonies, Gouyen and Victorio's other sisters, including Lozen, reenacted White Painted Woman's first menses and impregnation. They made four symbolic runs, which represented the four stages of life. His sisters were expected to make these runs without faltering. During the four days of the puberty ceremony, men, women, and children of within and outside the girl's rancheria placed corn offerings or other gifts before her. Each person received her blessings as the embodiment of White Painted Woman. The girl's family provided a great feast of venison, corn, and fruits for all who arrived. Each evening brought dancing. If the prayers proved successful, the Mountain Spirits might arrive to dance and thereby affirm that the girl was indeed blessed. On the final evening of the ceremony, dancing continued all night, and everyone who participated received presents from the host family.

Although not a ceremony per se, Victorio's dihoke period was nonetheless a sacred event. His family—indeed his people overall—held a stake in his success. When Victorio felt ready, he simply volunteered to join the next raiding or war party. Thus began the first of four novice missions completed under the strict codes and scrutiny of all men in the parties. In short, the dihoke had to demonstrate his physical prowess and spiritual readiness for manhood. In preparation—and with the assistance of his di-yin—Victorio had memorized an intricate warrior language, which had probably survived the migration south centuries earlier. While using this special language, the dihoke could not speak directly, for example, of lightning. He must instead say "thunder's friend." Death was called "that in which one comes again." Cattle were "ya-he-zine," or "those who stand facing downward," referring to the way livestock stand on a slope. In fact, nearly every object and action required distinctly unique terminology. Some Chiricahuas continued to use a form of this warpath language beyond the novice stage; others abandoned it after a dihoke became a full-fledged warrior. Regardless, all warpath language ended the moment the men returned to camp.

On each of the four missions, Victorio ate his meat cold and drank water through a special drinking tube—which girls also used during their ceremony—so that his lips would not touch the liquid and make his flesh weak. To satisfy an itch, he scratched with a specially crafted wooden scratcher because fingernails might similarly weaken the skin at this time. Like all dihokes, Victorio performed the most menial tasks on these missions. He tended the warriors' horses and made their beds. He chopped and carried the wood for their fires. At times, Victorio even cleaned the camp.

All the while, the adult men in the party watched the young novice very closely, looking for signs of laziness or any other negative behaviors. They taught him that hunting deer or elk, for instance, was more a spiritual endeavor than a skill. Overconfidence invited failure, and so the best hunter observed every ritual and taboo prior to the hunting expedition. He must never allow a pregnant or menstruating woman to touch his bows or arrows because such potent female power would dilute the male energy needed for hunting. Since Ussen provided the deer and elk, the hunt itself required fasting and prayer.

Following the actual kill, a hunter had to show utmost respect to the dead animal. He must skin and butcher the deer with head facing east. He must never straddle or step over the body or walk around the front of the head. Most important, Victorio learned, successful hunters always gave away large portions of the meat to widows, elders, or anyone else who asked for it and often ended up with only a little for themselves. The highly prized deerhide was, of course, also given away. Once the meat was consumed, the hunter must neatly stack the bones and not randomly discard them. Only after adhering to all of these conventions could a man attain skill as a great hunter.

The men whom he accompanied in those first four hunting or war parties also taught Victorio the importance of the Chihenne medicine hat. In fact, Victorio wore one for the first time on his dihoke missions. The medicine hats were sewn from soft buckskin. Each warrior made his own hat and adorned it with personal symbols. Sometimes these symbols represented the Mountain Spirits or, at times, celestial bodies such as the Sun, Moon, and Lightning. These hats grew more elaborate over time as the warriors added representations of their own personal power. So sacred were these medicine hats and the symbols upon them that when American John G. Bourke sketched one for an 1887 report to the U.S. Bureau of American Ethnology, Nan-ta-do-tash, its owner, claimed his hat was never the same afterward.

As Victorio progressed through his novice period, he learned many other expectations and taboos that he would carry forth into his adult life. For one thing, sexual intercourse before completion of his four missions would brand him unrestrained and weak. Even afterward, waiting until marriage was best. Instead, he should exhaust himself with physical activity. To bolster his resolve, the men reminded the fledgling warrior of the stories he had heard from childhood. "Women have 'teeth down there' to bite off a man's penis," he had heard often enough. Even Coyote had broken such teeth in a woman's vagina in order to have intercourse with her. Undoubtedly, lifelong disgrace and possible dismemberment proved powerful deterrents.

No records exist regarding how Victorio actually fared during his dihoke training. Nevertheless, his leadership role later on reinforces the assumption that he completed the four missions successfully. It is noteworthy that the elaborate male societies common to the Plains tribes were absent among the Apaches. Instead, after his dihoke period was over, Victorio would have turned his attention to seeking personal power, perhaps from an animal, a celestial body such as the sun or moon, or from a natural phenomenon such as lightning. A power might have approached him and asked him to serve as its di-yin. More likely, Victorio fasted for a period of days, prayed, and asked a di-yin how to obtain a desired power. Nana's power, for example, gave him the ability to locate ammunition, a skill on which Victorio would later depend. His little sister Lozen could locate an enemy if she turned her palms upward, prayed, and turned slowly in all directions. Her palms would change color when they faced the direction of the enemy. His mother's power was to dress wounds; Gouyen's power was to avoid wounds. Because Victorio succeeded in war, his power probably came from Lightning, but that is not certain.

Power could also enable a person to heal diseases such as owl or ghost sickness. Sometimes it allowed one to effectively heal wounds. Both Lozen's and Victorio's eldest daughter used their power to assist women in childbirth. Power might help a di-yin locate healing herbs and stones. Or it might permit an individual to specialize in warrior training. There were obviously many forms that power might take. Victorio's power, unfortunately, is lost to history. If it were possible to examine the symbols painted on his medicine hat, one might discover his power. However, Victorio's personal belongings were taken as souvenirs following the Tres Castillos massacre and were apparently never seen again. We know that at some point between 1835 and 1840, Victorio completed his novice period and was welcomed as a Chihenne warrior. He began this new stage of his life at a time of increasing violence between Apaches and Mexicans and between his people and the Americans.

Victorio's Larger World

Throughout his early life, Victorio witnessed a parade of Apache notables as they visited, traded, and sometimes went to war alongside members of his rancheria. Some historians have speculated that Chief Nana, a tall Chihenne leader with a decided limp and profound loyalty to Victorio, was his father. But Nana's grandson, James Kaywaykla, insisted that Nana was Victorio's uncle. Victorio, Kaywaykla claimed, called Nana "father" in part out of respect and also because Apaches often used the terms interchangeably.

The Chihenne or Bedonkohe leader Pluma frequented Victorio's region. Pluma was a major advocate of peace with white men and one of the last Apaches to remain camped near Janos presidio before Mexican independence. He returned to the Mimbres River country about 1821 and afterward spoke frequently of the steady migration streaming into northern Mexico. He had seen increasing numbers of white men, black men—some free and others seemingly enslaved—and unfortunately, even some strange Indian peoples from the East. Whether Pluma objected to these outsiders is not known. But, like most Apaches, Pluma disparaged the white man's thirst for gold and his obsession with mineral wealth overall. He and other Apache leaders worried that incessant burrowing into the earth might invoke the wrath of the Mountain Spirits. Nevertheless, Pluma and a Chihenne leader named Fuerte were probably the first Apaches to welcome a party of white men led by James O. Pattie and his father, Silvestre, who came to trap beaver in 1826. These were some of the first Americans to reach the Santa Rita del Cobre region located about fifteen miles from present-day Silver City, New Mexico.

James Pattie's journal fails to elaborate on a meeting with either Pluma or Fuerte, but clearly describes discovering what was undoubtedly a Chihenne camp. They found "maguey" or mescal still baking in the ground, sampled it, and reported that the concoction tasted a bit like "crab apple cider." The men in the Pattie party apparently found Chihenne country hospitable—again contradicting stereotypes of unfriendly, blood-thirsty Apaches—because, when furs proved less than profitable, they encountered no trouble in turning their attention to copper. The Santa Rita del Cobre mines would play a very important role in Victorio's life, even though they were not where he customarily camped.

The mines served as a magnet for Spanish and Americans hoping to get rich.

Archaeology suggests that pre-Apache peoples first extracted copper. The Spanish worked the mines on and off after 1600. In 1804, Francisco Manuel Elguea, a banker from Chihuahua, purchased a grant from Mexico City to work the mines. He built a small settlement and fort there. In 1807, American explorer Zebulon Pike estimated that the fully operational Santa Rita mines were sending some twenty-thousand muleloads of copper each year to the royal mint in Mexico City. Despite Pike's glowing account, however, the mines frequently shut down because of economic trouble and Indian raids. Even so, the Santa Rita mines continued to attract explorers, trappers, and travelers, including Pattie and his group. In 1826, Pattie negotiated a truce with three Apaches—Pluma and Fuerte were probably two of these—and opened the mines. But for a number of reasons that do not include the Apaches, after several months the party abandoned the mines and left for California. This experience suggests that, although chiefs like Pluma may have harbored suspicions regarding white men, the initial contacts were far from unfriendly.

In addition to Pluma, Victorio undoubtedly also met two Nednhi leaders, who would soon figure prominently in the deterioration of relations between Apaches and whites. Juan Diego Compá and his brother Juan José Compá were both fluent in Spanish and, like Pluma, traveled frequently to northern Chihuahua, bringing news from that region. Some believe that Juan José had once studied for the priesthood and this made him a favorite of Mexican authorities. The brothers also maintained good relations with a young Chokonen warrior named Cochise, whose land was in southeastern Arizona.

However, when Victorio was a child, it was undoubtedly Fuerte who impressed him most. Biographer Edwin R. Sweeney believes that Fuerte was none other than the celebrated Mangas Coloradas and that he obtained his new name around 1835. At six-feet five-inches, Mangas Coloradas towered over other men, and he reportedly weighed well over two hundred pounds. His

extraordinarily large head, deep-set eyes, and wide mouth made
him memorable. To watch such a man stride briskly across camp
or swing his huge frame gracefully onto a pony must have inspired awe. Frequently called a giant among his people, Mangas
Coloradas possessed great charisma and leadership abilities. He
also formed brilliant alliances. For instance, Mangas Coloradas
married one of his daughters to Cochise and hence solidified a
relationship between their bands. Later, as a warrior, Victorio admired and rode, raided, and fought with Mangas Coloradas. He
would also, therefore, ride with Cochise. Indeed, some claim
that he succeeded Mangas as principle chief, although others say
that it was the death of another Chihenne chief, Cuchillo Negro,
that left a leadership vacuum for Victorio to fill.

Victorio's rancheria would have learned a great deal from
their contact with these and other Apache leaders. For one
thing, they undoubtedly heard more about Americans and discovered that with these white men came virulent diseases. None
was more terrifying than smallpox. During the early 1830s Chihennes traveling between Janos and Mimbres country often
spotted eerie trail warnings: the head of a dead owl nailed to a
post with head pointing to the afflicted area or a sapling stripped
of all limbs except one. Both signs meant "stay away!" In addition, ghostly burned-out wickiups dotted northern Chihuahua
and New Mexico. Apache di-yins built piñon or juniper fires inside the wickiups, hoping to smoke out the disease. Afflicted
men and women remained inside until they could no longer
stand the massive smoke. But nothing seemed to work, adding
to the terror.

American Traders Enter Apachería

A new breed of white men brought trade goods and opportunities by the mid-1830s, and Victorio's people wanted very badly
to cash in. Benjamin Davis Wilson was fairly typical of these
Americans. He originally obtained a license from the Mexican
government to trap beaver, but soon found trade far more lucrative than furs. For one thing, white men had begun migrat-

ing into Texas after 1821. Like the existing haciendas and mining communities in northern Mexico, these newly established ranches and farms needed livestock and labor. Wilson also learned that Apaches and Comanches wanted American-made rifles and ammunition. Thus, an exchange began. When, for instance, the government in Sonora mobilized against American gun runners to prevent such trade from taking root, Indians took to raiding in Sonora but unloading goods in Chihuahua or New Mexico.

Out of this expanded trade came a tendency for Apache leaders to negotiate partial peace treaties with towns, haciendas, or individuals. This was not done because Indians failed to grasp the concept of larger political units, as is sometimes suggested, but because these treaties primarily served as trade agreements. Apaches probably upheld these treaties long enough to dispose of their plunder and abandoned the agreements when someone else offered a better deal. The Mexicans understood this; Americans did not.

A treaty signed on August 29, 1832, by twenty-nine Apache leaders and representatives from Chihuahua conveniently omitted any mention of Sonora. As expected, officials turned a blind eye when the Compá brothers raided goods from Sonora and distributed them to ready buyers in Chihuahua or north of the Rio Grande. Some merchandise even found its way to American territory through Bent's Fort in southeastern Colorado. By the time Victorio was enmeshed in his dihoke training, he had already frequently witnessed Chihenne warriors gathering in preparation for a raid. They first sang for hours to the haunting beat of the *esadedene* until eventually they drowned out the drumming altogether. Indeed, it is likely that at least one of Victorio's novice missions took him into Sonora to raid, trade, and return with weapons, bolts of cotton or woolen cloth, steel knives, metal pots and pans, and many other well-manufactured trade goods from the United States.

At the height of this trade the Sonora legislature reinstituted a version of the infamous ear-bounty policy of the late eighteenth century. In summer 1835, officials allocated some four thousand pesos to buy as many scalps as bounty hunters could bring in. It was not, however, a policy that set well with all. A year later, authorities reversed their extermination rhetoric and revoked the bounties, and in an effort to join rather than beat the Indians opened peace talks at Fronteras. Raiding shifted to Chihuahua. By September 1836, it was that state's turn to place bounties on Indian scalps. These policies came as one response to a federal government that could spare no troops or funds whatsoever to curtail illegal trade or to protect settlers in the northern reaches of the territory. The scalp bounties would continue in effect across northern Mexico until 1891, primarily in Chihuahua but to some degree bounty payments were still possible in Sonora and Durango as well. Indeed, it was under the scalp-bounty policy that the examining committee in Chihuahua City would in 1880 pay two thousand pesos for Victorio's scalp and fifteen thousand pesos for the scalps of sixty-one warriors with him at Tres Castillos. Over time, of course, the scalp bounties generated an intense hatred on the part of Southwest Indian peoples. They did not, however, put a dent in the illegal trade but, in fact, prompted acts of extreme cruelty on both sides for the remainder of the nineteenth century.

The actions of the Kentuckian John James Johnson clearly illustrate the savagery that this policy encouraged. Johnson, like Benjamin Wilson, originally arrived in Mexico to seek a fortune in the fur trade. As the law required, Johnson declared himself a citizen of Sonora, theoretically converted to Catholicism, and went forth to get rich. Also like Wilson, he quickly turned to trade as the more lucrative endeavor. Two of his favorite trading partners were Nednhi leaders Juan Diego and Juan José Compá, both of whom conferred extensively with the Chihennes. Traveling with Johnson in 1837 were two Americans, James or Santiago Kirker and Charles "King" Woolsey, both of whom would later become synonymous with the scalp trade.

On April 20, 1837, Johnson first contacted the Compá brothers, who were at the time camped near the copper mines, probably with Mangas Coloradas. As per the customary practice, the two sides came together and traded over a period of several days.

Neither Juan José nor Juan Diego had any reason to suspect the Americans more than usual as they exchanged their livestock and captives for manufactured knives and tools. But it was the store of American-made rifles that the brothers really wanted and that encouraged them to continue trading.

On April 22, Johnson invited the Nednhis and Chihennes to trade one more time. His men passed around a sack of piñole — a toasted and sweetened corn meal — and liberal amounts of *talupai*, a corn beer made from sprouted kernels. There was also much whiskey. Juan José or Juan Diego perhaps remarked that some of the Mexicans who had traded with them the night before were now missing from Johnson's group. "Too much drink!" or maybe a knowing shrug that suggested "Mexicans are unreliable" was the response. Indeed, the Mexicans were absent because they had learned what would happen next and fled rather than participate.

A small swivel cannon filled with scrap metal lay hidden behind the remaining sacks of trade goods. According to a Mexican captive just ransomed from the Apaches, one of the Americans suddenly drew his pistol and without warning fired point-blank at Juan Diego Compá's head, killing him instantly. Then the swivel gun open-fired. Fifteen or more Apaches, including Juan José Compá and one of Mangas Coloradas's wives, were murdered. Other Apache men and women lay bleeding from their wounds. Those Indians who could do so ran for their lives. They later returned to an even more gruesome sight. Two days later Johnson turned in twenty-five scalps at Janos, took half of the bounty for himself, and distributed the rest to his band. Ironically, Mangas Coloradas always blamed Sonorans and not Americans. Although there is no proof that Victorio was there on April 22, he almost certainly heard the stories. The massacre gave him even greater incentive to complete his novice training.

James Kirker and the Scalp-Bounty Trade

One individual whom Victorio came to hate was James or Santiago Kirker, another trapper-turned-trader. In 1821 — the same

year that William Becknell had opened the Santa Fe Trail—
Kirker worked for McKnight & Brady, the largest mercantile
business in St. Louis. That spring Kirker and John McKnight
piled trade goods into their wagons and departed for New Mexico Territory, hoping to cash in on Mexican independence and
the longtime dearth of trade among Santa Feans. Along the way,
Comanches intercepted the wagons and raided most of their
goods. Farther along the trail, Mexican soldiers caught and
threatened to imprison them. Kirker and McKnight straggled
into Santa Fe with most of the investment lost. They were the
third American trade group to arrive, and had they managed to
get through with goods intact, would have made a fortune.

Kirker realized, however, the potential in Mexican territory.
He left St. Louis for the West in 1822, careful to maintain close
ties with Missouri. Obtaining permission from the new Mexican government to trap beaver, he used the wagon trains heading in and out of Spanish territory to carry his furs back to St.
Louis. He began to mine around Santa Rita and by 1828 was also
trading copper for mining supplies. He bought himself a ranch
near Santa Rita and in 1834 used this as a headquarters to trade
contraband guns, powder, and lead to Apaches and Comanches
in exchange for stolen horses and mules. Then he sold these animals to wagon trains heading south into Mexico and north to
Santa Fe. After 1849, wagon trains would also head to California, nearly all of them in dire need of livestock.

The August 21, 1832, treaty augmented Kirker's trade because
it specifically designated the Santa Rita area as Chihenne land
(the treaty called them Mimbres) and conveniently shifted Indian trade north. Kirker's ranch became the perfect hub for
dropping off stolen merchandise. At one point, Juan José and
Juan Diego Compá were major players, as were Pluma and, of
course, Mangas Coloradas. Chiefs such as Cuchillo Negro, Itan,
and Delgadito, who would become known to Americans at a
later date, could all be seen heading towards the Kirker ranch and
herding horses and mules ahead of them from time to time.

Frustrated Chihuahua officials tried to shut down such operations. In February 1835, they imposed fines on any citizen who

purchased stolen livestock, prison terms for anyone selling whiskey to Indians, and execution to gun runners. Within two years, however, authorities made the decision to turn contraband dealers into mercenaries. Officials in Chihuahua City charged owners a fee for the recovery of their livestock, forcing them to subsidize the very traders who stole them in the first place or, at least, who profited from the Indian raids. In 1837, authorities began to enter into formal contracts with Kirker, Johnson, and others to create small guerilla armies to recover stolen goods. This action had caused the April 22 massacre.

On July 29, 1837, the Chihuahua War Tribunal passed a *proyecto de guerra*, or war policy, against the Indians. It was signed by the secretary of the tribunal Angel Trías and supported by some of the wealthiest men in Chihuahua. However, the president general of Chihuahua, a military man by the name of Antonio Bustamante, called the policy barbaric and unconstitutional. In October 1837, Bustamante ordered Johnson arrested. He accused Johnson, Kirker, and other foreigners of conspiring against Mexico. Although he could not prove it, Bustamante apparently believed that Kirker, in particular, had helped instigate the rebellions against Mexico that had gripped Texas in 1835–36. Moreover, Bustamante suspected Kirker and Johnson of running guns to the Pueblos, Apaches, Navajos, and Utes.

By 1839, Indian raids on Mexican lands increased. Over Bustamante's objections, the new civilian governor José María Irigoyen signed a contract with Kirker. Irigoyen was also the editor of *El Antenor*, Chihuahua City's newspaper, and used his editorials to support the proyecto and proposed contract with Johnson. The municipal council of Chihuahua City supported Irigoyen. It levied a tax on merchants to pay Kirker, who by this time had assembled a gang of more than one hundred Americans, Mexicans, former African slaves, and Indians. Even *El Antenor* described this band as "vicious, corrupted, haughty, and undisciplined." As a result, Irigoyen was voted out and Kirker's contract was cancelled. Chihuahua City made the decision to build up the state's presidios and local militias. This was not, however, the last time Chihuahua or Sonora would sign such a contract with Kirker.

When contracts were in effect, the sight of Americans and Mexicans riding into Chihuahua City with the scalps of Apache men, women, and infants dripping from their saddles became commonplace. Sometimes the scalps were not Apache at all, but those of peaceful Tarahumaras or Opatas. Indeed, so greedy were the bounty hunters that some Mexicans suspected there were non-Indian scalps as well. By the time Victorio completed his dihoke training, Kirker's death squads were scouring northern Mexico and as far north as Colorado. On at least one occasion they had killed Chihennes living near Warm Springs. As a warrior, Victorio would necessarily have to deal with this new breed of white men. As a leader, he would try to make sense of them. Despite the brutality of the period in which Victorio came to adulthood, it appears he recognized that there were vast differences between men like Pattie and men like Kirker.

CHAPTER 3

Encountering the Americans

THE year 1846 was a watershed for Victorio. He married, and within two years, he took on the role of father as well. This year also marked the beginning of the United States occupation of New Mexico, and again, two years later, the imposition of American government and laws. It took a few more years, however, before any of the Apaches felt ramifications from the American takeover. So in 1846, life for Victorio and the Chihennes continued in much the same manner as it had for the past decade. Deer and elk still abounded in the Gila and Mimbres river valleys. Trade continued. Gathering cycles persisted, and in most instances, the Indian campsites went unmolested.

Scalp-bounty hunters sporadically spread terror across Apachería, but seldom reached Chihenne country. It is noteworthy that, despite the abominable practice of scalping carried out against them, the Chiricahuas as a group generally refrained from retaliating in kind. Contrary to the stereotypes put forth in Hollywood movies, scalping was not customarily an Apache enterprise. This is not to say Apaches never scalped, especially once the practice grew so prevalent. Period accounts, however, liked to exaggerate so-called depredations and often assumed that all such deeds were naturally done by Apaches. One reason Apaches were loathe to scalp was their fear of the dead. They were especially afraid of contracting ghost sickness, a deadly wasting disease that only a special di-yin and a lengthy healing ceremony could cure. As a chief, Victorio reportedly permitted no scalping whatsoever, regardless of the provocation. It was altogether too easy, he believed, to involuntarily conjure the dead. A person's spirit naturally clung to the physical body after death.

In addition, the humiliation of having to enter the Happy Place without one's hair made the mutilated remnant even more of a magnet for ghosts. On those rare occasions when other Apache bands required a scalp for some ceremony, they took one and disposed of it immediately afterward. During the Apache wars of the 1870s and '80s, some Apaches may have taken scalps to retaliate against American depredations.

As more American outsiders moved in and began to displace the wildlife, the importance of subsistence raiding intensified. At the same time, as the population increased, trade markets expanded. Miners and farmers alike needed livestock, and some did not care from whence the animals came. Young Bi-duye inevitably launched his share of raids. He undoubtedly captured one or more of the small, lonely wagon caravans lumbering southward from Santa Fe or north out of Chihuahua City. Keeping well out of sight until the very last minute, he and his party would study the procession for hours as the oxen plodded toward that fearsome strip of waterless desert, which Spaniards had long ago dubbed the Jornada del Muerto. If he captured the wagon train where the road dipped into a small canyon, the teamsters were sitting ducks, and the warriors hit from above with lightning speed. Victorio drove the wagons away and left the doomed drivers dead or afoot with miles to walk to the nearest settlement.

Because raiding was a purely economic affair, it required no formal send-off. Warriors fasted as they did before hunting; they knew the powers pitied a hungry man. Everyone kept his eyes open for crows because the sight of a crow hanging around a camp before a hunt or raid augured success, although it was usually considered bad luck to see one. Raiders gathered the night before departure to sing, but there were no formal ceremonies, prayers, or ritual dances that must be perfectly performed. Naturally, each man carried a small pouch of hádndín for daily prayers while away.

During the 1840s, Victorio's name was increasingly linked with that of Cuchillo Negro, a Warm Springs Chihenne who attained the status of chief during that decade. His territory ultimately spanned the entire region between the Mimbres Mountains and the Rio Grande, including the Cañada Alamosa and the Warm Springs. Like Mangas Coloradas, Cuchillo Negro stood well over six feet tall, but, according to written records, he was plagued with a deficiency of muscle in his arms and legs, possibly a deformity or sort of muscular deterioration. John Cremony, who accompanied the International Border Commission as translator in 1851, affectionately called Cuchillo Negro the "gigantic savage." Cuchillo Negro maintained friendly relations with Mexicans and stands out as a primary advocate of peace between Chiricahuas and Americans. Young Bi-duye undoubtedly rode with Cuchillo Negro on many raids—he may have married into his band—and possibly became the chief's *segundo* or successor. Victorio's association with Cuchillo Negro offers another explanation for his lifelong alliance with Mangas Coloradas. During the 1840s and 1850s, Cuchillo Negro and Mangas Coloradas frequently raided and warred together, and their rancherias camped adjacent to each other most of the time.

There was also Nana, who was probably a member of Victorio's Warm Springs band. Oral history seems to reinforce the notion that Nana married one of Victorio's older sisters. Therefore, he may have joined Victorio's band at that time. Such was the fluidity of the Apache political and social structures, and it became even less structured over time. The lack of a formal organization proved almost as baffling to officials as the U.S. government bureaucratic labyrinth was to the Apache. It is nearly impossible to pinpoint some of these rancherias more accurately.

Even when Cuchillo Negro or Mangas Coloradas, for example, accompanied a raiding party, he did not necessarily lead it. Although a chief's main responsibility was the safety and well-being of his people, it was logical to the Apaches that whoever organized the party also oversaw it. Raiding parties were usually small, but depending upon circumstances, could contain one hundred or more men. These might later break up into smaller groups as they approached a target. The men would hobble their horses, using strips of buckskin or yucca fiber and usually would steal forward on foot, camouflaging themselves within the rough

Portrait of Nana, Warm Springs Apache and Victorio's second in command. Courtesy of Western History Collections, University of Oklahoma Libraries.

sagebrush or hiding among boulders. They sought no engagement with the enemy. The best targets were isolated haciendas or tiny Mexican villages, especially at siesta time or after dark. Experienced raiders could cut a dozen horses or mules from a

herd or lure them out of a corral and put several miles behind
them before the hapless owner realized he was a victim. As Victorio saw it, raids resembled a kind of harvest. His people never
took everything. In fact, if the farmer replenished livestock and
food stores, he could provide booty for another day. Hence, it
was foolish and counterproductive to destroy a victim or thwart
his ability to recover losses.

Afterward, the victorious Chihennes might butcher a few
steers or horses on the spot and feast, but most livestock was
traded. Janos served as their favorite hub, and until a smallpox
epidemic struck in 1843, hundreds of Nednhi bands and Chokonens camped there as well, drawing rations and offering hospi-
tality to their visitors. Janos Apaches eagerly shared food, gossip,
and maybe a little tulapai or whiskey. It was not difficult to find
a game of chance where Victorio might gamble away a captive
or a couple of horses just for fun.

Indeed, trade was conducted amid a festive climate. Raiders ate
and crowed over their success. With other Indians, they might
laugh and mimic those poor villagers who had spotted the
raiders, yelled out, or tried ineffectually to stop the theft only to
find their corral woefully depleted or themselves choking in a
cloud of dust. Victorio's people often traded with men such as
José María de Zuloaga, James Kirker, or others of their ilk not because they trusted such individuals but because these men offered
the guns, bullets, knives, and tools that Cuchillo Negro and
Mangas Coloradas so very much desired. Sadly, the traders also
possessed whiskey, a popular item. Warriors might ransom an
Apache boy or girl or purchase a young Mexican slave during the
trade process. They might take home bolts of red woolen and calico, eating utensils, coffee and sugar, and maybe a frivolous item
or two such as perfume or a mirror. If they met other Indians on
the way home, the men might barter for pottery. Apache women
made few if any clay containers. Their own twined burden bas-
kets were sturdy and their pitched basketry was well made for water storage. But clay pottery was best for cooking over a fire.

With trading over and goods wrapped securely in hides and
tied across their horses' backs, Victorio's people followed the

well-traveled trail that led directly from Janos up to the copper mines and branched off toward the Cañada Alamosa. They often trailed a dozen or so cattle and horses, some gathered on the way home in impromptu raids. With the return of a victorious raiding party, the feasting, dancing, and distribution of goods began. Generosity was expected. Besides, women, children, and elders had all played a part in the success. While the raiders were gone, they had all prayed each morning and evening. Mothers and wives said special prayers when they cooked meat. Thus, the raid, like every other aspect of Apache life, entailed the assistance and sacrifices of all. It is worth noting that Apaches did not raid for the purpose of taking another's territory or expanding their land base.

The Kirker Attacks Increase

Mexican officials heard the complaints of villagers and ranchers who demanded that their government somehow stop the never-ending raids. Nothing seemed to work. Treaties with the Apaches lasted about as long as it took the ink to dry. For example, for several years the Gileños, including Victorio's people, and the Mescaleros had pressured Chihuahua authorities to end the scalp bounties and recognize exclusive Apache occupation of the copper mines. In February 1842, Chihuahua gave in on both counts and wrote a treaty with these groups. Before the year was out, however, the raids resumed, primarily because the very men who protested raids were often the first to purchase stolen property. For their part, Apaches found the raids too lucrative to give up, and besides, the Mexicans seldom honored the territorial restrictions. Chihuahua authorities contracted with the graying, steel-eyed Kirker once again and unleashed his band of nearly 150 mercenaries. Thus, another wave of terror began.

Described as a fearful set to behold, the bounty hunters armed themselves to the teeth with the newly invented Colt repeating revolvers, Sharps and Winchester rifles, and for hand-to-hand combat and mutilation purposes, they used tomahawks and knives. Reportedly, the mercenaries were perpetually drunk as

well. On May 24, 1846, Irigoyan was again governor of Chihuahua, and this time went even further than before. He handed
Kirker the authority to call upon state militia when he needed assistance. In essence, the governor placed official troops under a
civilian commander for the first time. Soldiers were now eligi-
ble to collect the scalp bounties, and the Irigoyan policy obliged
livestock owners to pay recovery fees and thereby subsidize the
entire operation.

Although raiding continued, the northern frontier grew increasingly bloody. In an event eerily similar to the Johnson
massacre of 1832, Kirker and the Mexican trader José María de
Zuloaga precipitated a July 6, 1846, massacre, which Apaches
called the "time when Mexicans were laying in wait to double-
cross us." The pair invited a group of mostly Chokonens, who
were camped near Janos, to visit and conduct some trade. Believing that they were under the protection of the latest treaty,
the Indians felt safe.

As custom dictated, Kirker and Zuloaga passed around huge
bowls of piñole and cooked meat to begin the proceedings.
Then out came the jugs of mescal and whiskey. Sated and ine-
briated, the Indians slept. As they did, the bounty hunters—who
had consumed far less alcohol than they made it appear—sav-
agely shot and clubbed to death 130 people, including women
and children. They scalped the dead and paraded the bloody tro-
phies before cheering crowds in Chihuahua City.

Victorio's people heard of this and picked up rumors describ-
ing how citizens in that town had strung ropes across their plaza
and hung Indian scalps as if these were drying laundry. Mangas
Coloradas vowed right then and there to kill any scalp hunter who
ventured into the copper mines region. For the time being, at
least, he would turn his attention to the newly arriving white settlers. These Americans also aroused Victorio's curiosity.

The Army of the West Makes Contact

On May 12, 1846, the U.S. government declared war on Mexico,
and on a steamy August 18th, Stephen Watts Kearny, a veteran

of the War of 1812 and popular military leader, marched his Army of the West into Santa Fe. The stern-faced colonel raised the Stars and Stripes over the Palace of the Governors and declared New Mexico a territory of the United States. A man generally adept at dealing with Indians, Kearny had successfully met with some of the Pueblos before entering New Mexico's capital. However, many of those who accompanied him carried preconceived notions, especially regarding Apaches. Susan Shelby Magoffin, who traveled down the Santa Fe Trail with her trader husband in 1846, entered Santa Fe with Kearny's troops. She had never encountered an Apache before in her young life and exhibited a common yet false belief when she wrote in her diary that Apaches "always want . . . scalps." Similarly, Lieutenant William H. Emory, who wrote the official regimental record, called Apaches "Negro-like" with "smirking, deceitful-looking countenances."

Like Americans across the country, Magoffin and Emory were imbued with the new spirit of Manifest Destiny. John O'Sullivan, editor of the popular *Democratic Review*, coined the term in 1845 to describe an evolving ideology of expansionism and American exceptionalism, a blusteringly aggressive mix of republican pride and religious fervor. Under the banner of Manifest Destiny, Americans boasted about their God-given destiny to expand American values from coast to coast. They pressured Congress and the president to seize British- and Spanish-occupied territory in the West. Expansionists also advocated removal, confinement, or even outright eradication of Indian peoples in these regions.

Kearny's army was the vanguard of Manifest Destiny in New Mexico. He occupied Santa Fe just long enough to secure the territory and establish a temporary government. Because Santa Feans feared that the rowdy Missourians, who composed much of the Army of the West—some of whom were even slave owners—might assault their religion, attack their women, and appropriate their meager material possessions, Kearny took great pains to maintain discipline among his troops. He personally attended a Catholic mass and with the help of lawyers wrote a provisional Bill of Rights in English and Spanish commonly called the Kearny Code. He appointed Charles Bent—one of the Bent brother traders of Colorado—as provisional governor. After six weeks in Santa Fe, Kearny divided his troops. He sent Colonel Alexander Doniphan to negotiate a peace treaty with Navajos and then head south into Chihuahua as part of the war strategy. Colonel Sterling Price remained in Santa Fe to maintain order and uphold the Code. Kearny himself marched to California to assist in the conquest of that territory. Most important to Victorio's story, Kearny's westward movement took him straight across Apachería.

From afar, Mangas Coloradas, Cuchillo Negro, and Victorio watched Kearny's army advance slowly towards Santa Rita del Cobre. But it was the former trapper and trader Christopher "Kit" Carson who arrived there first. Traveling from California, Carson and his companions carried messages for President James K. Polk from adventurer John C. Frémont, whose antics had provoked a rebellion against Spanish forces in California that came to be called the Bear Flag Revolt. Mangas Coloradas welcomed Carson. The Apache perhaps noted with a bit of inner satisfaction Carson's surprise on learning that an American general had recently taken possession of Santa Fe. "He is at this very moment heading in this direction," Carson was told. Thanking Mangas, Carson rode forward to meet Kearny, whose delight at Carson's sudden appearance was obvious. Kearny persuaded the experienced guide to send a contingent of his men to Washington with Frémont's message, but to remain behind and pilot Kearny into Apache country.

Carson agreed and led the line of soldiers into the Black Mountains. As they threaded their way down narrow trails and over treacherous arroyos, Lt. Emory observed dense stands of cottonwood shrouding the now swollen riverbanks. He wrote in his official journal that walnut, ash, cedar, and mountain mahogany grew in profusion along the river bottoms. The Mimbres River, he later noted, spanned about fifteen feet wide and ran three feet deep; it was perfect for irrigating American fields. As they neared the deserted Santa Rita copper mines, Emory realized that the place was a ghost town. Buildings were silent and windswept. Although deserted, there was evidence that white men had once lived there.

At Santa Lucia Spring, about thirteen miles from the copper mines, Kearny met his first Apaches. Emory's colorful account accurately describes Indian men dressed in a typical hybrid costume of Mexican-made cotton shirts and white trousers and Apache-style buckskin breechcloths and leggings, obviously the result of extensive trade and two centuries of living side by side. In classic Chihenne fashion, all wore the distinctive tall buckskin moccasins that could be pulled up to cover most of the leg if necessary, but were usually folded to just below the knees. A rounded, turned-up toe—commonly called a nose—provided added protection against cactus thorns and spiny desert brush. Because soles in particular wore out quickly, Victorio's Chihennes always carried pre-cut rawhide to make emergency repairs.

Although Emory saw clearly that each warrior was armed with full cartridge "boxes" strapped to his waist, he undoubtedly missed the multitude of knives carefully concealed in moccasin folds. Emory noted that none of the warriors wore feather bonnets, which he apparently had expected to see. Instead, they sported what he described as elaborately plumed, intricately decorated helmets, which reminded him of the headgear of Grecian warriors. These were undoubtedly the Chihenne medicine hats.

The awe-inspiring and gregarious Mangas Coloradas now greeted Kearny. He expressed his affection for Americans, but wanted to know if they were allies of the Chihennes since they were enemies of the Mexicans. Mangas presented mules, ropes, and mescal to Kearny's men, and in return, Kearny passed around red shirts, blankets, needles and thread, and brightly colored handkerchiefs. The American colonel informed Mangas Coloradas that his people could become allies only if the Apaches stopped raiding. The more introspective Victorio, who was probably there, must have felt his heart sink. These Americans, he undoubtedly reasoned, were not necessarily friends. And they appeared far better organized than the Mexicans. Mangas, however, forever remained hopeful.

Two years later, the Mexican War ended. On February 2, 1948, the United States and Mexico signed the Treaty of Guadalupe Hidalgo, thereby agreeing among other things to halt Apache raids into Mexico. Still, Victorio undoubtedly shrugged if off. What was a border, after all? Gouyen's prophetic observation was more accurate: "Nothing good has ever come from Washington." Nevertheless, in October 1846, when Kearny concluded his meeting with Mangas Coloradas and continued west, the treaty was still two years in the future, and for the time being, at least, Chihennes could return to life as usual.

Victorio Gets Married

According to oral histories, Victorio married for the first time in 1846. Sadly, just as the name of his mother is lost to history, neither did the name of his first wife survive in written records. According to his descendants, however, young Bi-duye first laid eyes on his future wife at her puberty ceremony. He was one of the many visitors who brought gifts and asked her to bestow White Painted Woman's blessings upon him. Bi-duye did not see her again until after he had completed his dihoke training and established himself as a warrior.

Victorio was described as tall, "but not nearly as tall as Mangas Coloradas," and some considered him handsome. A single photograph of him is said to exist. It was taken at the Ojo Caliente or Warm Springs Agency circa 1877, when he was about fifty years old. His hair was noticeably streaked with gray and also a bit disheveled. He reportedly did not want his picture taken and struggled with agency officials to avoid the camera lens. In the end, he lost the skirmish as well as the headband that always kept his hair in place. Given his serene expression—and the fact that in 1877 a person had to sit immobile before the camera lens for nearly three full minutes—this story is somewhat unconvincing.

According to his great-granddaughter, Victorio was instantly smitten with the woman who would become his first wife. Apache convention prevented the two from speaking privately

Lesser-known photograph of Victorio and perhaps taken under duress.
Courtesy of Arizona Historical Society, Tucson (AHS 19748).

to each other. Her people always chaperoned when they met.
But eventually Victorio felt certain that she might seriously consider accepting him as her husband. At that point, he offered his
most valuable possessions to her parents. His future in-laws

took the gifts and thereby agreed to the marriage. Because marriage took place in the heart—especially a first marriage—they arranged no formal ceremony. The girl's parents did, however, announce the union and begin immediately to gather the venison, corn, fruits, and maybe a little freshly brewed tizwin to feed guests for four days of visiting and late-night dancing. Tizwin was made from the heart of the mescal plant. Sometimes mistakenly confused with tulapai, tizwin required a long time to brew and for that reason was used primarily for ceremonies such as wedding feasts. It also spoiled easily and therefore was usually drunk rapidly and in large quantities. At sunset on the fourth day, the wedding feast was over and the marriage was considered completed. The marriage union was sacred and, except in rare instances, permanent.

Unless his father was a warrior of some status—and we do not know if this was so—Victorio left his own rancheria to live with his wife's people. His mother-in-law painstakingly constructed the couple's first wickiup, and then she and Victorio never spoke directly to each other again. Victorio hunted, fought, and raided with his new father-in-law and wife's brothers, and his skills contributed to the well-being of this band. We do not know for certain if he lived with Cuchillo Negro's band. His name is sometimes linked with Ponce, a Mexican-educated chief, whose local territory was the farthest east of all Chihennes, and who, like Victorio, always maintained good relations with the Mescaleros. Less frequently, we see him with Delgadito, a warrior whose ultimate rejection of Americans would attract warriors of like mind. Or Bi-duye could have married into the rancheria of any number of subchiefs whose names never made it into the history books.

Still, as a married man, Victorio interacted regularly with Mangas Coloradas, who camped regularly at Warm Springs. His children remembered the six-foot, five-inch giant as quick to laugh and willing to hoist child after child high over his head in thrilling play. Mangas traveled with several wives and often a captive Mexican girl or two. He was a master at using marriage to create strong alliances. The most important of these was the marriage of his daughter Dos-the-she to Cochise. Later, his son

Mangas married Victorio's eldest daughter, Dilth-cleyhen. Another Copper Mines Chihenne leader named Itan sometimes accompanied Mangas Coloradas to the Warm Springs. Therefore, Victorio's name is linked, albeit less frequently, with Itan. Mangas Coloradas and Itan regularly warred and raided in Sonora, and both made Janos a sort of second home. Although Victorio undoubtedly accompanied them from time to time, he is most often associated with southern New Mexico and Chihuahua.

Victorio endured a periodically volatile relationship with his cousin Loco, whom some dubbed "feeble-minded" and whom Kaywaykla claimed was never truly a chief. Dilth-cleyhen called Loco crazy because he had done the unthinkable; he had killed a bear in his youth, and even more incredibly, using only a knife. Loco's face bore the disfigurement of that long-ago grizzly attack. His left cheek was deeply scarred and his left eyelid hung limply over the eye, giving him a rather sinister expression. Because the bear had gouged a chunk from one leg, Loco limped noticeably. By killing the grizzly, Loco transferred some of bear's power into himself, including a fiery temper. Everybody agreed that he was entitled to wear the bear's claw on a string around his neck, even though virtually no other Apache dared touch even a dead bear. It made Loco feared as well as respected.

Both Loco and Victorio excelled at raiding and frequently went together. But, despite their blood ties, Loco's outbursts alienated Victorio. Worse, the two vehemently disagreed over how one was supposed to treat slaves. Loco once beat a captive Mexican girl to death. Outraged, Victorio avoided his cousin for months. They reconciled, but soon after, Loco stabbed and killed a Mexican slave who belonged to Victorio. A hard worker, the girl was learning to speak the Apache language and teaching Apache children a little Spanish. Victorio and his family liked her. One day while Victorio was away, Loco ordered her to gather his firewood. She refused and reminded Loco that she belonged to Victorio's family. Livid, Loco pulled his knife and drove it into her heart. When Victorio returned, he fiercely confronted his cousin. "Shi-zooleh-ne-ee!" he snapped, meaning "You make me so angry, the blood goes to my throat!" Loco's people quietly folded up camp and moved away, and it was a long time before the two met again.

Mostly, when the various Chihenne bands came together, they visited. The men might satisfy their hunger with venison meat and corn and afterward hand-roll a concoction of tobacco and dried leaves into makeshift cigarettes. Sitting around a warm evening fire watching the smoke curl upwards, they told tales of their war party adventures and boasted of their most successful raids. Most important, they planned future missions. As talk continued, the men undoubtedly laughed about the strange mannerisms of the Mexicans with whom they traded and wondered when white men would return once more to the copper mines. These intrusions into Mother Earth, they believed, caused the small earthquakes that occasionally shook the ground in that region. During these gatherings, women shared their work, gossiped, and talked about their children.

Victorio's first child, a daughter named Dilth-cleyhen, was born in 1848, somewhere in the Cañada Alamosa. Like all Apache parents, Bi-duye and his wife adored and pampered their child, sometimes jokingly calling her "One Who Really Gets Around" because she proved an extremely active toddler. Dilth-cleyhen lived to be more than seventy years old. Victorio's first son, Washington, was born a few years later. His last son, Charlie Istee, was born in 1872. Although we know little about them, there were two middle children, probably daughters.

Dilth-cleyhen later told her own daughter that food was relatively plentiful during her childhood days. Her mother taught her that most of the things they ate grew in a special place and in a special season, and she came to love the complex but free hunting and gathering lifestyle of the Apaches. Women, she said, took the lead in obtaining food. It was their responsibility to keep everybody fed. However, they seldom made direct demands. An older woman might say "I'm hungry for mesquite," knowing that right then plenty of it was ripe for harvesting along the Rio Grande. She meant that it was time to move camp, a decision which required the men's participation. Later, when Victorio's people were restricted to reservations, a small contingent of women with only a few boys to protect them as they worked would slip away to gather the wild crops. But when Dilth-cleyhen was a child, gathering food still involved everyone.

"The mescal is ready to harvest!" meant a trip of several weeks to Mount Graham in Arizona, where the women and children gathered maguey heads, lined a dug-out pit with them, and cooked the plants down to a pulp. Afterward, the mescal was cooled, dried, and sliced for the trip home. Along the way the band might stop briefly to harvest wild strawberries, onions, or greens. The women brought most of what they gathered back to camp, but stashed the more durable surpluses in remote caves for when they traveled. Nana's grandson recalled, "We also left cooking utensils . . . blankets, bales of calico, and other commodities." By the 1870s, these became emergency rations, which meant life or death to those fleeing American soldiers. Even Apache children kept a small buckskin pouch of dried meat and perhaps mescal or nuts tied to their waists. To do otherwise could mean starvation.

Dilth-cleyhen learned her lessons well. She understood the importance of generosity. One day when she was old enough to help her mother sew her father's buckskin leggings and quiver, Victorio returned from a raid. He trailed a wagon full of groceries and bolts of colorful cloth. He said something like, "This is your first booty to be divided, my daughter," but cautioned Dilth-cleyhen, "divide it fairly among the people." She took great pains to give calico cloth to each woman and first to distribute the food to widows and elders. Victorio was proud of her. The wagon, Dilth-cleyhen recalled, came from a raid on a small wagon train, but with the arrival of the Americans after 1848, trade grew more lucrative and large-scale raiding increased.

Raiding-and-Trading Finds Expanded Markets

Once news of gold discoveries at John Sutter's mill near Sacramento, California, leaked out, adventurers calling themselves forty-niners streamed west. Hot on their heels came the merchants, prostitutes, gamblers, and ne'er-do-wells out to profit from the gold seekers. Many followed trails across southern New Mexico to avoid the high Rockies farther north. Everyone seemed to need livestock, and traders turned to their Indian partners for merchandise. Consequently, Chihuahua and Sonora experienced a new flurry of raids, and greater stores of contraband weapons and whiskey found their way into the hands of Apaches and Comanches.

Kirker guaranteed himself a profit on both ends. The Chihuahua legislature passed the Kirker Bill, or Fifth Law, on May 25, 1849, again giving him carte blanche to slaughter Indians. The law stipulated that the government pay 200 pesos for each "barbarous" Indian warrior killed, 250 pesos for any warrior taken alive, and 150 pesos for women and children captives. Sonora and Durango bore the brunt of these raids, which grew so frequent that at least twice Sonoran militias invaded Chihuahua in an attempt to retrieve the stolen goods.

In June 1849, Sonora and Durango enacted their own versions of the Fifth Law. The federal government declared all such laws unconstitutional on July 20, but the three states defied Mexico City. Worse, Mexican villagers and Opata and Tarahumara farmers discovered that they could earn more money from a single scalp than from a year of back-breaking farm labor. As scalps accumulated, authorities, as before, doubted that all of them belonged to Indians.

Janos was, as usual, the primary distribution hub, and Sonorans accused Janoseros of harboring thieves and stolen goods. The region grew more violent as a result. In summer 1850, for instance, Victorio heard of another attack on peaceful Apaches, this time on a group of Bedonkohes—Geronimo's band— camped there. En route to Casas Grandes, they had camped outside Janos for a few days. While some of the men went into the old presidio to trade, citizens attacked the camp, killing women, children, and elders. At first, Geronimo believed that his mother, wife, and children were taken captive. When he searched for them, however, he found their mutilated bodies in a pool of blood. The upsurge in violence moved right up into Chihenne country as well.

Some forty-niners stopped long enough to scour the hills of New Mexico and Arizona for traces of gold. They found the Piños Altos region in the heart of Chihenne country promising. Some prospectors stayed and others returned when placer gold played out in California, often invading Chihenne land and sparking occasional conflicts with Victorio's people. The federal government, which was now in charge, never seemed to see the urgency of the situation. Another problem was that the Treaty of Guadalupe Hidalgo obliged the United States to protect Mexicans from the Indians, but not the Indians from Mexicans, gold-seekers, or even Kirker's bounty hunters.

A third difficulty concerned the very nature of New Mexico. Formally organized as a territory in 1850, New Mexico had the sixty thousand population required for statehood, but the majority of these were Mexicans and Indians, hence the wrong kind of people. Thus, New Mexico remained a sort of poor relation within the United States. Governors were appointed and served at the pleasure of the president. They were also commanders-in-chief and, until 1857, superintendents of Indian Affairs as well. Most were eastern and unfamiliar with western ways. James S. Calhoun, an amiable Georgia businessman, was the first governor under the formal territorial setup.

Calhoun arrived with instructions to negotiate treaties with all of the Indians. He discovered, much to his dismay, that it was unsafe to travel more than ten miles from Santa Fe. Blaming traders who provided guns, ammunition, and liquor, he issued regulations requiring that all those operating in the territory obtain an official license. However, just as Calhoun could not safely travel outside of Santa Fe, neither could he enforce his regulations. Furthermore, far-off Washington, D.C., afforded no support. For one thing, the annexation of Spanish territory had intensified the slave-versus-free state debate, and throughout most of 1849–50 Congress worried about avoiding a civil war.

Calhoun tried an alternative approach. He began to organize a territorial militia under Kit Carson and another experienced mountain man named Ceràn St. Vrain. The problem was that the newly appointed commander of the U.S. military in New Mexico, Lieutenant Colonel Edwin V. Sumner, arrived in 1851 determined that only the regular military would deal with Indians. Sumner pulled most of the soldiers out of the towns and stationed them in forts on the so-called Indian frontier. He established a military headquarters at Fort Union, but smaller forts and outposts went up in Apache and Navajo country as well. By 1860, there were some sixteen established posts, many of which closed when the Civil War broke out in 1861. Sumner wanted no assistance from local militias and no interference from the governor. This relationship set a precedent between military and civilian authorities that would be repeated many times over the next several decades. However, in 1852, Calhoun became gravely ill and died. Sumner considered himself acting governor until the arrival of a new appointee, and thus, for about a year, headed up both the U.S. military in New Mexico and that territory's highest civilian office.

The United States Draws a Border

Victorio and his Chihenne people received their first extended look at Americans from the International Boundary Commission, which arrived in April 1851 to survey and establish the political border between the United States and Mexico in accordance with the Treaty of Guadalupe Hidalgo. From a distance, Victorio, Cuchillo Negro, Ponce, and Mangas Coloradas studied the commission under John Russell Bartlett. They watched eight-five infantrymen escort a parade of heavy wagons and livestock and deposit nearly three hundred men, including prison labor from Chihuahua, at the copper mines. The white men took up residence in the abandoned adobe shacks and what remained of a decades-old triangular-shaped structure, which was once a presidio headquarters and jail for their Indian labor. The Chihennes knew the place well because Santa Rita del Cobre was the heart of Mangas Coloradas's country, and Victorio visited it regularly.

Bartlett called his camp Cantonment Dawson. He noted the occasional untended orchard or farm in the vicinity and sensed an uneasy lull hovering over the copper mines. They were deep in Apache country, he told his men. "There is scarcely a family in the frontier towns but has suffered the loss of one or more of its members or friends," he wrote. "No American can possibly conjecture the terror felt by the people of all classes, whenever it was announced that the Apaches were near," the official interpreter of the party, John Cremony, added. For some reason, Bartlett immediately singled out Mangas Coloradas, Delgadito, and Ponce as the worst of the lot, but to his credit, acknowledged that many flagrant acts of injustice had been committed against them as well. In ten months, Bartlett must have met Victorio, but perhaps the Chihenne's quiet manner made him less visible.

Mangas Coloradas was first to greet the commissioners. Eventually, most Chihennes ventured forth, and the visits grew more frequent. The Copper Mines and Warm Springs Apaches brought food to share and offered trade goods. Once they became comfortable with whites, the Apache men and women liked to congregate around the interpreter's tent in the evenings. Cremony's account praises their soft voices. They never interrupt each other as white men so often do, he wrote. He noticed a great deal of laughter among the Apaches.

Although Cremony also failed to notice Victorio, he found one woman especially intriguing. She rode with the men and boasted of her ability to steal horses: her name, in fact, meant Dexterous Horse Thief. Of course, all Apache women could shoot guns, wield knives, and ride horses, just as the men mastered cooking and sewing. With few notable exceptions, though, women did not raid with the men. One who remained unmarried all of her life and served her people as a warrior was Victorio's sister, Lozen, but it seems highly unlikely that Lozen and Dexterous Horse Thief were one and the same because Lozen was only eleven or so years of age in 1851.

Despite friendly relations, Chihennes and Americans clashed during the ten-month stay, and disagreements reveal deep cultural misunderstandings between Victorio's people and these newcomers. In one instance, three Mexican traders arrived at the copper mines with a young captive girl, whom they had just purchased. Appalled, Bartlett freed her, but his act gave thirteen-year-old Savero Aredia and eleven-year-old José Trinfan the courage to seize the moment. The two boys slipped away from their Apache captors and threw themselves on Bartlett's mercy in hopes of securing freedom. They belonged in Delgadito's band, but it was Chief Ponce who initially stepped forward to demand their immediate return. Translations went through Cremony. He blustered, however, that Ponce's was a ridiculous request. Delgadito interjected, "An elder of my people purchased these boys six years earlier with the blood of his relatives. You have no right to interfere!" Bartlett offered $250 for the boys. Delgadito refused, but Ponce—the cooler head at the moment—persuaded his fellow leader to take the deal, realizing perhaps that Americans did not understand the concept of taking and adopting captives.

A second disagreement erupted on July 6. Neither of these directly involved Victorio's band, but both taught him much about whites. Jesus Lopez, one of the Mexican laborers, shot and killed an Apache. Bartlett clapped Lopez in chains, but added that Lopez would be punished when they returned to Santa Fe. "Now!" Mangas Coloradas demanded. Apaches wanted to know if their American brothers would do them justice. Bartlett snapped that the commission needed his labor and offered trade goods as a substitute. Victorio must have reflected on how Americans could equate an Apache life with a piece of cloth or a few head of cattle. What Victorio could not have known—and what Bartlett left unarticulated—was that white men considered it unthinkable to allow the Native justice system to punish wrongdoers. As early as the Pilgrim's Treaty of 1621 with the Pokanokets of Massachusetts, the ethnocentric presumption that Europeans were the epitome of law and justice dominated Indian-white relations. To turn even prison labor over to Apache justice was, in the eyes of Americans, a preposterous notion.

Ponce again stepped in: The dead man's mother wanted blood, not goods. But Bartlett came up with a diversion. He told Ponce that a group of renegade Apaches had recently killed several white men unrelated to the commission. If you want us to punish

Lopez here and now, Bartlett told him, you must do something for us. He demanded that Ponce capture the culprits and bring them in to show good faith. Realizing the impasse, Ponce reluctantly took the equivalent of Lopez's wages—probably in food, metal tools, and cloth—for however long the Commission remained at the copper mines. But the Apaches, including Victorio, left with the knowledge that Americans did not trust them.

Much to Victorio's relief, the Commission left Cantonment Dawson in January 1852. They had done their job poorly, and in 1853, the federal government was forced to send James Gadsden to Mexico City to renegotiate. The resulting Gadsden Treaty, which annexed thirty thousand square miles to the United States—land which the Chihenne Apaches considered theirs—was ratified in 1854 and the transfer was made in 1856. The fertile Mesilla Valley—Mescalero country—and land south of the Gila River—mostly Chihenne homeland—now fell under American control. The treaty restricted American and Mexican troops from crossing the border without first obtaining permission from the other government, and although formal talks went on sporadically for decades, the matter remained legally murky. The treaty did nothing to curtail scalp hunters. Shortly after the Commission's departure, the army established Fort Webster on the site on September 9, 1852. Although, technically, Fort Webster occupied land that Mangas Coloradas considered his, for Victorio the encroachment was too close for comfort. He grew increasingly wary.

The Revolving-Door Bureaucracy

The International Boundary Commission was merely the first of many American intrusions. Next came the Indian agents. The Indian Office appointed the agents, and there was no agency in Washington more corrupt. In addition, its officials made decisions with glacial speed—something Victorio would soon discover—and slow communications with agents in the field only intensified the situation. Most agents were products of the spoils system, and the majority sent to Victorio's Warm Springs people would prove no exception. Adding to that was a sort of turf war between the Department of War, which had originally housed the Indian Office, and the Department of the Interior, where Congress transferred the office in 1849. For most of his time dealing with Americans, Victorio would feel the impact of this jurisdictional battle. In a very real sense, he would find himself caught between civilian and military policies.

Interior created agencies and superintendencies across Indian country, often with little attention paid to need. An agent was usually responsible for a single tribe or for several bands within the same tribe. In the case of the Apaches, such an arrangement proved challenging. An Indian agent negotiated treaties and suggested reservation sites, distributed supplies, and oversaw the tribe's welfare. Apaches blamed the agents when Congress cut rations or when supplies never arrived at all, and indeed, too many corrupt agents siphoned off government money or contracted for substandard products.

A superintendent was in charge of all agents within a given state or territory, but ultimately the Indian Office made the final decisions and Congress approved or disapproved the budget and controlled the purse strings with the generosity of an Ebenezer Scrooge. There were always too few agents, especially good ones as Victorio would find out, too much corruption, and in the case of New Mexico, a chain of command stretched two thousand miles. Needless to say, few remained very long, and it is doubtful that Victorio laid eyes on many of them. Jack Hays was the first in 1849, but he came and went even before the border commission arrived. His report of January 3, 1850—which also served as a notice of resignation—blamed Kirker for his inability to meet with the Apaches. One band, possibly Loco's, had approached the agent's camp on the Cañada Alamosa, but before making contact, they reportedly spotted a large group of riders approaching their location. Fearing bounty hunters, the band quickly dispersed and never returned. Hays apparently felt he had seen enough to call Apaches treacherous, warlike and cruel, but thought they could be made to "observ[e] good faith with the white people." Nevertheless, the job proved frustrating for him.

After Governor Calhoun's death and before the next governor arrived, Edwin V. Sumner was both military commander and unofficial acting governor. John Greiner was acting Indian agent and superintendent. On July 1, 1852, Greiner and Sumner summoned Chihennes and Bedonkohes to Acoma Pueblo to negotiate a treaty. The Senate ratified this treaty on March 23, 1853. It called upon Apaches to acknowledge U.S. jurisdiction over them, permit military posts on their land, return captives, and stay out of Mexico. Although Itan and others attended the negotiations, Mangas Coloradas was seemingly the only Chihenne to actually sign the treaty. One reason is that at the same time, a large war party that included Ponce, Cuchillo Negro, Delgadito, and Nednhi leader Laceres had ridden into Mexico to avenge an attack on one of their camps. It is probable that Victorio was with that war party. When they returned in August, however, Greiner was waiting for them at Fort Webster. He noted that three chiefs—Mangas Coloradas, Ponce, and Itan—seemed to wield primary control. Although these men reportedly agreed to sign the treaty, their names do not appear on the final copy.

William Carr Lane was named to replace Calhoun in September 1852 and arrived in New Mexico later that year. During his one-year administration, Lane accomplished two things in the area of Indian affairs. He managed to spend all of the available money, and in April 1853, he negotiated a provisional compact probably intended to supplement the Treaty of July 1852, which Congress never ratified. The document was notable, however, because it was the first to bear Victorio's name—printed as "Victoria"—and his thumbprint. The eleven chiefs who "signed" agreed to "settle down," appoint chiefs to represent them, and select permanent campsites. In return, the federal government promised written grants to their land, but these would not convey military protection. Although this treaty seems on the surface to contradict the whole fabric of Apache custom, a closer look suggests otherwise. It committed the United States to supply corn, beef, and salt, brood mares, sheep, and cattle, all surplus trade items. Land guarantees meant fewer intrusions, and the absence of military protection probably led them to believe that the soldiers at Fort Webster would leave. From an American vantage point, the treaty seems lacking. To Victorio, it guaranteed land, freedom, and trade goods, and resolved to control scalp hunters. It is perhaps more curious that Mangas Coloradas signed the original Treaty of July 1852, which forbade incursions into Mexico, although there is some evidence that Sumner privately gave Mangas tacit permission to continue his Mexican raids.

The compact of 1853 suggested that the Warm Springs people establish their camps west of Fort Webster and well away from white settlements. It is almost certain that those who signed assumed the government would exclude whites from that region. Victorio's name on the document tells us that he was by this time serving as second to either Cuchillo Negro or Mangas Coloradas because one of the them—and probably both—held him in high esteem. Moreover, his signature brought him to the attention of Indian agent Michael Steck.

Steck was not the second Indian agent or even the third. After Hays's departure came Edmond A. Graves, who was named agent of what was now designated the Southern Apache Agency and included both Warm Springs and Mangas Coloradas's Copper Mines Apaches. He was not especially effective. On September 1, 1853—three agents later—an energetic young man named James M. Smith arrived. Over the next several months, he conducted a survey of the Apaches, moved the agency to newly established Fort Thorn (near present-day Hatch), and died suddenly on December 15. In May 1854, former military physician Michael Steck was named agent of the Southern Apache Agency. President Millard Fillmore had already appointed this Jefferson Medical College (Philadelphia) graduate as Mescalero Apache agent in 1852. This was his first appointment to the Indian Service.

Dr. Steck jotted a brief question onto a morsel of paper one day while looking over the unratified compact: "Why is Lucero Victoria?" Bi-duye's name was frequently misspelled as Victoria—as it was on that treaty—so there is little doubt about whom Steck was referring. Just as Mangas Coloradas was probably called Fuerte before 1835, is it possible that at one time Victorio was dubbed Lucero? If so, it gives us one more glimpse into Victorio's hidden life, and it suggests that the water hole called Lucero Spring was one of Victorio's frequent campsites. Maybe it was his favorite.

Steck proved one of the very few dedicated agents assigned to Victorio's people. Honest and hardworking, he gained their trust despite Congress's failure to ratify the provisional compact and, consequently, his own inability to supply rations. Named to the position in May, the new agent was not able to begin until August 1854. But upon his arrival, Steck immediately swept through Chihenne country to meet the principal chiefs. They at first refused, sending word to him that they had settled into permanent camps and were no longer raiding. But where were the gifts? What happened to the rations? Steck appealed to Governor David Meriwether, whom President Franklin K. Pierce had appointed in 1853 to succeed Lane, only to discover that Governor Lane had exhausted nearly all of the Indian funds. So, he would receive no help from Santa Fe. Steck later got word that Chief Ponce had died earlier that summer, killed at the hands of his own people in a "drunken frolic." Given the anti-Apache rhetoric of the day, it is difficult to know whether Ponce indeed drank to excess. Regardless of how he died, another conciliatory voice was gone.

When Victorio rode into the agency in May 1855, he found the doctor demonstrating to a few old men how to plant corn using hoes rather than the Apache digging stick. Victorio also noticed that as Steck built mounds of soil and placed the seeds in rows, he forgot to pray. What a foolish man, he must have muttered. How did Steck think corn would grow without spiritual assistance? But the agent had summoned him. The new governor wanted the Apache leaders to meet him at Fort Thorn.

Thus, on June 7, 1855, most of the chiefs assembled, as per the request. Two notables were missing: Mangas Coloradas was ill, and Cuchillo Negro was in Mexico. Itan, Delgadito, and several Mescalero chiefs were there. Meriwether described the building in which they met as twenty-five feet by eighteen feet, with two windows, one door, and a temperature inside of about 106 degrees. Onlookers crammed into the tiny room, adding humid-

Site of the Warm Springs Apache Reservation. Courtesy of Center for Southwest Research, University of New Mexico. Indians of North America Collection (negative #994-002-0008).

ity. An elderly Chihenne woman, whom the Americans called Monica, translated. As talks began, a fight broke out between a Mescalero and a Chihenne, and the latter was killed. Such violence did not bode well for a good outcome.

The Apaches quickly discovered that the Americans wanted land. This came as no surprise to Victorio. Those who eventually signed ceded 15,000 square miles of land in exchange for $67,000 paid over twenty-six years, health care, and education. The Indians retained about two thousand square miles. In the end, Congress refused to ratify the new treaty because, as the Senate deliberated, rumors of gold, silver, and copper discovered on Mimbres land reached their ears. Thus, they opted not to act for fear of giving away valuable mineral lands. It is doubtful that anyone reported the failed treaty to Victorio, Itan, or Delgadito. But one result of that failure was that Steck continually ran short of rations. Moreover, Steck began to realize that he had better finalize a permanent reservation before it was too late.

For now, Victorio's people hunted. But it was imperative that they secure rations before winter, because even Steck could see that wildlife was becoming harder to locate. If Victorio obeyed the agent's request to remain in one place, the ability of his people to find wild foods was compromised. Naturally, some women had made the usual trip for mescal, piñon nuts, and yucca flowers, but Victorio could spare fewer warriors to protect them these days, and hence that meant less time spent gathering the crops and preparing them for travel home. It was not at all certain that there would be sufficient food to sustain Victorio's people throughout the winter.

There was still raiding, and in summer 1855, Chihennes and Bedonkohes swept into Galeana for livestock and captives. They fled with their goods to the copper mines, but this time Sonoran troops followed them right over the border and captured forty-two Apaches. In October and November, Delgadito led two small raiding parties to La Mesilla, but New Mexicans protested to Santa Fe authorities and 121 ranchers and farmers turned to the federal courts with a $500,000 lawsuit that attorney John S. Watts demanded be paid out of Indian appropriations. The secretary of the interior eventually denied their suit, and relations between Americans and Apaches became increasingly volatile.

Some New Mexicans took the law into their own hands. The Mesilla Guard went into the field. Modeled after the old Spanish mobile cavalry units, the Guard had formed in 1851 in large part to protect the area left out of the original border survey. The Mesilla Valley had become prime for malcontents, debtors, deserters from the army, smugglers, and fugitives of all kinds. Conflicts with the Apaches sometimes resulted. Furthermore, over time Texans and southerners dominated this region and, in fact, would petition for separate territorial status in 1856. Sadly, too many of these men exhibited no respect for Indians or Mexican Americans. On the other hand, the Guard also had its share of ne'er-do-wells, and in 1855 Steck accused members of stealing Mescalero livestock. In January 1857, some of the Guard murdered innocent Apaches in the Florida Mountains and in the streets of Doña Ana itself. "Mesilla complains, but brings it on itself," Steck wrote.

In fall 1855, Captain Joseph Eaton, commander at Fort Thorn, decided to personally pursue the Apache leader Delgadito. Eaton and sixty-one of his soldiers marched straight into the copper mines country, hot on the trail of innocent Chihennes, not Delgadito's raiders. Somewhere along the line, Eaton had crossed trails, a mistake that occurred too frequently. All this activity heightened tensions in southern New Mexico. In early 1856, Victorio, Mangas, and a young warrior named Negrito, who seems to have succeeded Ponce, raided in Mexico and upon their return showed Steck their new inventory of recently acquired Sharps rifles, Colt revolvers, and a modern invention—matches—which they had carefully wrapped in buckskin. If Steck could not provide rations and supplies, Victorio told him, they would help themselves.

In 1855, after leading Copper Mines Chihennes for more than twenty years, the aging Mangas Coloradas moved his camp closer to the agency, in part to distance himself from Delgadito and those who challenged the Americans. With Ponce dead, Mangas and other moderates like Cuchillo Negro would have to figure out how to coexist with whites. Then, suddenly, on May 24, 1857, Cuchillo Negro was killed accidentally by American soldiers under Benjamin L. E. Bonneville. They were seeking those responsible for the murder of Navajo agent Henry Linn Dodge, and Cuchillo Negro was an innocent bystander. With his loss and with Mangas Coloradas taking a less active role, Victorio assumed greater leadership. He was considered moderate in his views and actions at this time.

The Need for a Permanent Reservation

Although willing to deal with whites, Victorio did not curtail his raiding activities. For one thing, they were quickly becoming his primary means of survival. In summer 1857, he and Mangas Coloradas joined Cochise to raid and trade livestock with none other than Zuloaga. While at Janos, Mangas's band suddenly came down with a mysterious illness that killed many of them. Steck later diagnosed the ailment as either strychnine or arsenic poisoning. To avoid further affliction, Mangas Coloradas and Cochise struck out for Sonora, while Victorio's Chihennes, still healthy, stayed on at Janos until early 1858. The selective nature of the poisoning episode caused Steck—and later some historians—to speculate that somebody targeted Mangas Coloradas. The cloud of suspicion, without much proof to back it up, most often falls on Zuloaga. If correct, the fact that Victorio's band was not poisoned reinforces his role as a moderate.

Afterward, Steck tried harder than ever to entice Victorio and Mangas to remain in their permanent camps and begin farming. His request deepened in early 1858 when Leonard Secaurus reopened the Santa Rita copper mines. A permanent reservation could wait no longer, Steck concluded. "This valley is large enough to locate the Mimbres and Mogollon Bands . . . with the Mescaleros," he wrote to Washington. He established a new agency on the southern bank of the upper Alamosa River near Fort Craig in 1859 and called it the Warm Springs or Ojo Caliente Agency, but got little cooperation from Meriwether, who, Steck seemed to believe, took every opportunity to interfere with his work. Significantly, one of the previous agents, Edmond Graves, had subsequently married Meriwether's daughter. Never a friend of the Indian, Graves had voiced little hope for them in his June 1854 report to the Indian Office. "All that can be expected from an enlightened and Christian government, such as ours is, is to graduate and smooth the pass-way of their final exit from the stage of human existence." Like agent Hays's in 1850, Graves's report and resignation was written as a single document. Was Meriwether's relationship with the former agent part of his difficulty with Steck? It is almost impossible to determine. It was, however, a happy day for Steck when Meriwether resigned as governor in late 1857 and left New Mexico. Still, the ultimate decision regarding a permanent reservation for the Chihennes could come only from Washington, not from Sante Fe. Steck could not have predicted that his simple request would take the Indian Office more than twenty years to address and ultimately cost Victorio and most of his Warm Springs people their lives.

CHAPTER 4

The Civil War in Apachería

AS the United States edged closer to civil war, so, too, did Victorio's warriors engage in more frequent fighting, sometimes against other Indian bands but most often against Mexicans or the occasional local militias. Dilth-cleyhen recalled one night in 1860 when the men prepared for war. The specially selected di-yins had fasted and begun a prescribed ritual of prayer and songs as was their custom. As the time for battle grew near, women gathered piles of wood and brush and built a roaring fire in anticipation of the war or "angriness dance." Around the fire, di-yins and elders seated themselves in a circle. Then the warriors joined them. Mothers, wives, and daughters sat in an even larger circle behind the men, praying and softly chanting.

Dilth-cleyhen remembered that night because the elders always chose one warrior to begin the war dance, and on this particular evening they called upon her father. Although a child at the time, she remembered that this was when relations between whites and Apaches were starting to deteriorate, so perhaps the Chihennes planned to retaliate for some depredation with a surprise attack on a company of soldiers. Bi-duye, she said, was naked from the waist up. He wore only the wide breechcloth that hung to his ankles. He stood up and moved slowly into the center of the circle. Victorio then tucked the rear flap of his breechcloth between his legs and into the front of his belt. Now free to move about, he solemnly began to dance in place. After a while, three warriors joined him. All danced in place, changed sides, and repeated the steps. They carefully performed each sequence four times, while behind them rose the steady and hypnotic drumbeat and chant of the singers. Nobody shouted,

Dilth-cleyhen said. Nobody called out. Mostly the people seated around the fire uttered prayers that to an outside listener might sound a bit like "wah, wah."

Victorio's people also clashed with white men in the year or so before the American Civil War. Contrary to later movie stereotypes, however, war was not a constant, and in many instances came about only after whites encroached. By 1860, Victorio undoubtedly realized that treaties did not protect his Chihennes and that the whites kept arriving. The Americans, for example, made no attempt to thwart Jacob Snively when in May 1860 he found placer gold in Bear Creek on Chihenne land and established the village of Birchville. Nor did officials protest when hundreds of prospectors trekked straight across Victorio's land to join Snively's diggings. Birchville became known as Piños Altos, and its presence created a perpetual thorn in Victorio's side. So, too, did the new town of Silver City, also founded in 1860, challenge Apache patience. Also by this time, the mines at Santa Rita del Cobre operated regularly. This was Mangas Coloradas's favorite region and one to which Victorio frequently traveled. Thus, both had to endure prospectors setting up camp in the heart and on the fringes of their land.

Agent Steck on the Eve of War

Victorio heard rumors that agent Michael Steck was hoping to avert further conflict by creating a permanent reservation site for the Warm Springs bands. In fact, Steck had for years realized the need to establish such a reservation, and in the years immediately before the war, found the need becoming even more pressing. He noticed that the Warm Springs bands were gravitating away from the agency. He discovered an increase in the amount of liquor traded to the Apaches as well. Also, with liquored-up miners in the area came assaults on Apache women and fights with the men. Ironically, many of the prospectors demanded military action when their actions led to Apache retaliation. Increased contact, Steck noted, brought an upswing in diseases as well. Dozens of Victorio's Warm Springs people, children and adults alike, had come to him coughing until they could barely breath. Whooping cough was only one of many diseases from which the Apaches suffered. They also went to his Southern Apache Agency for treatment of tuberculosis, pleurisy, pneumonia, influenza, and measles. There was always the fear of a sudden smallpox epidemic. It is interesting that there is no record of Victorio himself ever having come to the agency with an illness. Perhaps he left cures to his medicine men.

Despite all of this, Washington ignored Steck's requests, and Congress failed to appropriate adequate funds for rations. Thus, Victorio continued his active raid-and-trade subsistence patterns. As always, his favorite trading partner was the Mexican village of Monticello located in the Cañada Alamosa. Agent Steck frequently admonished authorities in Santa Fe and Washington, D.C., for their inattentiveness and may have secretly understood Victorio's plight. Not only was there a constant shortage of rations, but the whites had also depleted the area of most of its game. If Apaches left their land to hunt, settlers cried "foul!" Steck noted that Victorio mostly stayed on his land, although he was not growing corn.

Then Steck heard frightening rumors that the Interior Department was considering a concentration policy—moving several tribes to one reservation—and was entertaining the notion of relocating Warm Springs entirely. Members of Congress seemed easily intimidated when St. Louis and San Francisco newspapers accused them of coddling the Apaches. Editors sent their stringers to Silver City and Piños Altos to collect firsthand reports of Apache depredations. As Steck pushed for a permanent site, Captain Richard S. Ewell of Fort Buchanan cautioned him, "If [you pursue] the Warm Springs site you must be prepared to hear the dogs howl ... as there are several here who are paid by the newspapers for their howls." In addition, citizens petitioned Steck to move the agency far from where whites wanted to live.

Steck realized that the longer Americans occupied the area, the easier they would find it to trump Indian claims. He sent letters to Commissioner Alfred B. Greenwood, who seldom bothered to reply. As this point, Steck experienced what Americans today call burn-out. When Sylvester Mowry vacated the post of territorial delegate to Congress in 1860, Steck threw his hat into the ring and was elected. His preoccupation with politics inadvertently led to a disaster, however. As Steck busily prepared to leave for Washington, he apparently agreed to meet Chief Elias, a Chihenne leader and peace advocate. According to historian Dan L. Thrapp, Steck forgot about the appointment. On December 4, 1860, as Chief Elias camped near the agency waiting in vain for Steck to show up, a former Texan named James Tevis led twenty-eight Piños Altos miners in an attack on the Apache leader's temporary camp. The miners killed four Chihennes, including Elias. Oddly, Steck failed to report the event for several months. When he finally did write the report, he seemed, uncharacteristically, to blame Elias for the attack, suggesting that the chief had foolishly attempted to trade with Texans. Why he did this nobody seems to know.

Tevis later admitted that one of the miners discovered a mule missing and naturally presumed Elias's hungry band camped nearby had stolen and eaten the animal. Instead of attempting to resolve the issue peacefully, Tevis admitted, the miners got liquored up and assaulted the Indian camp. As usual, their actions went unpunished. In the wake of the attack, some pro-Confederate newspapers printed stories inciting an already tense public against the Indians. Those articles blamed Victorio, Mangas Coloradas, and sometimes Cochise for every missing horse, mule, or cow. Newspaper articles even included instructions telling settlers to keep brown sugar laced with strychnine on hand, give some to any Indian encountered, and return a few hours later to collect the scalps for the bounty. Such was the antidote to Indian troubles, writers claimed. Of course, these same accounts were silent regarding attacks on Warm Springs villages.

This rhetoric led to inflamed Apache-white relations, but it would be inaccurate to characterize all relations as violent. Beginning in the 1850s, a small company calling itself the San Antonio-to-San Diego Mail Company had carved out a route across Apache territory. Its trail cut through some of the most rugged canyons and badlands in the Southwest. Best known were Apache Canyon, which lay between Cochise country and the copper mines, and Cooke's Canyon, located on Chihenne land. Both places guarded precious springs of water. The Butterfield Overland Mail Company took over the route in 1858 and built stage depots at both locations with small arsenals for their station masters because these narrow passes were ideal for ambushes. Between 1858 and 1861, however, Victorio and Mangas allowed stagecoaches to travel unmolested, and Cochise even regularly supplied hay and wood to the depot at Apache Canyon. Nor did Victorio complain—at least not to whites—when the military established the outpost of Fort Craig on the southern bank of the Alamosa River, allegedly to better protect his people from area miners. So, although conflict and war were more common in the years preceding the Civil War, they did not dominate Victorio's life.

Dilth-cleyhen Completes Her Puberty Ceremony

More important to Victorio at the moment were preparations for his eldest daughter's puberty celebration and passage into womanhood. Her mother and other female relatives had already carefully selected a perfect piece of doeskin for the dress. They stitched it into shape and painted the dress with circles that represented the sun, rainbow arcs, stars, and a crescent moon. Her mother chose a special di-yin—probably a woman—to bless Dilth-cleyhen's dress with her sacred songs and prayers. These arrangements had to begin several months in advance of the ritual itself. Another woman was chosen to educate Dilth-cleyhen regarding her duties as a woman and teach her White Painted Woman's sacred instructions. Dilth-cleyhen's mother gave the teacher an eagle feather as a token of respect and gratitude.

In 1860, life was such that families might still plan ceremonies months, possibly a year, ahead of the scheduled event. Within a decade or so, that would all change. Dilth-cleyhen's ceremony was held at a special site, but in the years following the Civil War, families frequently found it impossible to freely chose a desired location. Moreover, when they were on the run—as they were more and more often after about 1875—even the luxury of planning ahead was seldom possible. At times, a band might be forced to take time out in their flight from soldiers and stop just long enough to give a girl an abbreviated version of the ceremony. Still, the ritual was so sacred that, regardless of their circumstances, Apaches believed it was imperative to carry it out.

Nana explained why. Victorio had undoubtedly head the story many times, but liked to listen as Nana related it yet again. One could always learn from a story no matter how many times one heard it. "Long ago," the story began, "some Warm Springs [Apache] had visited their brothers [the Mescaleros] and were told of a cave." A di-yin named E-son-knh-sen-de-he, whose power was strong, visited the cave. Afterward, she found that her cures were many. But Ussen also directed her to scale Mt. Meteor in Warm Springs territory with special prayers. Fearful for her safety, her people went, too, and prayed at the base of the mountain while E-son-knh-sen-de-he climbed the cliffs. She discovered toeholds in the side of the rock that had just appeared for her benefit. At the top stood another cave. Inside, she encountered two fierce mountain lions, then two giant poisonous snakes, and the two beasts "that we do not name." Afraid but determined, she bowed her head and walked between them. Only then did E-son-knh-se-de-he notice the Mountain Spirits. "What does our daughter seek?" each asked. All possessed different powers.

The final spirit was an aged women. E-son-knh-se-de-he said to her, "Mother ... in your infinite wisdom you know what will bring the greatest good to my people." The female spirit replied:

> What you ask I shall give. It is this: at times your people may have direct communication with the Mountain Spirits.... When your young girls have attained womanhood you are to make a feast for the worthy—the chaste. You will observe the rite of which I tell you. It is for the maidens, their sponsors, and the medicine men.

She gave E-son-knh-se-de-he the ritual. Medicine men must sing a minimum of 174 prayers during the four-day ritual. The men in the tribe were to retire to a secret place, don buckskin skirts, moccasins, and masks "surmounted by a high crown of sticks, painted with sacred symbols." No red, she ordered. Red was the color of war and never intended for other uses. The men would dance and through them would come messages from the Mountain Spirits or Gááns to the maidens. The maidens, in turn, would interpret these messages to the medicine men, who could decide for whom each was intended and how to best carry it out. "All who attend the dances will receive good. . . . Even though an enemy be present he is to participate in the blessings." The maiden would also receive personal power to prolong her life and help against the dark forces. Every part of her life—grinding corn, finding water, building shelters, hunting, taking long journeys, childbearing and rearing, and reaching the status of elder—was affected by this ceremony and the messages she received. "All along the way, the puberty ceremony was her benefactor."

As the time for Dilth-cleyhen's ceremony neared, women gathered all the special foods needed to feed the many visitors who would call and ask for White Painted Woman's blessings. A di-yin wove a distinctive basket to hold the pollen, ocher, deer-hoof rattle, and grama grass that she would use. The basket also marked the far point of her traditional runs. Dilth-cleyhen's grandmother made long strands of beads, fastened together with eagle feathers, to adorn the girl's hair during the ceremony. Grandmother obtained the drinking tube, which was used so that water would not touch the girl's lips, and procured the wooden scratcher. She inspected the dress with its long fringe and gathered plenty of pollen.

The ceremony continued for four days. Victorio proudly observed and participated in the blessings. One must wonder if he thought back to the puberty ceremony of his first wife, Dilth-cleyhen's mother, and when he was first smitten and hoped he might one day marry her. According to the oral stories, the Gááns indeed visited during Dilth-cleyhen's puberty ritual and carried messages to and for her. She never faltered in her four runs. The people of her band danced each night, and all obtained the hoped-for blessings. Thus, the puberty ceremony was a success. Later,

Dilth-cleyhen observed, "At the time of my Feast, it was then that our family first used white flour to make our bread. Before that, we used ground corn." It is not likely, however, that white flour was used in any of the foods made for her ceremony.

Cochise and the Bascom Affair

About the time that Victorio celebrated his daughter's passage into womanhood, Abraham Lincoln was elected president. In the next few months, seven southern states, including Texas, seceded from the Union. Thus, when the new president took office on March 4, 1861, ringed by federal troops who were present in case of a Confederate attack, the only remaining recourse was war. William Dole, Lincoln's commissioner of Indian Affairs, saw in the president an empathy for Indians and pushed Congress for a well-managed reservation policy, but impending war put Indian affairs on the back burner. An Illinois politician with no experience dealing with Indians, Dole was probably not in a position to design a far-reaching policy anyway.

Although distant from the battles, Victorio and the Apaches were dramatically affected by the Civil War. Soldiers with southern sympathies resigned and made their way back to the Confederacy. Others waited to receive their orders to move east. Meanwhile, an event occurred that did not involve Victorio but profoundly affected him. The Bascom affair, as it was called, turned Cochise against whites, and this would later impact decisions regarding Victorio's reservation site. In January 1861, a ne'er-do-well named John Ward and his mistress, Jesusa Martinez, discovered some livestock stolen from their corral and realized that her nine-year-old son, Felix Ward, was missing, too. Felix, who as an adult would scout for the U.S. Army under the name of Mickey Free, either ran away from what was probably an abusive home or was kidnapped by the same band of Pinals who took the livestock. Ward reported the livestock and the boy's disappearance to nearby Fort Buchanan. On February 4, a young, inexperienced lieutenant named George N. Bascom led fifty-four soldiers straight into Cochise country.

Cochise agreed to parley with Bascom. He told the lieutenant that, although he disliked Mexicans, he felt no animosity towards Americans. In fact, he reminded Bascom that he was supplying hay and lumber to the Butterfield mail line. He had no reason to take the boy or to lie, Cochise maintained. To show good faith, Cochise agreed to assist the army in tracking both. Then, for some reason, Cochise suddenly sensed danger. He yanked a knife from one of the folds of his moccasin, slashed a hole through the back of the tent, and fled. Caught off-guard, Cochise's companions were not fast enough, and Bascom seized them. From afar, Cochise negotiated for their return. Three were blood relatives, and one was his beloved brother, Coyuntura.

Bascom refused all offers. He wanted the boy. Cochise reiterated that he knew nothing of the child's whereabouts. Hoping to break the stalemate, Cochise proceeded to attack a wagon train and take a group of Mexican and American passengers prisoner. He sent word that he would release his hostages when Bascom let the Apache prisoners go. Bascom, however, clung to his ultimatum. Now desperate and enraged, Cochise killed his captives and left their mutilated bodies on Apache Pass for all to see. In retaliation, Bascom hanged all six Indian prisoners. A broken-hearted Cochise burned with hatred towards what he saw as unreasonable and brutal Americans. Despite the provocation, Cochise made no further attack on the Americans. Meanwhile, Victorio remained at peace at Lucero Spring.

Civil War Comes to the West

However, by April, Victorio—and indeed all of the Apaches—watched the white men move out. Butterfield abandoned its southern route. Employees closed the depots. Reassigned to fight in the Civil War, the soldiers began to leave and with them went many of the contractors who had supplied goods and services to the forts. Agent Tully distributed rations to the Warm Springs people until May 1861 and finally had to leave. As the white men departed, Victorio rejoiced and joined Cochise and Mangas Coloradas to retake their territory. On

May 7, Victorio helped the others attack a wagon train near
Piños Altos, and on May 22, he led a raid that removed every
head of stock from Fort McLane. Victorio, Mangas, and
Cochise recaptured the old stage depots and unearthed whatever was left in the nearby arsenals. They established camps at
Apache Pass and at the highest point overlooking Cooke's
Canyon and appropriated the water sources. From these vantage points, they forced many of the now unprotected ranchers and farmers to pull up stakes. For the fun of it, they sometimes harassed whites, pinning them against the canyon walls
with bullets or showering them with a hailstorm of arrows as
they tried to maneuver wagons and pack horses through these
passes. The farms and ranches that had sprung up since 1848
were suddenly vacated. Piños Altos and Silver City became almost ghost towns. As military camps shut down entirely, Victorio, Mangas Coloradas, and Cochise watched in glee as the
Americans packed up and left.

By late spring, Geronimo joined the chiefs. Historians have
debated whether Goy-ah-kla—meaning One Who Yawns—was
his childhood or baby name, or whether as Apaches told biographer Angie Debo, the name pronounced with a different
infection means "intelligent, shrewd, and clever." More of a
medicine man than a chief, Geronimo gained in stature among
his people about the time of the American Civil War. Nevertheless, Victorio did not entirely trust Geronimo, and Dilth-cleyhen's mother often said, "I think he does not tell the truth. He
looks out only for his own interests."

Occasionally, the Nednhi chief Juh came up from his stronghold in the Blue Mountains to bask in the newfound freedom as
well. The influx of whites after 1849 had persuaded Juh that
Sonora was the safest place for his people. Whites, he argued,
were more difficult to understand and to deal with than Mexicans. Juh, whose name meant "He Sees Around," had the power
to see into the future, which perhaps contributed to his decision
to retreat to Sonora. Those who met him noticed immediately
that Juh stuttered badly. Juh maintained close ties to Victorio
and Mangas Coloradas, perhaps because the Nednhis and Chi-

hennes had ridden together for so long. But he allied frequently
with Cochise and Geronimo as well, and in fact married Geronimo's sister, Ishtan. Ishtan, reportedly Juh's favorite wife, was
said to accompany her husband on raids and in war parties.

By holding Cooke's Canyon, the Apaches were able to isolate
Piños Altos and restrict the miners' movements for most of September. The stranglehold on the canyon resulted in a virtual
siege, and on the 27th of that month, Victorio's people watched
as Arizona volunteers tried to maneuver around them and
move in supplies to the harried miners who found their food
supplies dangerously low and their livestock dwindling. The
Apaches held their position and kept the volunteers at bay.
Furthermore, during the late night hours, Victorio himself
positioned Chihenne warriors along the crests of the hills surrounding the town, and at dawn they fired into it. While Victorio kept the miners pinned down with gunfire, Cochise's
Chiricahuas swept in. Hand-to-hand combat raged throughout
Piños Altos. The miners were able to unload a small cannon and
fill it with scrap metal. They managed to light the fuse and spew
the metal into the fray, finally repelling the Indian attack. As
usual, technology won the day. Edwin Sweeney claims that the
Apaches sieged Piños Altos less to run the miners out than to
show them who was in control. Having seen the backs of the
military and many civilians, they may have entertained the notion of clearing out the region altogether, but did not attempt
to do so, another challenge to existing stereotypes.

Now largely in control of southern New Mexico, Apache
bands continued to travel freely in Chihuahua as well, sometimes
showing up in Janos for medical attention or to trade. They
abandoned their permanent, agreed-upon camps and their gardens and returned to the lives they had always loved. Chihennes,
Mescaleros, Chiricahuas, and Nednhis closed most of the roads
between La Mesilla and Tucson and freely raided the camps of
the settlers who dared to remain in the area. It seems that Victorio, Mangas, and Cochise honestly believed that they had run
off the white invaders. To their way of thinking, the Americans
had finally given up.

The California Column Arrives

Victorio's joy was short-lived. Despite the war and general movement eastward, Americans had not abandoned the region altogether. Within three months of the April 1861 attack on the federal arsenal at Fort Sumter, fighting commenced in Virginia. During this brief interim, Dr. Steck returned to the agency at the Cañada Alamosa and attempted to reestablish governmental control over Victorio's Chihennes. He remained only a couple of weeks, however. On July 13, Steck fled to Santa Fe in the face of extreme pro-southern sentiment and the threat of an invasion. Confederate sympathies were rampant in southern New Mexico, but the invasion did not occur there until winter 1862. Henry H. Sibley, previously second in command at Fort Union, had resigned his commission in the U.S. Army before the war began, but returned with twenty-five hundred rowdy Texans. His mission was to march up the Rio Grande, swing east and take the route over treacherous Raton Pass, and take the Colorado gold fields. Afterward, Sibley planned to march his men west to Sacramento and appropriate the gold there as well. Jefferson Davis and the Confederate legislature envisioned millions added to the Confederate treasury and sea ports opened on the Pacific Coast, thus offering economic and diplomatic advantages for the South. This route lay east of Victorio's land, but Sibley's invasion of New Mexico and the Confederate threat would occupy the few soldiers who remained for almost a year.

Sibley garnered support in the Mesilla Valley, where pro-southern Democrats dominated and where Steck was trying to reestablish the Warm Springs Agency. On January 18, 1862, the Confederate Congress proclaimed Arizona a territory of the South. Then Sibley began his march north. He successfully engaged troops at Fort Craig and then at Valverde, located just south of present-day Socorro. He swept relatively unmolested through Albuquerque and Santa Fe. He was stopped on March 27, 1862, at Glorietta Pass when he clashed with a combined force of New Mexico and Colorado volunteers. Soundly defeated, the Texans straggled back to Mesilla, ending the military threat but not the southern influence in New Mexico. Moreover, Arizona's secession by proxy brought New Mexico to the attention of Washington, and the military responded.

To secure the territory, the War Department ordered now General James H. Carleton and a column of 2,300 volunteer cavalry and infantry from California—hence dubbed the California Column—to leave Los Angeles and invade Arizona. As Victorio's people continued to hold the land around Piños Altos, Carleton reached the mining community of Tucson on June 7, 1862. He proclaimed Arizona a territory for the United States and imposed martial law. He at first ignored the Apache presence because the first job was to seek out and arrest southern sympathizers and conduct military tribunals. Sylvester Mowry, for example, was arrested for his part in the Sibley plot. His newspaper, the *Weekly Arizonan*, had regularly spewed southern views and severely criticized the United States. Mowry was ultimately imprisoned at Fort Yuma.

Still, Carleton did not remain in Tucson for very long. His next mission was to make contact with Colonel Edward Canby at Fort Craig and to regarrison some of the forts, especially Fort Stanton in the heart of Mescalero country, and build others to protect strategic places like Apache and Cooke's canyons. Carleton then intended to occupy Mesilla and eradicate any pro-southern sentiment that still threatened the region. With that accomplished, he would turn his attention to the Indians. Apache runners brought word to Cochise, Mangas Coloradas, and Victorio of an impending movement out of Tucson. The soldiers planned, according to the messengers, to follow the old stage route and march directly over Apache Pass.

What Victorio and the others did not know was that Californians in particular nursed such a deep hatred for Indians that that state's history remains one of the most brutal. The forty-niners had almost immediately displaced the Californios—native-born residents of Mexican heritage—and brutalized the Chinese, but if they resented these so-called foreigners, they loathed the Indians who sometimes worked in the gold fields for the Californios and whose villages dotted the land. Many Californians

saw nothing wrong with shooting Indians down like deer or en-
slaving them and selling their Indian women and children.
James H. Carleton was no exception. Born and raised in Massachusetts, he was a staunch, no-nonsense Christian, a domi-
neering leader, and an avowed Indian hater. Although some
historians argue that he adopted his anti-Indian views only after
spending a few months in the Southwest experiencing Victorio
and Cochise's assaults, that seems unlikely. He later explained his
callous attitude when he asserted that Indians would rightfully
become known only in history and at length be "blotted out, of
even that, forever." But first Carleton had to make his way
through Chiricahua country, and Cochise, Mangas Coloradas,
and Victorio guarded the only reliable water source in the rugged
Chiricahua Mountains.

Carleton sent three messengers ahead to inform Canby of his
imminent arrival. One of these messengers was an express rider
named John Jones, and with him were Sergeant William Wheel-
ing and a guide called Chavez. Cochise's warriors killed Wheel-
ing and Chavez a few miles east of the pass. Jones escaped and
was subsequently captured by Confederates. He reportedly
smuggled word to Canby that Carleton was in Tucson and that
Apache Pass was still closed to Americans. But only six days after Jones's departure, Carleton sent young Colonel Edward
Eyre to scout the Tucson-to-Mesilla road. On June 18, Eyre ran
squarely into an impressive line of Apaches chiefs including
Victorio, Nana, Cochise, Juh, and Geronimo. "We seek peace,"
Eyre assured them. The chiefs nodded and let Eyre continue,
knowing that he would soon discover the two messengers' bodies "stripped and lanced" on Apache Pass. When Eyre reached
Fort Craig on July 4 and raised the American flag there to the
cheers of volunteer troops, he undoubtedly thanked God that he
was alive to tell the tale. Oddly, Eyre did not send word back to
Carleton, who was ready to march.

Thus, on July 9 or 10, one contingent under Captain Thomas
L. Roberts left Tucson with 126 soldiers, twenty-five civilian
teamsters, and two hundred head of stock. He also carried two
howitzers. Without having received a warning from Eyre,

Roberts could not know that Victorio and the others, now including Mangas Coloradas as well, waited to ambush them at Apache Pass. Roberts' orders were to locate the Puerto de Dadao, a clear, abundant spring of water and the only adequate water source in the region, and to secure it for Carleton's main column, which was about a week behind. Roberts saw no Apaches as he approached the dreaded pass. Believing all was well, he ordered his men to approach the spring cautiously. Suddenly, the Apache warriors open-fired from behind rocks along the canyon walls. The Americans fired back, but the canyon walls served as a formidable fortress, and they were unable to dislodge the Chiricahuas. According to historian Jay J. Wagoner, the Battle of Apache Pass was one of the largest-scale engagements between federal troops and Apaches in Arizona history.

Surrounded and thirsty, Roberts unleashed his howitzers. Heavy charges blasted against the rock walls. Mangas Coloradas was injured, and his men had to carry him to safety. Former border commission interpreter, John Cremony, who had returned from California with Carleton's column, said that Mangas Coloradas caught a carbine ball in his chest and was taken to Janos for medical attention. Cochise, Victorio, and Juh fell back. They had never before encountered heavy artillery such as these howitzers. Victorio for one, felt humiliated by their retreat and then furious. But, despite army reports to the contrary, the Chiricahuas claimed that not one warrior was killed in the encounter.

On July 28, Victorio and the other chiefs reluctantly allowed Carleton's main column over Apache Pass without resistance. He ordered fortifications constructed there to guard the pass and water, and the new post was named Fort Bowie. By mid-September, Carleton relieved Canby of his command. As for the Apaches, not only had they experienced new and powerful weapons used against them, but they had watched American troops arrive from the West for the first time, rather than from the East. Anthropologist Richard Perry argues that the combination of heavy weaponry and strange arrival from the opposite direction undoubtedly convinced the Apaches, probably for the very first time, that Americans surrounded them and were there to stay. Certainly, Victorio and the others realized they had not run off the whites as they had previously thought.

American Hegemony and Apache Losses

As Carleton initially crossed southern New Mexico, he spotted devastated fields and orchards and empty corrals. The charred timbers and adobe foundations of many burned-out and unoccupied shacks and jacales stared back at him. He heard rumors, too, of at least one hundred Americans killed since 1861, many of them attempting to flee across Cooke's Canyon. Victorio could have taken Carleton to other sights like the deserted and skeletal Indian villages that told of dawn attacks or late night retaliatory raids upon his Chihenne people. The commander asked neither Victorio nor the other chiefs for such a tour or for a peace negotiation. Instead, Carleton sent messengers to as many of the leaders as they could find to demand unconditional surrender. Although Carleton may have originally intended to arrange some type of communication between his men and the Chiricahuas, in the end he did nothing of the kind.

Like those before him, Carleton also had a passion for gold and even petitioned the federal government for funds to build a road to the gold fields. The more developed the land, the less room for Indians, he reasoned. In addition, perhaps the commander thought such a policy reflected the views of President Lincoln, who claimed that one of his primary concerns was to make the West safe for settlement following the war. Regarding natural resources, the president believed they were "unexhausted, and, as we believe, inexhaustible." Lincoln apparently looked forward to exploiting the land, its timber, and its vast minerals for years to come.

Carleton stationed some of his soldiers at Piños Altos to protect the remaining miners and the gold and silver deposits there. He allowed the men to prospect on the side if they wished. Because he felt no empathy towards Victorio's Warm Springs people, the commander saw little reason to curtail the brutality of his soldiers towards them. And the savagery indeed escalated. John Cremony, who remained at Piños Altos, related an event that, if it really occurred, shook the Chihennes to their very core. In late 1862, he wrote, some miners at Piños Altos took Mangas Coloradas captive on one of his visits there. They subsequently tied him to a tree and flogged him or, in Cremony's words, "administered a dose of strap oil." Mangas Coloradas's biographer, however, found no evidence to support the story. Neither Jason Betzinez nor Geronimo so much as mention it in their autobiographical accounts. Nevertheless, the story has over the years found acceptance in popular literature.

There is no question about the next event. In January 1863, Mangas Coloradas indeed went to Piños Altos to negotiate a peace with the whites. This time it was Daniel Ellis Conner who recounted the story. Mangas Coloradas had, as usual, expected to eat, exchange gifts, and then talk. His people—especially Victorio and Nana—warned Mangas that this was an unwise course of action. For one thing, the Apaches had made up their minds as a group not to negotiate with the miners. Mangas must have believed that he was under a flag of truce. Besides, the old man wanted to return home to Santa Lucia Springs and live in comfort and harmony. That would prove virtually impossible without some type of agreement between the white men and him. Instead of welcoming the elderly chief, the miners presented their guns and ordered Mangas to stand still and surrender. Mangas reportedly did as they asked.

General Joseph R. West was in charge. Like Carleton, West had no love for Indians and declared that instead of negotiating a treaty, "the old 'brave' [would account for] the loss of two plundered government wagons and teams," or remain a prisoner. West put a group of his soldiers in charge of the Chihenne chief. That night as Conner watched from afar, he noticed strange movements coming from where Mangas Coloradas lay on his blanket. It was about midnight. Each time a sentinel stepped close to Mangas, the old man seemed to thrash about, draw up his legs, and try to tuck the lower end of his blanket over one foot with the other. Whenever Conner edged closer for a better look, the sentinels walked off. So he watched from a distance and recorded what he saw.

> I could see them plainly by the firelight as they were engaged in heating their fixed bayonets in the fire and putting them to the feet and naked legs of Mangas, who was from time to time trying to shield his limbs from the hot steel ... [after a while] Mangas raised himself upon his left elbow and began to expostulate in a vigorous way by telling the sentinels in Spanish that he was no child to be played with. But his expostulations were cut short, for he had hardly begun his exclamation when both sentinels brought down their Minnie muskets to bear on him and fired, nearly at the same time through his body.

Mangas Coloradas fell back onto his blanket. The sentinels shot him repeatedly with six-shooters. Then the soldiers scalped him and the next day cut off his head, which was washed, boiled, and sent to a museum in New York City, where it was subsequently lost.

When Mangas Coloradas's people heard of the murder and desecration, they were outraged. His band began to mourn, but many of them also asked if there was powerful witchcraft afoot. When word of his father-in-law's murder got to Cochise, he angrily swore revenge upon those guilty. Meanwhile, Victorio was similarly horrified. The murder, he thought, was barbaric, but the mutilation of the remains was an act that far exceeded even that. Connor wrote that he saw Apache smoke signals nearby and apparently believed that some of Mangas Coloradas's cohorts were waiting for his return. Thus, it is possible that Victorio saw from afar some of the commotion going on at the camp. But oral histories say that scouts brought word of Mangas Coloradas's death to Victorio. The Chihennes reportedly retrieved the old chief's body after the soldiers discarded it.

The physical condition of the body at death was how the deceased would travel through eternity. Beheading was the worst depredation possible, and for whites to treat an esteemed leader in such a manner proved that they were uncivilized. During even the heated battles in Cooke's Canyon or Apache Pass, the Chiricahuas had refrained from mutilating the most worthy warriors. However, Americans in 1863 would have argued that the enormous head of Mangas Coloradas was of great scientific value back east. General George Crook later maintained that such intensified brutality suggested military discipline had badly eroded under Carleton. Certainly this event opened a new era of brutality between Americans and Apaches in New Mexico.

Mangus, Mangas Coloradas's twenty-three-year-old son, was too inexperienced to take over leadership of his father's band. Hence, Victorio, Loco, and Nana stepped in. During this period Victorio emerged as a leading Chihenne chief. Two days after the great Mangas Coloradas's death, West sent his troops to seek out and destroy whatever Apache rancherias they could find. In one encounter his men killed nine Chihennes, all from Victorio's camp. Nevertheless, these events were only the beginning of Carleton's war on the Apaches.

The Bosque Redondo Experience

With the Confederate threat diminished, Carleton turned his attention to subduing the Indians living in New Mexico. Settlers in the Mesilla Valley, for example, had bitterly complained of Mescalero raids for years. Similarly, Mexican farmers whose lands were located in northwestern New Mexico lived in almost constant fear of the Navajos. Of course, the ranchers and miners in southwestern New Mexico wanted Victorio's people removed. Conveniently, Commissioner Dole had already advocated a concentration policy for Indian reservations. In fall 1862, Carleton ordered Kit Carson to begin the round-up of the Mescaleros. By summer 1863, Carson had impounded nearly three hundred. The Warm Springs Apaches, however, were temporarily left unmolested. Carleton ordered the Mescaleros removed to a consolidated Indian reservation, which he selected himself, called the Bosque Redondo. It was a barren, windswept tract on the eastern New Mexico llano or plain. The soldiers at Fort Sumner were assigned the duty of overseeing the new reservation. Carleton defended his site as ideal, even though

summers were hot and dry and winter ice storms plagued the region with some regularity. Measles, smallpox, and influenza
devastated the Mescaleros, and they were easy prey for Comanche warriors who swept in from Texas periodically. On June
30, 1864, Carleton abolished the Southern Apache Agency,
which had ministered to the needs of Mescaleros and other
Apaches living in southern New Mexico.

In summer 1863, Carleton turned against the Navajos, sending Kit Carson to subdue and relocate them to the Bosque. Carson's orders were to "lay waste the prairies by fire." During a
cold winter campaign, he destroyed at least five thousand
Navajo sheep, goats, and mules, and burned their winter food
stores and orchards. By spring 1864, the first of 8,474 Navajos
prisoners arrived at the Bosque. That Navajos and Mescaleros
were longtime enemies mattered not at all to Carleton. In summer 1865, fields at the Bosque were abundant with corn, wheat,
and beans, but a prolonged drought caused crops to fail every
year thereafter. Carleton awarded supply contracts to his friends,
and as a result, prices soared and quality plummeted. Often the
rations never arrived at all.

With the situation deteriorating rapidly, Michael Steck, who
was appointed superintendent of Indian Affairs for New Mexico
on May 23, 1863, censured the Bosque Redondo experiment and
Carleton's treatment of the Indians living there. Steck also noted
that in the first year alone, the reservation operation cost the government nearly one million dollars. He judged this a massive
waste of funds. Steck reported that the tribes of the Southern
Apache Agency were no longer cohesive, but rather were fragmented. He now referred to them as simply the Gila Apaches. Although Steck's assessment of Carleton's performance was accurate,
it is more difficult to analyze his statement regarding tribal frag-
mentation. Perhaps without Mangas Coloradas, the rancherias
split up and fell under myriad chiefs such as Victorio, Loco, Nana,
and Delgadito, to name a few. With the general unrest, there was
undoubtedly a major shift in alliances. Delgadito, for instance,
had, become less conciliatory and tended to attract Apaches eager
to fight Americans rather than to negotiate with them. As several

of these chiefs were killed in rapid succession, the Chihennes obviously also experienced a period of tremendous leadership change. Not having visited the region since 1861, Steck probably did not know the extent of these changes. But he apparently heard rumors. Victorio, it seems, was gaining in prestige among many of the Copper Mine Apaches, and it was during this period that he began to gain a more sizable following. Closing the Southern Apache Agency only exacerbated the chaos.

Carleton, however, refused to back down. The animosity between Steck and the autocratic military commander intensified. In March 1865, Carleton made the decision to remove the so-called Gilas and impound them at the Bosque Redondo along with the Mescaleros and Navajos. Realizing that the Chihennes still lacked a permanent reservation, Steck reluctantly agreed. He reminded Carleton, though, that the Chihennes had kept the peace since 1854. "Treat them with respect," was Steck's implied message. The superintendent also reminded Carleton that it was his own failure to enforce military discipline that had resulted in the death of Mangas Coloradas.

Carleton became furious when, as he claimed, Victorio agreed to negotiate but never showed up. Victorio countered that he, Loco, and Nana had indeed waited, but it was the general who never arrived. The chiefs remained as long as they could, he said, but fearing a trap, fled. Hence, Carleton used this impasse to declare a policy of unrelenting war against "the rattlesnakes."

Again, Steck tried to intervene. As before, he reminded Carleton that Victorio, in particular, had always kept the peace and, in fact, had continued to live at his chosen campsite long after the other Chiricahuas went on the warpath. Steck offered to negotiate a peace treaty with Victorio and repeatedly requested a military escort to the former Southern Apache Agency. Steck sent word to Victorio, who was allegedly camped somewhere around Piños Altos at the time. The Apache chief reportedly waited for two months to parley with the former agent.

Carleton brusquely refused Steck's request for an escort: "I am of the opinion that when we are at war with a band of Indians, the Military department ... should and must manage all affairs connected with them," he wrote. Carleton denied the Chihennes' peaceful overtures and instead sent troops to find Victorio. As far as we can tell, Victorio flatly refused all demands that he go to the Bosque Redondo. There were no mountains there. He did not intend to give up their lives at Warm Springs for a piece of barren land. Nor did he want to live with the Mescaleros and Navajos. Victorio made his position clear: "I and my people want peace ... we are tired of war ... we are poor and we have very little for ourselves and our families to eat or wear." But he would sacrifice only so much to please the Americans.

Steck protested Carleton's appropriation of his treaty-making responsibility. So, too, did Mesilla newspaper editor A. E. Hackney and at least one justice of the peace voice their concerns regarding Carleton to Washington. But the focus back east was still the war. Then came the sudden assassination of Abraham Lincoln in April, and for the next decade Congress debated southern reconstruction. Complaints were again pushed aside. Besides, Carleton was presenting his own version of events. He proclaimed victory over the Indians, which pleased Commissioner Dole. He claimed that the Bosque Redondo contained good land and water, and in his opinion, the Indians were "the happiest people I have ever seen." So, concerns regarding Indians and New Mexico Territory remained low priority.

Arizona Complicates American/Apache Relations

However, the war had brought major changes that would complicate Apache/white relations after 1865 and directly affect Victorio's future. On February 24, 1863, Congress had admitted Arizona to the Union as a separate territory. Colonel John R. Baylor, the Confederate governor of Arizona, had before the arrival of the California Column espoused complete extermination of the Indians and, in March 1862, went so far as to order the Arizona Guards to gather Indians using whatever means possible, kill the adults, and sell the children to defray costs. Because Jefferson Davis reportedly stripped Baylor of his command shortly thereafter, the order was never carried out.

It is not surprising that territorial governor John Goodwin told the first Arizona legislature meeting on September 26, 1864, in Prescott, that extermination was the only possible Indian policy to pursue. The legislature passed a resolution to exterminate Apaches during this first meeting. Moreover, as miners moved rapidly into Tucson and Prescott, Arizona newspapers openly advocated the eradication of Indians and the silencing of anyone who favored coexistence.

Thus, Arizonans exhibited no tolerance for Apaches. When King S. Woolsey, an old Indian fighter from Alabama, a former scalp-bounty hunter, and member of Arizona's first legislature, encountered Apaches near present-day Miami, Arizona, on January 24, 1864, he found nothing wrong with outright murder. Strangely, he made a flimsy attempt to rationalize his actions, claiming that the Indians had planned to kill his party. Whatever the Indians' intentions, Woolsey and his companions had apparently decided it was safe enough for them to spread a red blanket on the ground and lay out tobacco in anticipation of trade. He passed around piñole laced with strychnine, as the regional newspapers recommended. According to the accounts, Woolsey said something like "keep laughing and talking!" But he also ordered that each of the six Indian leaders be targeted.

The Apaches relaxed. Woolsey gave the signal. Each white man fired, instantly killing all of the Apache chiefs. The other Apaches were caught momentarily off guard, but soon rallied. A running fight that covered one-half mile reportedly ensued. This event—sometimes called the infamous Piñole Treaty—was simply a version of the old scalp-bounty policy removed from Sonora to Arizona. Indeed, a resolution implementing $100 scalp bounties was proposed in Arizona, but failed to pass the legislature only because citizens refused to fund the measure. They also expressed fear that such a policy might unleash violence against non-Indians as well. Coupled with the brutal death of Mangas Coloradas, Woolsey's Piñole Treaty represented a shift toward heightened brutality, a fact that was not lost on Victorio when news of the event filtered to the Warm Springs camps. It seemed the ex-Confederates put Indians on a level with

African Americans. In short, white superiority justified killing both races at will and without fear of the courts. On May 20, 1865, the U.S. War Department even encouraged the recruitment of volunteer regiments in Arizona to fight Apaches. By winter, Arizona had recruited five such companies.

The End of Carleton

Meanwhile, the Indian Office and members of Congress finally got around to questioning Carleton's reservation policy. As Steck had noted, the Bosque Redondo cost nearly one million dollars in the first year of operation. In May 1864, at about the time that Victorio was pondering the Woolsey massacre, Congress had reluctantly approved another $100,000 for the project, but questioned the extravagance. Secretary of War Edwin Stanton ordered an investigation of Carleton's supply contracts, but it took three investigations before he relieved Carleton of command in September 1866. Nevertheless, the general's actions had also helped convince the Interior Department that military control of the Indians was not going to work. Moreover, Carleton had almost single-handedly undermined the fragile trust that Steck had painstakingly built up with Victorio's people during his five years at the Southern Apache Agency. Carleton probably did more damage to Apache and white relations than the Bascom affair and the murder of Mangas Coloradas combined. His support for mining on Indian land, his permission to soldiers to prospect for gold while on duty, and the Bosque Redondo failure had dramatically increased unrest, distrust, and violence. As editor Hackney accurately predicted, the treachery manifested during the Civil War years would have a lasting impact on the Apache's fear of the military.

In the midst of the chaotic postwar turmoil, however, Victorio returned to the Warm Springs. His daughter Dilth-cleyhen joined him. She had married a young warrior a few years after her puberty ceremony. But her husband was killed in a raid in 1865, leaving her alone and with an infant daughter named Beshad-e. In keeping with Apache customs, Dilth-cleyhen returned to live with her parents, her hair cut in mourning. She also possessed a new power, the ability to assist women during childbirth, which she would possess for the rest of her life. Meanwhile, Victorio had taken a second wife and sired two more daughters. He continued to petition Steck to make the Warm Springs Reservation permanent, but received no reply.

On May 4, 1866, Victorio's Chihenne warriors ran off thirty head of cavalry horses from Fort Craig, and on June 6 drove another thirty-six horses from Camp Mimbres. One sheepherder was killed near Fort McRae. Afterward, the citizens around Piños Altos reported stolen stock with some regularity. More and more, they blamed Victorio. After the war, whites grew increasingly intolerant and settlers were quick to cry "Apache depredation!" A permanent reservation was an absolute necessity, but how could one force the Indian Office into a decision?

Agent Michael Steck had grown exhausted trying to extract a decision from Washington regarding a permanent reservation for the Chihennes. Shortly after Carleton's departure from New Mexico, Steck resigned from the Indian Service. He retired shortly thereafter to a farm near Winchester, Virginia, where he died on October 6, 1880, just four days before the slaughter at Tres Castillos. Thus, when Steck left New Mexico, he turned the quest for a permanent reservation over to others. Sadly, nobody after him was as eager for a favorable solution.

CHAPTER 5

Victorio and the Peace Policy

VICTORIO took a third wife in 1870, and by January 1872, she bore him a second son, Charlie Istee. The boy was only slightly younger than Victorio's first granddaughter, Beshad-e, whose mother, Dilth-cleyhen, helped bring him into the world. Despite Dilth-cleyhen's power over childbirth, Charlie Istee's mother died a few weeks later. Charlie was, according to tradition, handed over to Victorio's second wife, allegedly a sister of the third wife. But, suddenly, Victorio lost his second wife as well. Several months after Charlie's birth, while Victorio and some of his warriors were away hunting, the women walked a short distance from the camp in order to dig some of their favorite roots. While the women worked, a band of white men appeared; they shot and killed most of the women, including Victorio's second wife. A grief-stricken Victorio handed Charlie over to another female relative of his second wife in a nearby rancheria, and asked her to raise the infant. Throughout his entire life, Charlie never lost his fear that whites might kill him because he was Victorio's son.

In the decade immediately following the Civil War, Victorio repeatedly told Indian agents he wanted to make a lasting peace. Peace meant a permanent place to live, one far from white settlements. But although he remained firm in his desire for peace and a reservation, Victorio experienced pangs of apprehension over how to overcome the smothering web of dependency that seemed to wrap itself more tightly around the Apache people with every year that they endured reservation life. Before long, his Warm Springs bands would need the white man's rations for their very survival, and once that happened, there was no longer any freedom for them.

Victorio's great-great granddaughter claimed that after his two wives' deaths, he vented his grief in a wave of raids across southern New Mexico. It is equally likely that he continued to see raiding as the one guaranteed alternative to starvation and to the stifling boredom of reservation life. To idle around the agency for food and blankets belied every value he had ever learned. A lucrative attack on an isolated ranch or army post brought his people beef or horsemeat, and with any luck at all additional horses or mules to trade for guns and cloth. Of course, fleeing the reservation exposed the Chihennes to scalp hunters on the prowl, miners eager to shoot an Apache, and military patrols seeking so-called renegade Indians. But it honed one's skills, kept his people fed, armed, and mounted, and fostered communication with other Apache bands along the way. As long as this opportunity remained, the Chihennes could operate in a sort of middle ground between true independence and utter dependence.

There was yet another obstacle in Victorio's path to peace, and that was the federal government. Following the Civil War, Congress demanded major changes in Indian policy. These included a hard-line reservation policy, replacement of military Indian agents with civilians, and the concentration of many bands onto a single piece of land. Although these were intended to streamline affairs and generate more humane treatment of the Indians, in the end they simply encouraged greater indecision, buck-passing, and graft. These policies also undermined this fragile Chihenne middle ground. They contributed to increased anti-Indian racism, especially in Arizona, and cultivated a hydra-headed approach to decision making with myriad individuals trying to control the process and nobody seemingly in charge. Such failures would eventually prove fatal to Victorio's dreams of peace.

The Revolving Door Swings Again

In spring 1867, Victorio found newly appointed agent Luis M. Baca in residence at the old agency. Victorio quickly realized that, like agent Tully before the war, Baca had no rations to distribute

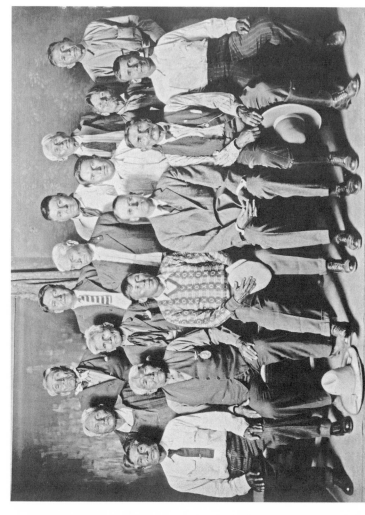

Group of Warm Springs elders, including Charles Istee, Victorio's only known surviving son (bottom row, far right). Courtesy of National Anthropological Archives (negative #44767).

and no decisions from the Indian Office. As always, Victorio took his rancheria to higher ground for the summer to avoid the endless ninety-plus-degree days and the clouds of mosquitoes and flies that hovered over the muggy river bottoms. There his Chihenne people remained until it was time to return and collect wild strawberries and then piñon nuts. By the time Victorio returned to agency headquarters in the fall, he discovered a different man sitting behind the desk.

Baca was gone. A. Baldwin Norton was there in his place. During his brief tenure as Indian agent, Norton petitioned Congress for $27,000 in appropriations, but Congress failed to act on his request, and Norton took no further action. The following summer, John Ayres sat in the agent's chair, but he departed before the summer was over. In August the Indian Office appointed Jonathan B. Hanson, but it is doubtful that Victorio so much as laid eyes on Hanson, because he resigned in September. By midautumn Charles Drew, an energetic and dedicated military man with an unfortunate proclivity for the bottle, was running the agency. Despite his addiction, Drew was one of the best agents the Apaches ever had, second only to Michael Steck.

Throughout early fall, when Apache men and women went into the agency for rations or medical treatment, they returned with news that the agent wanted to meet with their chief. At first, Victorio hesitated. Baca had wasted his time. The other agents had barely stayed long enough to unpack. What did this new man have to offer them? How long would he remain? Victorio and Loco conferred night after night. They finally agreed that it would not hurt to find out, and in October both rode into the agency to speak with the new agent. Like whites before and after, Drew described Victorio as restrained in his conversation and so aloof that the agent feared the Chihennes might be on the verge of war. Loco was the more gregarious of the two and more to Drew's immediate liking. Before long, however, the new agent grew less suspicious of Victorio's reserve and quiet demeanor. Victorio was not disposed to war, he finally concluded. After the talks, Drew cautioned the secretary of the interior that his Chihennes desperately needed food, blankets, and clothing.

Mostly, he concluded—as Steck had determined years before—they needed a final reservation site. Game was scarce, rations were sporadic, and the people bordered on starvation.

Victorio and Loco even decided to relocate their individual camps closer to the agency until Drew could arrange more rations. That way there could be more communications between them. The fact that the chiefs lingered near the Cañada Alamosa agency for at least a month suggested an acute need for food. As they waited, Victorio rode into the agency frequently to remind Drew of their absolute need for a permanent home. But it was not just any site that his Chihennes sought. The Warm Springs people needed their sacred land and the springs. The faceless officials in far-off Washington seemed not to understand this. However, Victorio inadvertently got their attention when he suggested that Cochise might agree to join his people at Warm Springs. This was not a promise, but it does indicate that the two chiefs had discussed the possibility. The Indian Office saw the offer as a way to solve its Cochise problem.

Finally, after no word regarding a reservation and no end to starvation-level rations, an exasperated Victorio took his people farther from the agency to set up their winter camp. Throughout that winter of 1869–70, some three hundred or more hungry Apaches gravitated towards Victorio's camp. Instead of wondering why so many otherwise healthy Apaches needed food, blankets, and shelter so desperately, New Mexicans complained about their presence in the area. Grant County residents confronted agent Drew with accusations that his Indians were stealing their livestock and horses. For an explanation, Drew turned to Victorio, who replied that it was probably Navajos, or maybe Mexicans, who were to blame. But Victorio also questioned how long the Americans intended to keep hundreds of hungry, bored warriors in one place without feeding them. Was the plan simply to starve them to death?

Partly out of boredom perhaps, Loco and one of Mangas Coloradas's sons named Salvador agreed to help track cattle taken from a small community called San José. They managed to locate the stock, and Salvador announced that he could tell immediately that Mexican rustlers, not Apaches, had taken the herd. The area was a hotbed of cattle and horse rustling, Drew acknowledged. There was a growing number of Anglo and Mexican outlaws eager to take livestock and herd it into Arizona or to Mexico. Nevertheless, he could do little about the lack of rations and even less to protect the Chihennes from such rustling accusations. "I cannot so much as feed your people. I still hope you will remain here," he told Victorio, "but I can promise nothing."

Reluctantly, Victorio agreed. Even if he and his warriors were inclined to bolt, there were the women, children, and elders to consider. Besides, Victorio liked and trusted Drew. Sadly, in June 1870—about the same time that Victorio married for the third time—Drew rode out from the agency alone to investigate yet another report of stolen cattle. Unlike Victorio's Chihenne people, the agent knew little about the rugged mountain range in which he found himself. He became hopelessly lost and ran out of water. By the time a rescue party of soldiers finally found him, Drew was already exhausted and dehydrated beyond revival. He died as a result of that misadventure. Victorio had considered Drew a friend as well as an Indian agent, and three years later would ask General Oliver O. Howard for an agent like Drew.

With Drew gone, Victorio wondered if Washington would forget all about the Warm Springs people. His men had resigned themselves to planting and were even now hoeing corn and thinning young squash and chili plants. In fact, they were carrying out the very activities that the agents wanted them to do. Still, he had Dilth-cleyhen, her hair cut in mourning for her deceased husband, in his wickiup, along with his first granddaughter, Beshad'e. His son Washington would soon marry, but there were three wives, three daughters, and his unmarried sister Lozen to feed. Victorio wanted some assurance of aid.

A New U.S. Indian Policy

Unknown to Victorio, the departments of war and interior were undergoing tremendous change. On July 28, 1866, Congress had slashed the number of military troops in the United States and created four African American regiments of infantry and two of cavalry, all of them with white officers. Former Iowa native Edward Hatch and Benjamin H. Grierson of Illinois organized the first two cavalry units. Grierson's Tenth Cavalry was ordered to Texas, while Hatch's Ninth marched to New Mexico. Both would become embroiled in chasing down Victorio. For a time, Congress seriously contemplated returning the Indian Office to the War Department—at least until hostilities concluded—but Interior retained control. Exactly where military control ended and civilian jurisdiction began, however, was anybody's guess, and this made Victorio's situation a political hot potato as well.

The War Department placed Arizona operations under the Division of the Pacific, but kept New Mexico, which included Victorio's Chihennes, under the Division of the Missouri. This sliced Apachería right down the middle and left no uniformity of command or responsibility. Now, the jurisdiction for Cochise's people was different from that for Victorio's. But things only got worse. Spurred on by the November 1864 Sand Creek massacre, when Colorado militia slaughtered and mutilated nearly two hundred Cheyennes, influential Quakers set about to reform Indian policy. In response, in March 1865, Congress authorized a series of surveys of Indian conditions, and these found disease, alcoholism, and despair rampant. The invasion of railroad crews and the loss of buffalo and other game exacerbated the problem across Indian country. A Joint Special Committee recommended that the Indian Office remain in the Interior Department.

In July 1867, Congress sent peace commissions comprised of military and civilian representatives to hear Indian complaints and write new treaties. Although the government was considering sending the Navajos to Indian Territory, on June 1, 1868, commissioners concluded a treaty that allowed them to return home. For tribes without "logical" reservation sites, such as Victorio's people, the commissioners would select areas. These peace commissions discovered two things. First, they determined that most Indians had become too dependent on the federal government to merit the category of nation. Thus, they

Colonel Edward Hatch. He commanded the Ninth Cavalry in New
Mexico during the Victorio Campaign, 1879–80. Courtesy of Palace of
the Governors (MNM/DCA) (negative #128134).

suggested a downward status of Domestic Dependent Nation, a description which Chief Justice of the Supreme Court John Marshall had coined in 1831. In 1886, the Supreme Court would designate tribes as "dependent communities" and assert Congress's absolute authority over them. Second, they saw a clear division between peaceful and so-called hostiles. Agents, they decided, must separate the two, assimilate the willing, and leave the others to the military. The commissioners again recommended transferring the Indian Office to the War Department, but this suggestion was ignored. For now, Victorio remained at the Cañada Alamosa.

Victorio and the Peace Policy

When Ulysses S. Grant was elected president in 1868, most Americans assumed he would favor military control of Indian affairs. Nevertheless, influential Quakers stepped in. Still reeling from the Sand Creek massacre and other depredations carried out against Indians in the West during the Civil War, they wasted no time asking the president-elect to adopt their plan. This became part of a larger reform movement sometimes dubbed Grant's Peace Policy, or simply the Peace Policy. Grant appointed full-blooded Seneca Ely S. Parker to head the Indian Office. A lawyer and civil engineer and one of General Grant's aides during the war, Parker was also the first Native American commissioner of Indian affairs.

In addition, a Board of Indian Commissioners was created on April 10, 1869, to oversee the Indian Office. All of its members had strong Christian ties—although the board did not represent any denomination per se—and all strongly believed in reform. Vincent Colyer, who would one day meet Victorio face to face, was a leader of the new Young Men's Christian Association and had held the position of secretary of the U.S. Christian Commission, which during the war, had provided church services and Christian literature to soldiers. William Welsh, a wealthy Quaker, was perhaps the single most important member of the commission. He and his nephew, Herbert, would play leading roles

in shaping Indian policy from the end of the Civil War until
Theodore Roosevelt's administration. As a group, the board
heard Indian and civilian complaints, inspected all Indian Office
budgets and reports, and oversaw agents and superintendents.

The board was also instrumental in ending treaties between
the government and Native peoples. Existing treaties remained
valid, but the legislation—a rider attached to an appropriations
bill—substituted fiats, resolutions, and presidential executive
orders for the ineffective and perpetually broken treaties. The
Peace Policy went even further. On July 15, 1870, Congress replaced the military agents with civilians. Thereafter, thirteen
Christian denominations divided up the agencies. These changes
complicated Victorio's situation. For one thing, they continued
the revolving door and fragmented decision-making even further. After Drew's death, Argalus G. Hennisee, a military man in
charge of the Mescalero Agency became acting agent for the Chihennes. Then on October 17, 1870, civilian Orlando Piper was assigned to the Cañada Alamosa agency.

Eleven days before Piper took his oath of office, special agent
William Arny—appointed by Commissioner Parker himself—arrived from Washington to tour Apache country. A deeply religious
member of the Disciples of Christ Church and a confirmed advocate of the Peace Policy, Arny hoped to accomplish three things.
He intended to make an official tally of their numbers. He planned
to recommend a permanent reservation for Victorio's people.
And as part of the selection process, he would determine what, if
anything, was required to make the site a more suitable reservation. Hennisee escorted Arny to the Cañada Alamosa agency,
where they met Victorio, Loco, and Nana. The next day, Cochise
rode into the agency with ninety-six of his warriors. After con-
ferring with this formidable group, Arny concluded that the
Cañada Alamosa was an ideal spot. The government could fund
a small reservoir to irrigate upwards of two thousand acres, he
wrote to Commissioner Parker. Cochise promised to consider
moving his own people there as well. His Chiricahuas were also
tired of war, he said, and with food and blankets provided, perhaps a thousand or more Apaches would move to the reservation.

Arny toured the valley and counted fifty-two Mexican families in the Cañada Alamosa area and a total population of 193 people. He found forty-six homes and two mills. Moreover, most were willing to move, and he estimated that it would cost the government only $11,000 to remove them. Hence, the reservation site was not only an ideal location, it was also a bargain. Arny also suggested four alternative sites, including the isolated Tularosa River Valley located about eighty miles west of Socorro; Camp Thomas in Arizona; Santa Lucia, established before the Civil War; and the Mescalero Reservation. He urged a rapid decision, given the Apaches' desperate need for protection from whites as they made the transition from what he called barbarity to civilization.

The Indian Office took more than a year to respond. Cochise's people, who had returned to Arizona to prepare for the move to the Cañada, soon heard rumors that, instead of living at Warm Springs, all of the bands were now slated to move in with the Mescaleros near Fort Stanton. Under those circumstances, the Chiricahuas opted to stay in Arizona. Again, Victorio waited anxiously. He had bid farewell to Arny convinced that the decision was final or nearly so. Now a new Presbyterian missionary agent named Orlando Piper was in charge and had no answers. Nor did Nathaniel Pope, New Mexico superintendent of Indian affairs, who visited Cañada Alamosa in April 1871 and begged Victorio to remain patient. Pope managed to increase rations temporarily, and Piper moved his office to the Cañada permanently. But nothing else changed.

Pope also traveled to Arizona to try to persuade Cochise to leave the territory. He found the Chokonens half-starving, but Cochise was nowhere in sight, possibly away raiding or attempting to hunt for ever-dwindling game. One of the men riding with Pope was a former trader named Thomas Jeffords, who before the Civil War had driven the mail wagons through Chiricahua territory. In fact, it was Jeffords who had negotiated an arrangement with Cochise to secure safe passage through Cooke's Canyon. Because a degree of trust existed between the two men, Jeffords went out alone to locate Cochise. When found, he refused all entreaties to return to camp and talk, but sent word via Jeffords that the influx of whites in the area worried him.

So, too, did the recent attack on Aravaipa Apaches concern him. The Camp Grant massacre, as the event came to be known, forced Apaches to question how well the U.S. government intended to protect them. A Lieutenant Royal E. Whitman had granted the Aravaipas permission to settle at the Camp Grant outpost on a temporary basis and tried to make it permanent. Six weeks later, his unopened letter came back with a note stating that he had not submitted it properly. But Tucson residents, Mexicans, and some Indian allies objected and attacked the Aravaipa camps. They clubbed 144 Indians to death, all of them technically under army protection. As a result, Cochise grew even more suspicious of whites and refused to leave the safety of his mountain stronghold. Thus, Arny's visit left Victorio in the same precarious position as before, in limbo because his permanent reservation hinged on Cochise's decision. To make matters worse, in 1870 many of the Apache bands suffered from another smallpox epidemic as well. As his people grew ill, Victorio asked over and over why there was no word.

Vincent Colyer Selects the Tularosa Valley

Word came in the form of Vincent Colyer, a member of the Board of Indian Commissioners. For more than a year, the board had engaged in a power struggle with the commissioner. Whereas Parker had chosen Arny, the board sent one of its own. Vincent Colyer arrived at the Cañada Alamosa on August 17, 1871, at a time when Victorio was in Mexico. In Victorio's absence, the naïve and woefully misinformed Colyer concluded that the chief no longer wanted to live at Warm Springs. Pope cautioned the commissioner against making such a foolhardy assumption, but Colyer decided that the Tularosa Valley was the better site anyway. Loco did meet with Colyer and stressed the Chihenne position. When Loco pointed out that already miners from Silver City and Piños Altos were attacking them with some regularity, this seemed to reinforce Colyer's decision. Had Victorio met with Colyer, things might have turned out differently.

Blissfully unaware of the ramifications of his decision, Colyer journeyed on to Arizona without waiting for the most important leader in the Warm Springs region to return. In Arizona, Colyer found the Pinals and White Mountain Apaches cultivating corn, beans, and pumpkins. All Victorio's people needed, he maintained, was a liberal distribution of hoes, spades, and seed, plus a few years' time to do likewise. Victorio could have told Colyer that agent Steck had already introduced farming at Warm Springs, but the tools and seed never arrived with any regularity. While in Arizona, Colyer got a taste of the newly arrived and brusque General George Crook, recently appointed as commanding officer. Crook curtly informed the unwelcome commissioner that the War Department had issued him no orders to cooperate. Moreover, nobody under his command possessed such an order, either.

Arizona newspapers branded Colyer a do-gooder, and Crook sarcastically dubbed him "Colyer the Good." Governor Stafford asked citizens to treat Colyer kindly, but letters to the editor were revealing. One reader wrote: "That the President's 'peace policy,' so popular in the states, does not meet with much approval out here is unquestionably true; and any one who comes here to execute it must expect to meet with Disapprobation."

A staunch abolitionist before the war, Colyer was used to controversy. Besides, in addition to resettling Victorio's Chihennes and Cochise's Chiricahuas, Colyer had an even more unpopular mission. He planned also to document the corruption he found among the many contractors who supplied reservations and military forts. He could expect little thanks for his efforts because the fragile economies of New Mexico and Arizona depended heavily upon these contracts. Back in April 1870, Charles Drew had accused two contractors—Thomas Jeffords and Elias Brevoort—of stealing timber from Apache land and got the government to revoke their licenses. Brevoort retaliated by charging Drew with supplying whiskey to the Indians and claiming he was frequently drunk on the job. As a result, Drew's fate was in limbo at the time of his death.

With so much government money up for grabs, fraud, mis-representation, and corruption remained widespread. Bootleg-ging was rampant, and this was yet another problem Victorio faced. Nor had he ever had much luck with agents. Victorio of-ten complained about the lack of food and the poor quality of the beef and flour handed out to his people. Those, like Drew, who fought on behalf of the Apaches usually lost. Others co-operated and lined their pockets. The result was always the same: Victorio's people teetered on the brink of starvation most of the time, and it was only the ability of his warriors to slip off the reservation and raid that kept them supplied with meat. Things had changed little in the twenty years since a frustrated Michael Steck first noted that nearly eighty percent of the money paid out for supplies was going into the hands of corrupt agents and contractors, most of whom clearly did not want the Apache wars to end. Peace with the Apaches posed an economic threat. Nor did they especially want Victorio and Cochise's people as-similated and independent. Although Victorio perhaps accu-rately realized that whites were perpetuating war, he probably did not know why. He thought Americans just wanted his peo-ple exterminated; he did not know they sought to make money from the Apaches' misery.

When Colyer returned to New Mexico, his decision was final. Significantly, he made his decision without listening to the most important leader in the region. Although the Cañada Alamosa contained pure spring water and fertile land, every acre of it was occupied by the Mexicans, "including a town of three hundred," he incorrectly wrote. To even think of buying them out was pre-posterous. Victorio would have pointed to his trading partners in the village of Monticello and asked if these were the Mexicans to whom Colyer was referring. They were not intruders, Victo-rio would have told him. The farmers were his friends. In fact, even after 1879, when Victorio's people were on the run from American soldiers, the people of Monticello kept them supplied with food, clothing, and guns. In return, Monticello was always exempt from Chihenne trouble. The preferred reservation, Colyer determined, was the Tularosa Valley, approximately ninety miles northwest of Warm Springs. He notified Pope, then Washington, of his decision. Suitably isolated with sufficient wood, water, land, and game, the valley was large enough to hold Cochise's band as well. On November 11, 1871, the Indian Office handed down orders for the move to proceed, and nine days later, the preparations began.

Victorio Refuses to Move

Victorio heard the news at about the time that his son Charlie Istee was born and as he mourned the death of his third wife. He was furious, then defiant. Loco agreed. Moreover, Cochise flatly refused to consider Tularosa as a permanent home. He took the last of his band back to Arizona in March 1872 and vowed to safeguard his own territory from all removal attempts. Victorio brusquely informed agent Piper that the new site was unhealthy. It bred fevers and disease, he told the agent. Piper replied that the decision was now out of his hands.

   Victorio refused outright to go. Piper closed down the Cañada Alamosa agency and sent word to Victorio that he would hand out no more rations from that location. Still, Victorio did not budge. They were a mountain people, he exclaimed. Ussen had given them the springs as a source of power. How could they remain a people if they neglected the one thing asked of them? An unsure Piper cautioned the military not to use force against the defiant Chihennes. It would only intensify an already delicate situation. He pleaded with the superintendent and, through him, with the Indian Office for more time. Army columns watched Victorio's people more closely than before. Then, as noted above, tragedy struck when women out digging roots were attacked and killed, one of them Victorio's second wife. Now, his mourning increased.

   The War Department sent representatives to assess the matter. Victorio stayed away, undoubtedly on account of his grief. Those who had come to scrutinize the situation noted that prospectors were already invading the Tularosa Valley. Thus, it was less attractive than Colyer had indicated. For the time being, therefore, the move was put on hold. But again, the delay only complicated matters. The troops had already garrisoned Fort Tularosa, and on May 9, Piper had formally established the new agency. Moreover, a few Chihennes had already settled there. Disgusted at the whole situation, Loco departed for Mescalero country. Victorio hid most of his people deep in the Black Mountains. A stalemate ensued.

However, in late May, Victorio abruptly rode onto the Tularosa reservation and sent word to Piper that if wagons arrived at the Warm Springs to transport elders and supplies, his people would make the ninety-mile trek to the Tularosa reservation. What changed Victorio's mind? His great-granddaughter suggested that it was the need to obtain rations. Babies such as Charlie and Beshad-e would never survive if the Chihenne hunters kept returning without game. Whatever the reason for Victorio's decision, approximately three hundred Apaches left the Cañada Alamosa in late spring in army wagons, on horseback, and on foot. They moved across the northern Mimbres range and down into the valley of the Tularosa.

Their new home was heavily forested, and the land was poorer than at Cañada Alamosa. Crops had more difficulty taking root. The corn and pumpkins raised at Warm Springs had proven far superior. For years afterward, whenever the Chihennes returned, they found crops growing in profusion along the Cañada Alamosa. Maybe these crops continued on their own. It is more likely, however, that a small contingent of men and women always secretly remained behind and tended the plants. The Tularosa Valley experienced more extremes of temperature than did the Warm Springs area. Nights were often frigid even in spring and autumn. As Colyer had noted, the valley was isolated, which made transportation of supplies more difficult and increased the costs significantly. Rations were slow to arrive, and because of that, hungry raiding bands trickled out of the valley. Some abandoned Tularosa altogether, heading back to the Warm Springs or to Cochise country. Those who stayed largely abandoned farming after the first summer and turned instead to gathering wild foods to supplement whatever rations arrived. At times, they took the rations they did not care to eat, such as white flour, to the scattered Mexican villages and traded for venison, beef, and corn.

While living at Tularosa, Dilth-cleyhen remarried and moved out of her father's wickiup. Within a few months, she was pregnant again. But before she could even tell her husband about the baby, he was shot and killed in a raid. In 1873, she gave birth to another daughter, and at about the same time the woman taking care of Charlie Istee grew desperately ill. Victorio returned from her camp with his infant son, and by summer 1873, Dilth-cleyhen was raising three children, two of her own and her brother, whom she treated as her own child. Later that year, Carl Mangas—one of Mangas Coloradas's sons—asked Victorio if he thought Dilth-cleyhen might accept him as her new husband. She agreed. Thus, for the third time in just a few years, Victorio's eldest daughter was newly married. Afterward, a worried and brooding Victorio left the reservation at frequent intervals. He often rode south into Old Mexico to raid and trade. Sometimes he conferred with Cochise. He had a permanent reservation, but his people scarcely had enough food to eat and nothing much to do each day.

What Victorio did not know, of course, was that General Crook was preparing for a winter campaign against all off-reservation Apaches. As military officials had predicted, the wind was blowing in a new direction. Colyer had lost favor with the Interior Department. His reports on corruption had found too "many avenues of fraud ... to watch them all at once," and the Board of Indian Commissioners began to examine accounts presented to the Indian Office for payment. In 1873 alone, they turned down thirty-nine vouchers totaling $426,909.96. They forced a congressional investigation of Commissioner Parker, and although he was absolved of complicity in the corruption, he resigned. Still, Colyer crossed swords with the secretary of the interior once too often and in 1873 resigned from the board altogether. But even as Colyer's influence waned, a third peace mission was taking place.

Mangus, son of Mangas Coloradas. Courtesy of Palace of the Governors (MNM/DCA) (negative #16327).

Oliver O. Howard Betrays Victorio

Oliver O. Howard, a Civil War veteran whose one arm revealed combat and military honors, headed this final mission. Howard had overseen the Freedman's Bureau at the end of the Civil War and generally seemed a good choice for dealing with Apaches like Victorio. For one thing, he combined military service with an evangelical Christian zeal. He outranked Crook and carried instructions directly from Secretary of the Interior Columbus Delano himself. His piety irritated many, but Indians tended to like Howard. He regarded himself as especially gifted in dealing with them. And he listened. In addition, he absolutely believed that Apaches needed fertile land, protection under the law, and some viable means of assimilating into mainstream society. In Victorio he saw a victim who needed a friend. Unfortunately, his romantic, Cooperesque image of the long-suffering Noble Savage clouded Howard's ability to truly fathom Victorio's situation. Still, the forty-five-year-old Victorio discovered a rare empathy in Howard's approach and attitude.

Howard arrived at Tularosa in July 1872, and Victorio met with him soon after. Both Howard and his assistant, Lieutenant Frank J. Sladen, took notes of the meetings. Their observations often stand in stark contrast, but between them we get a glimpse at the otherwise elusive Victorio and perhaps a touch of the dilemma he faced. Interestingly, Howard described Victorio as neither aloof nor wily, but sincere and soft-spoken, a good man who "was troubled for his people." Sladen saw a face stamped with cunning and cruelty, but Howard concluded that Victorio "made my mission successful." Victorio made it clear from the start that he hated Tularosa and wanted to return to the Cañada Alamosa. Howard sensed that Victorio spoke not only for himself but as a strong force against the young warriors who favored an all-out attempt at war with the Americans. Thus, he cultivated the Chihenne's friendship and concluded that Victorio was at heart a man who desired peace.

Victorio escorted Howard around Tularosa and then Cañada Alamosa. As he did so, Howard also received a first-hand view of Apache camp life. They "are deliberate" in their speech, though garrulous once they get started, he observed. Reticent to speak in front of whites, they loved to play practical jokes on each other, and they laughed a lot among themselves. They were so polite that even when men and women were on the verge of starving, they did not eat unless invited. Their dietary mainstay was an unappetizing flour pancake, which weighed about a pound and was as sodden as a cake of putty, Howard noted with distaste. However, this was the result of insufficient and terrible rations, he claimed, and not an Apache choice.

Finally, Howard agreed that Warm Springs was superior to Tularosa. The water was more plentiful and better tasting. The land was more fertile and had better irrigation possibilities. Besides, "we want to live here," Victorio repeated many times. The cost of buying out the few Mexican families residing in and around the Cañada Alamosa region was still negligible. Yes, Tularosa was the more isolated location, but, as already discovered, living there meant astronomical transportation costs and lengthy delays in receiving necessary supplies. In nearly every sense, Cañada Alamosa was the more sensible reservation site. Before Howard left, Victorio also asked for a new agent. He disliked Piper—they all did—and said of him, "He's getting old, and he had better go home and see his children and take care of them." His people wanted an agent like Drew. Everyone had liked him.

Exactly where communications broke down is uncertain to this day. Perhaps Howard simply overstepped his authority. When Victorio bid good-bye to Howard, he was utterly convinced that he and his people would soon be returning to Warm Springs. For the remainder of 1872 and well into 1873, he awaited final word. Howard, on the other hand, claimed that from the start the agreement depended on Cochise, so after leaving Tularosa, the former general visited the Chiricahuas. Thomas Jeffords and twenty-one-year-old Chie, the son of Cochise's brother Coyuntura, escorted his party. Along the way they picked up two Chiricahua warriors—Sancho and Ponce, a nephew of Cochise and married to Chie's sister—and some of their band. Ponce agreed to help Chie locate the elusive Cochise, and while Ponce was gone, Howard, for some reason, allowed Sancho and the others to camp at Warm Springs. This so enraged whites that a group of Silver City residents mobbed Howard's party as they rode through town. Even worse, Victorio soon discovered that, while his band waited patiently at Tularosa for official instructions, Sancho's people were already living at Warm Springs indefinitely. Victorio also heard that Sancho did not hesitate to raid, which prejudiced whites even further against Apaches. It jaded them against any thought of Victorio's people returning there.

Ponce, Chie, and Jeffords found Cochise, but the Chiricahua chief told Howard that he still refused to move. He liked New Mexico, but his warriors overwhelmingly favored Arizona, and so he, in a sense, was outvoted. Cochise reminded Howard that he, indeed, wanted whites and Indians to drink of the same water and to remain friends, but he would stay in his own territory. As a result, Howard recommended a new reservation later called the Great Chiricahua Reservation to house all of Cochise's Chiricahuas. There was enough land for them to hunt and live in relative isolation. Fort Bowie would serve as their military protection. Jeffords, whom the Chiricahuas dubbed Stag-lito or Red Beard, agreed to stay on as agent. Everyone parted "with utmost good feeling," and the Chiricahua reservation was confirmed by presidential executive order on December 14, 1872. Because it abutted the Mexican border, there were constant rumors regarding Apache raids into Sonora. But Cochise remained there, and even after his death on June 8, 1874, his son Taza tried to live up to his father's promise.

However, the creation of the Great Chiricahua Reservation cost Victorio dearly. The deal negated the agreement that he believed he and Howard had made. As Victorio waited in limbo in the Tularosa Valley, Howard sent word to the agency explaining that the president would not set apart the Cañada for "a few Indians," nor would Congress allocate the money to buy the land. But the agent in charge did not pass the information along to Victorio. Howard also claimed, "Victoria [*sic*] knows that I believed Cachise [*sic*] would go to [the] Cañada but he did not go."

Apparently, Victorio knew nothing of the kind. He was again be-
trayed, and by a white man he had dared to trust. Howard sent
instructions to the superintendent in Santa Fe to authorize the
addition of coffee, sugar, and one-half pound of flour per day to
the regular rations. He approved Piper's leave of absence for
"reasons of health," and the agent left with a great sense of relief.
However, it was John Ayers who replaced Piper in November
1872, and it was Ayers who kept Howard's letter out of Victorio's
hands. Consequently, it is not at all clear that one agent was better than the other.

Conditions at Tularosa Deteriorate

On November 11, settlers blamed Victorio for attacking the isolated Brown Ranch not far from the Cañada Alamosa. Victorio
reminded Ayers that Sancho, not he, was living at Warm Springs,
and his own people remained at Tularosa, awaiting word of their
impending move. Perhaps whites or Mexican outlaws had taken
the livestock. Most likely, it was Sancho, Victorio snapped. His
people could not patrol the region or police other Indians!
Wasn't that the job of the military? He did, however, offer to
hunt down Sancho if doing so would help his own people. It apparently did not.

In the spring, Victorio slipped out of the valley and rode to
Chiricahua territory. Indeed, he began to lead warriors back and
forth between the Great Chiricahua Reservation and Warm
Springs with some regularity. He also rode into Sonora occasionally to raid and trade. Whites along the border raised such
a noise that the secretary of the interior asked the military to consider transferring authority for the Chiricahuas to New Mexico
in order to unify the jurisdiction for Apaches. The War Department countered that it was not the jurisdictional split between
New Mexico and Arizona, but the Interior Department's inability to deal with the unsatisfactory Tularosa situation. At the
same time, Arizonans complained about Jeffords and his loose
methods in dealing with the Chiricahuas while New Mexicans
admonished Superintendent Levi Edwin Dudley for allowing

Victorio to migrate at will. Howard's actions had probably laid the groundwork for a policy called concentration.

The concept was not new. Actually, a Colonel James L. Collins had initially proposed a single Apache reservation near a military post back in 1857, but the idea was dismissed. However, the Interior Department came to favor concentration as a concept during the war years, but could not persuade Congress to act. The proposal reared its head again about 1870, and Fort Apache was named as an ideal place. In 1872, Howard formally delineated what would afterward be called the San Carlos Reservation, located near Fort Apache. In addition to the ideas taking shape in Washington, corporate interests were beginning to eye the large copper deposits in western New Mexico and around Bisbee, Arizona. Industry could not realize the potential wealth in these regions until the Apaches were removed. Hence, economic development provided a motive for quick action.

Conditions at Tularosa deteriorated rapidly. Victorio's people often found the commanding officer of Fort Tularosa drunk and the men allowed to do pretty much whatever they pleased. In January 1874, for instance, drunken troopers accidentally shot an Apache woman in the arm. The post surgeon amputated her arm, and she died. In addition, the post trader freely sold whiskey to troops and Apaches alike. Finally, in late February, Victorio, with support from Nana, Loco, and Ponce, informed Superintendent Dudley that they wanted to return to Cañada Alamosa right away. A shocked Dudley suddenly realized that Ayers had never read them Howard's letter. No wonder they kept talking as if the move were a certainty. Now, Dudley had to tell them the truth. He described their reaction as sulky and morose, but it was undoubtedly a combination of disbelief and sense of betrayal.

Afterward, the situation at Tularosa grew even worse. Frustration boiled over into "practical jokes" against whites. Dr. Henry Duane reported arrows shot at him as he answered a call at the agency. That they missed him suggests an attempt at intimidation rather than any real threat to his person. Although the doctor concluded that the Apaches fired the arrows for their own amusement, it is more likely that such actions revealed extreme frustration and even rage. Their contempt was compounded as disease increased among those living nearest to the agency. Duane reported treating fevers, whooping cough, dysentery, conjunctivitis, pleurisy and other types of lung ailments, as well as an unusually large number of abrasions and lacerations. That spring other white employees of the agency also dodged miscellaneous arrows fired at them as they walked from building to building. A frightened agent Thomas received reports that Victorio was raiding off the reservation and that some of his bands were secretly brewing tiswin or tulapai in the remotest sections.

In midsummer a band of Mescaleros attacked Shedd's Ranch in the Organ Mountains, a major stopping-off point in the stolen cattle trade. The Eighth Cavalry killed three of them and trailed the rest to Tularosa. They were, the cavalry concluded, heading straight to Victorio. When soldiers discovered that it was Sancho who was leading the raiding parties, Thomas demanded that Victorio help track him down. In an uncharacteristic show of anger, an enraged Victorio allegedly shouted that if the agent wanted to fight Apaches, he would happily oblige him and stormed out of the agent's office. Victorio reportedly quipped as he left that "the tiswin was about ready," and they would have to finish talking later. When several companies of cavalry plus Navajo scouts arrived the next morning to search for Sancho, Victorio at first sent word that he would meet them in a canyon, where nobody could surround him. Then, he apparently changed his mind and sent word that he was meeting warriors arriving from the Chiricahua reservation instead. Perhaps he wanted to make the military think he had large numbers of warriors available for battle. Or the excuse might have simply provided a cover under which to leave the area. As the troops waited, Victorio broke camp and melted into the mountains.

In response, a less than diplomatic Thomas herded as many of Victorio's followers as he and the soldiers could round up into the agency corral and held them hostage. "If they want war," the agent allegedly blustered, "let them have it." But Victorio did not want war. He simply wanted to go home to Warm Springs and ignore the white men. Moreover, what Thomas did not know was that one of Victorio's nephews had been wounded in a recent raid. Thus, he was protecting his nephew, not trying to instigate war. Victorio returned without explanation to the agency later that summer, but for the remainder of the year, he traveled out of Tularosa and into the Black and Mogollon ranges at will.

The Apaches who lived in the Tularosa Valley at this time numbered approximately 660 in the winter and 300 in the summer. Women, like the men, found themselves always on guard. They did not feel safe. Nor did they know when intruders might attack them. According to Dilth-cleyhen, such assaults occurred with uncomfortable regularity. Women and elders remained on alert to gather up children at a moment's notice and run away. Of course, that often meant losing whatever foods they were harvesting at the time, which made for even less to eat. The specter of starvation hovered over them. And without necessary corn, meat, and hides, it was impossible to plan events such as the puberty ceremonies, since one could not pay for di-yins to perform the rituals.

After months of waiting, Dudley inspected the Cañada Alamosa himself. By executive order of April 9, 1874, Victorio's people were allowed to return, and on July 21, Dudley ordered Thomas to open a new agency there. It was exactly what Arny had recommended four years earlier. Victorio was relieved. An immediate change came over his people. For one thing, arrows stopped flying. That summer Victorio led his people home. Agent Benjamin M. Thomas resigned, and in September, John M. Shaw of Socorro was named agent to the Southern Apaches. The problem was, of course, that all of this was still only a temporary solution.

CHAPTER 6

"Hell's Forty Acres"

AS Victorio moved his people back to Warm Springs, the debate over civilian versus military control of Indian affairs reached a climax. Former Commissioner Ely Parker, himself a former military man, condemned civilian agents as men who lacked experience and authority. They were, he believed, destined to fail, and once they did, the military would need to step in and fight or patch things up. The military, in turn, called Interior's policy of concentration impractical and unbusinesslike. Victorio would have described them all as, at best, a people who made no sense.

Several western state and territorial legislatures issued memorials demanding transfer of the Indian Office back to the Department of War. The Catholic Church pressured the government as well, especially when the Board of Indian Commissioners announced plans to divide reservations between the Protestant denominations only. Congress dutifully proposed transfer bills in 1876 and 1878, but neither passed. New secretary of the interior Carl Schurz launched an investigation of the Indian Office in an attempt to eradicate the worst problems. None of these actions helped Victorio and his people, who remained trapped inside the jurisdictional debate and subjected to the whims of Washington bureaucrats.

Back home at the Cañada Alamosa, a wary Victorio carefully established his camps atop buttes, which allowed his warriors to watch the valleys below and monitor every conceivable approach to his area. He stationed men on the towering rocks that lined many of the riverbeds. Following a rainfall, the rivers tended to flood and thereby prevented access from the outside altogether. But when these beds were dry, as they were for much

135

of the year, almost anyone could easily come through the narrow canyons and wreak havoc, if he wished, upon the unsuspecting camps. Thus, once they returned to the Cañada Alamosa, the Chihenne warriors stood ready to turn back any unwanted visitors.

Indian inspector E. C. Kemble described Victorio's favorite haunt to the *New York Times* as surrounded by high hills, approached from the side "nearest civilization" through a narrow pass, in which a hundred resolute Indians could keep an army at bay. It was a place where Victorio might hurry his women and children out of sight in seconds and barricade them from intrusion. However, his immediate difficulties did not come from the canyons surrounding his stronghold, but were caused by several peripheral events. One of these events was the death of the great Chiricahua chief Cochise, which occurred on June 8, 1874, following a long illness, which some believe was cancer.

How Cochise's Death Affected the Chihennes

With Chihennes again living at the Cañada Alamosa, a few Chiricahuas maneuvered past General George Crook's military patrols to join Victorio. It was from these men and women that he learned of Cochise's death. The esteemed chief had died about the time that Victorio was leaving Tularosa Valley. Shortly before Cochise's death, agent Jeffords and Superintendent Dudley had visited his village and found the chief sitting astride his horse in front of his wickiup. He was about to die, Cochise told them, and he wanted to sit on his horse one last time. At nearly seventy years of age, Cochise still possessed such tremendous strength that many Apaches, including Victorio, believed his illness and subsequent death could only be caused by witchcraft. Cochise's leading di-yin had even created a special and extremely powerful tonic called *zagosti* to thin the chief's blood and strengthen his heart, but to no avail. Its failure to work merely confirmed the suspicions.

Witchcraft was, of course, the worst crime an Apache could commit. It therefore warranted the worst punishment. Clearly,

Victorio agreed with Jason Betzinez, who said that once an Apache suspected witchcraft, his suspicion soon produced fear, then hatred, and finally the need to act. Thus, Victorio would have approved when Taza, Cochise's son, took twenty-seven warriors to hunt down the suspected witch. Taza dragged the witch back to the main Chiricahua camp and ordered him to cure the chief or face death by slow fire, a terrible but fitting way for a witch to die. Cochise died despite everything and, undoubtedly, so did the suspected witch.

With Cochise dead, Taza became the primary Chiricahua chief. Although well liked, an esteemed warrior, and possessed of an ability to get along with whites, Taza unfortunately lacked his father's charisma. He was unable to hold together a large following, as his father had. The young warriors increasingly challenged Taza's authority, especially men who resented having to live on a reservation. Skinya, one of Cochise's fiercest and most courageous warriors, and his brother, Pionsenay, led the unrest against Taza. Despite their new chief's pleas to stay on the reservation, they frequently skirted Crook's troops and raided in Old Mexico. Moreover, the brothers headed straight for Warm Springs when the authorities got too close.

Their activities created factions among the Chiricahuas. Some of the men followed Taza and others gave their allegiance to Skinya and Pionsenay. Still others transferred their loyalty to Victorio, who was sometimes in the middle of the factions. Some disgruntled Chiricahuas followed neither Taza nor the brothers, but moved instead to the Cañada Alamosa reservation and called Victorio their chief. This had the unhappy consequence of inflating the number of Apaches living at Warm Springs and keeping rations short. The new agent, John M. Shaw, noticed the expanding population, and this movement, which created instability on the Chiricahua reservation as well.

A second event also occurred during summer 1874. Geronimo showed up at Warm Springs with horses destined for trade into Mexico. He, too, began to use the Chihennes' reservation as a base of operations. Because rations were few, he raided frequently. Sometimes he hooked up with white and Mexican outlaws to trade. When asked about Geronimo's presence, however, Victorio's usual response was "these people are not bothering us." In fact, this was an understatement because off-reservation warriors such as Geronimo, Skinya, and Pionsenay brought livestock to help supplement the scanty rations. Moreover, they helped keep the Chihennes better clothed, armed, and mounted.

Victorio also left the reservation at frequent intervals in search of supplies. He, too, traded as far south as Janos, although more often with the villagers of Monticello. Inspector Kemble claimed that Victorio sometimes traded government-issued goods. Kemble's disdain for this practice is clear in his writings. If one cared to look around the town, he noted, one could see government property in the shape of camp kettles, axes, tin ware, and clothing. Even worse, he said, the cutthroat Mexican thieves "sauntered lazily about in blankets on which the brand U.S.I.D. [United States Interior Department] appeared in letters nearly half a foot long." Obviously, Monticello—which the inspector inaccurately referred to as Cañada Alamosa—supplied the Chihennes with what the agency could not. Every so often, the farmers gave candy or some sweet treat to the Apache children as well. But Victorio's dealings with them branded the villagers as cutthroats and the Chihennes as renegades.

During his off-reservation forays, Victorio sometimes went east to visit the Mescaleros, where he reportedly had another wife. If he crossed the Rio Grande during the summer, the riverbed was usually little more than mud. During the winter or spring months, however, runoff from the mountains to the north could make the river a torrent. At such times, Victorio, like all Apaches, tossed a piece of turquoise into the raging water as he prayed for assistance and a safe crossing.

The Mescalero Reservation, which was formally established on May 29, 1873, also fell short of rations. There were always some warriors who, like Victorio, escaped to the White or Guadalupe Mountains in search of wild game, or who raided the scattered farms around Lincoln County. Like Geronimo, the Mescaleros increasingly sold their livestock to the growing gangs of cattle rustlers operating out of La Mesilla or El Paso Del Norte. How

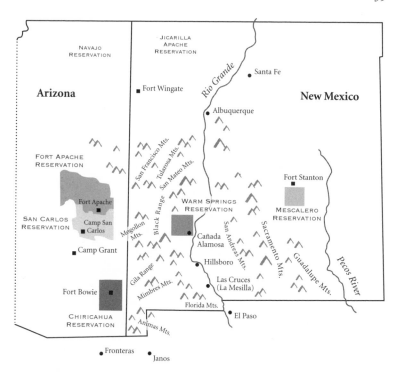

Warm Springs, Chiricahua, Mescalero, and San Carlos reservations

often Victorio accompanied these Mescalero warriors on their hunting and raiding expeditions is not known. Nevertheless, movement between reservations encouraged communications and trade between Apaches and gave warriors in particular something to do besides sitting idly near the agency. At the same time, such movement between reservations unnerved whites.

The Indian Office Selects San Carlos

For the most part, Dilth-cleyhen recalled the days at Warm Springs as some of the best. Women again used the summertime to harvest wild foods when they could find them, although now they always carried revolvers and as much ammunition as possible. Instead of warriors, it was usually the younger boys who accompanied the women, but they, too, armed themselves to the hilt. Although they constantly feared attack, Dilth-cleyhen fondly remembered how Victorio took her, Charlie Istee, and his grandchildren on extended excursions into the Black Mountains.

There he told them stories about their people's origins and showed them significant places. Over there were the petroglyphs left when the Gáans departed from earth. Right here Ussen told the ancient ones to stop their migration and seek their special powers. In those very mountains, White Painted Woman taught the first Apaches to locate the healing plants and stones that they would need. She explained to them which animals they might eat and which they must avoid. Every animal had something to teach humans, but they must observe carefully and patiently. Here White Painted Woman and Child of the Water handed down the sacred instructions for all of the Apaches to follow and for the first time gave them their ceremonies, prayers, and songs. Power came from these very springs. That was why the Chihennes must never surrender their land, he said. To do so was also to forsake their sacred responsibility. It was their job to care for all of this. In short, Victorio gave his children and grandchildren the lessons that would sustain them as a people even after they left this place. He must also have asked Ussen whether Killer of Enemies had somehow made his white tribe stronger than Child of the Water's Indeh.

While Victorio remained at Warm Springs, the government busily strung telegraph wire to Apachería to enhance communications between the Indian Office and its agents and between military commands east and west of the Mississippi. Moreover, by 1873, the Indian Office decided to concentrate all remaining Apaches onto a single reservation and chose San Carlos in eastern Arizona. General O. O. Howard had formally delineated this spot during his 1872 visit. Wedged between what today is the Tonto National Forest and the New Mexico border, San Carlos was located approximately one hundred desolate and often waterless miles north of Tucson. With the telegraph in place, however, San Carlos seemed less remote and more feasible as a reservation. Lieutenant Britton Davis, who would later command the Indian scouts and after Victorio's death negotiate a surrender with Nana and Geronimo in 1883, called San Carlos "Hell's forty acres." Soldiers assigned there considered it the worst place in the whole territory. Everybody claimed that if people had ever lived there on a permanent basis, no Apache knew of it. The area was denuded of all vegetation except for a few low-growing, viciously armored cacti. Temperatures soared to one hundred and twenty degrees in the summer and hovered over one hundred degrees from May through October. Water was stagnant and brackish, and in most places, there was none at all. Rocks heated to such intensity that their touch burned through moccasin soles. Rattlesnakes, tarantulas, scorpions, Gila monsters, and giant centipedes infested what little shade was available, and at night slithered forth, making even more danger for humans. Western novelist Own Wister later wrote: "Take stones and ashes and thorns, with some scorpions and rattlesnakes thrown in, dump the outfit on stones, heat the stones red hot, set the United States Army after the Apaches, and you have San Carlos."

Western Apaches had gone there on January 1, 1873. Next came the Yavapais and Walapais, followed by the White Mountain Apaches. Victorio escaped concentration for the time being. At first, these Western Apaches found a degree of isolation from each other, but as San Carlos filled up, it was less likely that the New Mexico Apaches would find satisfactory accommodations once they were removed there. San Carlos was governed by a parade of incompetent agents, but because of the strong military presence, most of these early agents managed the reservation using a prisoner-of-war model. However, after the Board of Indian Commissioners began to replace existing agents with missionary agents, the responsibility for San Carlos fell to the Dutch Reformed Church.

Thus, John Philip Clum arrived at San Carlos on August 8, 1874. He was twenty-two years old when he set foot on the reservation for the first time. A New York native, he had no experience whatsoever in dealing with Indians. In his teens, he began to suffer so badly from acute rheumatoid arthritis that he had to

Apaches waiting in line for the ration door to open at San Carlos Agency, Arizona. Courtesy of Center for Southwest Research, University of New Mexico. Indians of North America Collection (negative #994-045-0004).

quit Rutgers University before graduation and move to New Mexico's dry, hot climate. The Reformed Church needed an Indian agent, and in 1874 Clum was living and working in Santa Fe. The youthful Clum was brash, quick-witted, and hot-tempered, but to his credit, he was also honest and willing to learn Apache ways to some extent.

In contrast to the military, Clum adopted a civilian model. On August 10, just two days after he arrived at San Carlos, Clum created an Apache police force. This worked so well that by 1877 the Board of Indian Commissioners recommended tribal police systems on all reservations. In fact, on May 27, 1878, Congress appropriated $30,000 for Indian police, and by 1880, there were forces on forty reservations. Clum also established a tribal court, placing law enforcement into the hands of Apaches whenever feasible. Although he made himself the leading judge, he chose influential leaders to serve on a panel of justices so that it was an Indian court which sentenced wrongdoers. He would later make a point of inviting Victorio to participate on the court.

Clum confiscated weapons to cut down on the violence and to make Indians dependent on government-issued rations. He shut down the illicit brewing of tizwin and tulapai as much as he could. Convinced that idleness bred trouble, the new agent recruited Apache men to dig a sanitation system and to erect agency buildings. Clum's unique style allowed him to persuade the San Carlos Apaches to do things they would probably never have done for other white men. It is also reasonable to think that, for the first time ever, these Apaches were asked to do something besides sit around and remain inactive most of the time. However, there was still inadequate food and shelter, and the generally unhealthy conditions bred disease. Nor was the land productive for farming. Most frequently, Clum clashed with the locals. And he ran into trouble with the military assigned to protect the reservation.

Initially, Clum ran headlong into General George Crook, a former West Pointer who first fought Indians in 1856 in Oregon and since 1871 had commanded the military at Fort Apache. The general firmly advocated military control over what he called civilian interference. Crook had vehemently opposed Vincent Colyer's mission and tolerated Howard only because the one-armed general boasted a distinguished military background and outranked him. Crook's disdain for government Indian policy did not make him an enemy of the Indian, but he proved a thorn in the side of civilian agents.

That Crook was unconventional was shown even in his dress. He wore Chiricahua-style boots with a nose, dressed in canvas or corduroy suits and a felt hat rather than standard army garb, and in cooler weather, he sported an old army coat with a bright red lining. He set about almost immediately to streamline the long, cumbersome army pack trains that limited mobility and offered visible targets for ambush. He recruited Apache scouts who could follow trails and locate remote hideouts, and for the remainder of the Apache wars these scouts were a constant and very visible presence. Victorio hated the notion of using Apaches to trail Apaches and often thought them contemptible traitors. Still, he had to admire the strategy.

John P. Clum, San Carlos Indian agent, and his Apache tribal police escorts. Photo by H. Buehman. Courtesy of Palace of the Governors (MNM/DCA) (negative #70554).

More important, Crook, like Clum, discovered that a good many of the problems came not from the Apache people but from agents, post traders, and contractors who plundered the supplies intended for Apaches, and also from the Indian Office, which held remarkably short-term views. He believed that the Interior Department should have secured Warm Springs as a permanent reservation site when it had had the chance. Warm Springs, not San Carlos, was where Victorio's people belonged and there was no good reason, short of blind arrogance, why the Indian Office could not have secured that location. Later, Crook repeatedly cautioned Apaches to learn farming techniques and assimilate, but disagreed that they were savages. "The American Indian [is] the intellectual peer of most, if not all, the various nationalities we have assimilated to our laws, customs, and language," he later wrote.

During the first nine months of Clum's tenure as Indian agent at San Carlos, there were constant fireworks between the two men. Clum believed that Crook encouraged his officers to show disrespect toward him, or at the very least turned a blind eye to their antics. When Clum first arrived, he discovered that the parade ground was decorated with Indian heads, presumably about two weeks old. According to one story, a scout unceremoniously tossed a burlap sack containing a severed head at the new agent's feet. It was rumored that when Clum conducted a roll call, the post commander held a simultaneous roll call and threatened to send soldiers after any Apache who answered the agent's instead of his roll call. Sadly, with Clum, it is sometimes hard to tell where fantasy ends and the truth begins. Nevertheless, he claimed, probably accurately, that he had a difficult time establishing his authority. Once, when Clum made it clear that he, not the military, was in charge of the San Carlos agency, the post commander—with Crook's nod of approval—opened the guardhouse and released all Apache prisoners in retaliation.

This patronizing attitude carried over after Crook was reassigned to the Department of the Platte in March 1875 and left Arizona. He did not return until 1882, and therefore, it was Civil War veteran August V. Kautz who was commanding officer during the remainder of Clum's tenure and the entire time that Victorio lived at San Carlos. Needless to say, the fireworks between military and civilian agent continued. So, as Victorio's people moved onto "Hell's forty acres," they were also caught inside the jurisdictional turf battles between departments, ideologies, and personalities.

Concentration Reaches Warm Springs

After Cochise's death, the steady defection of warriors who refused to follow Taza, combined with what Crook called agent

Tom Jeffords's loose methods, made the Chiricahuas' situation tenuous. In late May 1876, Skinya and Pionsenay reportedly killed a stage keeper in Cooke's Canyon. Afterwards, they might have headed to Warm Springs, but in June they showed up again at the Chiricahua Reservation to recruit more warriors. Jeffords called in the military. Before troops could get there, a fight broke out between the leaders. In the scuffle, Taza wounded Pionsenay, and Naiche—Taza's brother—killed Skinya. Six other warriors were killed, too. When the cavalry rode in the following day, the commander relieved Jeffords of his responsibilities and frightened Taza into agreeing to move his people to San Carlos. Less than thirty years old, Taza simply did not command the same authority as his father or possess ability to challenge white dominance.

Clum, accompanied by Colonel Kautz, arrived to escort the Chiricahuas to San Carlos. Clum found Geronimo and Juh on the Chiricahua Reservation and tried to persuade them to move to San Carlos with Taza and the others. Both refused. So Kautz alerted Colonel Edward Hatch in New Mexico that these men, as well as some unhappy Chiricahuas, might attempt to slip away and seek refuge with Victorio's bands at Warm Springs. As Kautz had predicted, some Chiricahua families did in fact sneak to Warm Springs, hoping to live there permanently. Hatch intercepted dozens, but many more got through. With Great Chiricahua Reservation closed, Victorio's land became a magnet for off-reservation Indians and those seeking an alternative to San Carlos.

After the removal of the Chiricahuas, Clum decided that everything was calm enough to allow him to go to Ohio and get married. He decided to mix business with pleasure and took twenty Apaches with him, including Taza. The newly wed Clum and the Apaches visited the Centennial Exposition in Philadelphia and Washington, D.C. There, Taza contracted pneumonia and died. When the nineteen Apaches returned to San Carlos, Naiche became chief. Naiche was even less adept at leadership than Taza, causing even more Chiricahuas to consider Victorio their chief. Furthermore, Chiricahuas found the circumstances of Taza's death mysterious and again suspected witchcraft. As a result, Naiche watched helplessly as his father's once powerful Chiricahuas split into ever increasing factions at San Carlos.

In addition, Geronimo moved on and off the Warm Springs Reservation at will. Thus, the spotlight soon turned on Victorio. It got even brighter after agent John Shaw resigned amid charges of corruption. The Warm Springs agent since November 1874, Shaw primarily contributed a May 1876 census, which contained 916 names. Victorio's name headed the list, along with five dependents. The list also included his eldest son, Washington. The problem was that, although the Warm Springs Apaches generally numbered about 450, the census revealed more than 900. By later that summer, the number swelled to around 1,200.

It is possible that Shaw might have explained the discrepancy, citing the increase in Chiricahuas coming to Warm Springs. However, the Indian Office smelled fraud and sent Inspector Kemble to investigate. Kemble found a number of irregularities. For one thing, Victorio's young warriors sometimes raided the agency beef. Although Shaw at times recovered the cattle, he had to admit that usually he just recorded the loss as "issued to the Indians." He also confessed that neither he nor Victorio could control the young men who did not want to live on a reservation. In addition, he often allowed Victorio to issue the rations to his own band rather than doing it himself. Whether Shaw skimmed any profits off the top is unclear. However, he frequently ran short of rations. The Indian Office noted with some astonishment that Shaw had issued more flour and beef than any other previous agent, and yet the Apaches claimed they were constantly on the verge of starvation.

In his conversations with the inspector, Victorio admitted, "I am getting old," and agreed that he did not control all of the young men on the reservation. He knew that liquor flowed freely across parts of the Warm Springs Reservation, but was powerless to stop it. Whiskey came from outside traders, but the Apaches brewed their own tulapai and, if they were able, ceremonial tizwin. The next Warm Springs agent noted that the Indians frequently traded their cattle for corn in order to make their special concoction. He determined that they preferred to suffer hunger rather than thirst, although by some accounts tulapai has nutritional value. When the only available sources represent a single viewpoint, it is sometimes difficult to find the truth. For example, tulapai might have filled otherwise empty stomachs. Beshad-e insisted that, despite these problems, her grandfather always wanted peace. Sometimes that was just not possible.

Still, Shaw had noted that after the move back to Warm Springs peace, quiet, and order reigned. Victorio had kept faith with the government, even though Dilth-cleyhen recalled that ration lines were long and there was seldom enough food. The Chihennes were happy at Warm Springs, but it was a time of social stress. Idle young men with no way to achieve honors sometimes neglected their family duties. Victorio had trouble keeping tempers from flaring, and even he led them off the reservation now and then. Men and women sat each night around "a low-flamed fire [and] ... talked, discussing various policies, the advice of leaders, what the agents and military men were apt to do." Mostly, she said, they tried to cooperate and raided only when necessary. Beshad-e reported overhearing her mother remark how tired Victorio looked during that time. The lines had deepened at the sides of his mouth. His smiles were rare and fleeting. A few strands of gray hair streaked the black.

Kemble finally concluded that Shaw was a weak administrator and, with the exception of the census, had accomplished little. Worse, the agent had cost the Indian Office too much money. The inspector blamed both Shaw and Victorio for the waste and for allowing Chiricahuas and Geronimo's Bedonkohes to use the Cañada Alamosa agency as a stopping-off point in what he called their illegal trade network. Finally, Kemble claimed that the Mimbres were no further advanced toward "civilization" than when they first came upon a reservation. Shaw resigned June 19, 1876, and James Davis was appointed on August 31. Between those two dates, Lieutenant Henry H. Wright and some of his Navajo scouts attacked one of Victorio's largest villages and burned everything in sight, and a month later a group of citizens from Silver City stole horses from the agency and blamed the theft on Victorio and his Chiricahua allies. In February 1877, a military patrol found Geronimo at Warm Springs, and on March 20, 1877, Clum was finally ordered to take his San Carlos Indian police and arrest him. That order was the end of Victorio's stay at Warm Springs, even though Clum was not immediately told to take the Chihennes back to San Carlos.

Clum arrived at Warm Springs on April 17 or 20, depending on whose account one reads, at approximately 4 A.M. He immediately housed his police in the adobe buildings on the agency grounds and awaited Colonel Hatch's two companies, who were to assist in making arrests. According to some, Clum's police caught Geronimo red-handed in the act of taking supplies from the agency stores and clapped him in chains. Others claim that Clum sent for Geronimo, and when a group of the leaders arrived with him, he shackled all of them, including Victorio, Nana, and Loco. Agent Davis merely wrote that "on the 30th of April and the 1st of May 1877, 450 of these Indians were removed by Agent J. P. Clum, to the San Carlos reservation." Clum's report suggests that he had not heard much about Chief Victorio and perhaps barely noticed him at all. It fails to mention the primary chief of the Warm Springs Chihennes by name. In a letter written to Governor Safford in Tucson on April 26, Clum wrote, "I have Heronemo [sic], Ponce, Gordo and fourteen other prisoners. The worst are chained." Only later did Clum refer to Victorio and then as a chief who wanted his people to live peaceful and orderly lives. At San Carlos, he showed Victorio the utmost respect.

According to oral histories, Victorio received word that Clum sought a talk with him and showed up at the agency about May 1. He was shocked to find himself suddenly taken prisoner. Clum, it seems, had just received a telegram from the Indian Office ordering him to take the Warm Springs Apaches to San Carlos. He offered Victorio clemency and safe passage if he agreed to move, and with 103 Indian police and soldiers surrounding him, Victorio undoubtedly saw few other options. Still, he was allowed to return briefly to his camp. He allegedly announced to his people, "We must leave." But he also prudently counseled them to cache most of their arms before leaving because one day they would return.

Not all of the Indians living at Warm Springs left with Clum. About two hundred, it seems, escaped into the mountains. Some of these were probably Chiricahuas living there clandestinely. Those Chihennes who managed to elude the soldiers and watched their relatives taken away, reportedly followed the procession as it made its way into Arizona. They hallooed at their loved ones to flee, but to no avail. Some must have remained at Warm Springs legally because Davis's August 10 report states that "the Indians who did not leave this reservation on the arrival of Apache scouts from San Carlos and United States troops" were digging irrigation canals and farming, albeit without much enthusiasm.

With Geronimo in chains and Victorio, Nana, and Loco under arrest but not confined, the 453 Warm Springs and Chiricahua Apaches began the slow move to San Carlos. Smallpox broke out among the prisoners even before the caravan started, and along the way, eight Apaches died of the disease. The outbreak increased their desire to escape, and many of the men found themselves torn between freedom and remaining with their wives and children. It was a long and arduous trip, and Victorio knew that some of the elders moved with great difficulty. Most of his people walked over terrain that was hostile and rocky. Rainstorms pelted Victorio's children and turned the steep paths into unstable rinks of mud. The deluges made roads treacherous for wagons, horses, and those men, women, and children struggling on foot.

When the Indians finally arrived, Victorio saw San Carlos at its very worst. Summer temperatures were beginning to peak. Rattlesnakes competed for the paltry strips of shade. He must have felt almost ill. This was not the place Ussen had made for them. Indeed, it did not appear to be a place that Ussen had created for anybody. Their babies began to sicken and die almost immediately upon their arrival. Adults soon started to die as well. Years later, Victorio's granddaughter described the water as "salty—nasty" and the landscape as treeless with only a few mesquite bushes to provide shade. Victorio undoubtedly knew from the start that they could not remain. He resolved, however, to make the best of a terrible situation for the time being.

Existing at San Carlos

Victorio and his Chihenne people adjusted poorly to life on the new reservation. Because San Carlos was already too crowded, they received the former site of Camp Goodwin, abandoned earlier by the military because so many soldiers had died there from malarial fevers. Nevertheless, the place was deemed satisfactory for Apaches. In addition, the influx of Apaches at San Carlos guaranteed that rations were always in short supply, so Victorio again saw his people perpetually on the verge of starvation. Friendly Nednhis and Chiricahuas camped nearby. So, too, did White Mountain Apaches, whose antagonism toward Victorio's band produced frequent arguments and sparked fights. Victorio quickly realized that his children, grandchildren, women and elders, in particular, were in danger.

Victorio also discovered that Pionsenay had followed the Chiricahuas to San Carlos. Unwilling to live on the reservation himself, Pionsenay raided, harassed the military, and generally tried to lure unhappy Apaches away from their captivity. To make matters worse, Pionsenay was able to persuade some of Victorio's own warriors to bolt. Therefore, Victorio faced a dilemma. If he remained, his people risked starvation, illness, and social disintegration. His ability as a leader was compromised, especially among the young men. To flee, however, meant that the weaker ones must stay behind at least until he could sort out a place for them to live. This presented him with a difficult decision because he was not sure he could persuade anyone to let his people go home. Again, outside events intervened.

Since his arrival at San Carlos, Clum had treated Victorio with a rare deference. Fortunately, the agent's normally arrogant manner did not influence their relationship. Right away, Clum offered Victorio a seat on the council of judges, and Victorio accepted without hesitation. The Chihenne chief found Clum a strange but generally honest man. Instead of sending the military to scour the hills for suspected tulapai parties, for example, Clum led the Apache police himself. Yes, the agent was "encumbered by ego and a faulty memory," but he brazenly challenged the military and Indian Office alike on behalf of his charges. He hated Geronimo and regarded him as a ruthless renegade and "multi-murderer," but befriended the other chiefs and earned their respect. Clum even gave nicknames to most of the chiefs, calling Aravaipa chief Eskiminzin "Skimmy," for example. It is worth noting that Clum never contrived a nickname for Victorio.

When Victorio pleaded for improved rations, Clum listened to his complains sympathetically. He agreed that something needed to be done, but could not force Washington to give him more funding. In fact, whether the young agent realized it or not, he was losing the Interior Department's support—and that of the Reformed Church as well—in his continuing battle against the military authorities. After moving Victorio to San Carlos, Clum wrote to the Indian commissioner:

> If your department will increase my salary sufficiently and equip two more companies of Indian police for me, I will volunteer to take care of all the Apaches ... and the troops can be removed.

However, as the Peace Policy waned, so did the desire for missionary agents. Clum, in particular, represented a so-called bleeding-heart civilian and one who openly baited the military. Kautz made no effort to hide his animosity. The Arizona press called the young agent bombastic and impudent, and Tucson merchants complained:

> If you take the military contracts away from us, there [will] be nothing worth staying for. Most of our profits come from feeding soldiers and army mules.

When Kautz assigned an officer to watch over the Indians and to inspect incoming supplies at San Carlos, Clum became furious at what he considered an intrusion into his business. He got even angrier when he heard that Kautz had the tacit approval of the secretary of the interior. Clum had once before tendered his resignation when he felt support from Washington receding. But on July 1, 1877, he resigned for the second and last time. According to Arizona historian Jay J. Wagoner, he rode away, leaving behind a group of bewildered Apaches. This occurred barely two months after Victorio's arrival, and made the Chihennes' situation more uncertain. Clum had skillfully run a poorly planned reservation with little government support. He had kept diverse groups working together, often through sheer force of personality. He had built the agency almost single-handedly and run it virtually alone. Some Apaches, possibly including Victorio, hoped the government would appoint Jeffords, but afflicted with its usual myopia, Washington began to assign another string of incompetent, short-lived agents. One of these was H. L. Hart, who alienated many.

About September 1, two months after Clum's departure, Pionsenay returned laden with goods. He led twenty-two more Chiricahuas away from San Carlos. Fights on the reservation increased, and men periodically slipped into the mountains, allegedly to brew tulapai. Government accounts often report that these off-reservation Apaches consumed large quantities of liquor and returned home to their families drunk. However, whites seldom followed the Apaches into the remote regions and probably saw few of them interact with their families afterward. Thus, Anglo accounts are often unreliable. More than likely, the men who followed Pionsenay were trying to avoid the reservation conflicts. They undoubtedly hunted, perhaps raided, and returned with some trade items and news from other areas. Mangus, Dilth-cleyhen's husband, joined them at times. Victorio apparently did not. But, by mid-September, Victorio came to a decision. He told the other Chihenne leaders that they could not remain there. They thought through their situation. The people were hungry. The elders and children were dying, and fights got worse every day. The new agent cut rations even further. In addition, their children were by this time infested with insects. Malaria attacked young and old alike. Fevers were common. "Why do they want to keep us here?" he heard his people ask many times. The only answer Victorio could logically give them was, "So that we will die."

They would flee. But where? Loco asked the inevitable question. He knew that soldiers patrolled the trail between San Carlos and Warm Springs. Victorio did not know where to go, but anywhere was better than San Carlos. Loco agreed, but in the end, he remained at San Carlos with his family. They had a little food, but despite their starvation rations, Dilth-cleyhen and the other women had managed to hoard small bits of food each time the agent distributed meat, coffee, and flour. Fortunately for them, Apaches were used to going without. Besides, they had dried meat and corn, blankets, and weapons cached in the mountains not far from the Warm Springs agency.

Some of Victorio's warriors took a few horses from their old rivals, the White Mountain Apaches. It was rumored that before he left, Victorio singled out a White Mountain chief and his family and killed them as revenge for the earlier deaths of some of his people. Written evidence is scanty, but oral histories seem to verify the rumor. Once Victorio gave the word, more than three hundred people fled San Carlos. Some 143 Warm Springs Apaches, including Dilth-cleyhen and her children and Loco, remained behind. Redeeming those left behind would remain one of Victorio's primary goals. Those who escaped mostly walked, keeping to the high ridges whenever they could. Speed was vital, and when elders or pregnant women fell behind or could not keep up, they were hidden near a water source and left with one or more boys to care for protect them and, if possible, lead them to safety. The men raided horses and the occasional steer along the way, and they ate wild game when they could find it. They located some of the cached rifles, but ran out of ammunition and resorted to traditional bows and arrows—also left behind for just such a need—and sometimes used crude spears or even rocks. It would take time to recover those weapons stored closer to Warm Springs.

Victorio Seeks a Place to Live

Victorio and his people needed somewhere to live. Family members left behind could not stay at San Carlos one day longer than necessary, but to redeem them required a place to settle in peace. Worse, the soldiers pursued the escapees relentlessly. At first, Victorio thought to head down to Old Mexico, but realized that soldiers had cut off all trails to the south. Commanders had sent patrols immediately to surround Warm Springs and guard all of the trails leading into the Black and Mimbres ranges. So Victorio went north, and in late September, he surrendered at Fort Wingate on the Navajo Reservation. Nana took a smaller group farther east, skirted the search parties, forded the Rio Grande, and found sanctuary among the Mescaleros. In all likelihood, both Victorio and Nana considered these destinations a temporary solution. They were merely places to settle until the Indian Office finally made the right decision. After all, the whites in Washington were blind, but were they stupid, too?

Victorio asked military officials at Fort Wingate to help him secure a permanent reservation anywhere except San Carlos, but preferably at Warm Springs. As long as Clum had remained agent, there was a glimmer of hope that the situation might improve. No longer. Indian Inspector William Vandever, who had served as acting agent at San Carlos between Clum's resignation and Hart's arrival, traveled to Fort Wingate to meet with Victorio. He and his people could not return to Warm Springs, Vandover told the Chihenne chief. The agency had since closed. The land, he said, had been returned to the public domain some months before. But this place was promised to us by the men who came here from the East, Victorio reminded him, and reiterated that he would not go back to San Carlos.

Throughout October, Victorio alternately met with authorities and slipped away from Fort Wingate to hunt or raid for food. A few Chihennes moved back to Warm Springs without permission and remained hidden in the mountains and canyons, careful to avoid whites. But Victorio knew that he could not return there himself. Nor could his people illegally exist there for long. He remained with the Navajos and hoped officials would change their minds regarding Warm Springs. If not, Fort Wingate and the Navajo people offered an alternative. When no decision was forthcoming from Washington, officials in New

Mexico gave Victorio and his people permission to return to Warm Springs in November 1877. It was only temporary, they said. Victorio agreed, but reminded them that they would die before they returned to San Carlos.

The Chihennes returned once again to their mountains, sacred springs, and abandoned gardens and remained there until summer 1878. There in the place of his birth, where years ago his mother had buried his umbilical cord, Victorio found renewed strength. It is very likely that, thinking he had now twice persuaded whites that his people should return to Warm Springs and the Cañada Alamosa agency, Victorio would always believe that he could force this pattern to continue until the Indian Office gave up. Eventually, the Indian Office must tire of the game, and then they could remain in their homeland forever. But for the time being, his people hid and tried to molest no one while the chiefs negotiated for permission to stay there.

The Indian Office Holds Firm

Colonel Hatch, perhaps more than anyone, pressured to keep Victorio's people in New Mexico. He claimed that Warm Springs was the best place for the Chihenne people. As a precaution, however, he ordered the band disarmed, although he undoubtedly knew they kept some weapons hidden away. The Indian Office transferred Dr. Whitney from Fort Wingate to serve as acting agent. For six months, Hatch and Whitney tried unsuccessfully to persuade Washington to release the relatives still at San Carlos. Whitney, while he lived at the Cañada Alamosa, spoke often and for long periods with Victorio, who described the illness and starvation at San Carlos. Newcomers, the chief said, were crowded in with all the others. It was as if under the concentration policy the Indian Office wanted to cram as many Apaches as possible in one small and barren out-of-the-way space. They received no protection. But no matter how many times Victorio asked or Whitney wrote to Washington, months passed with no decision.

At one point, the Interior Department considered removing Victorio's people to Indian Territory in present-day Oklahoma, but the War Department argued against such a move, citing the high cost of a one-thousand-mile trek. Sherman, like Hatch, concluded that Victorio was better off in New Mexico. In addition, Sherman and General John Pope, commander of the Department of the Missouri, now agreed that the best solution was to resurrect the Southern Apache Agency, excluding, of course, the Mescaleros, who were now safely ensconced around Fort Stanton. But with the land around the Cañada Alamosa and the Warm Springs returned to the public domain, a few whites had already begun to settle there, and now Interior Department officials decided it was impossible to reverse the momentum. Warm Springs, they concluded at last, was not suitable. Even so, the final, inevitable decision moved forward sluggishly.

Meanwhile, Victorio repeatedly pressured to bring the children and elders to Warm Springs and worried at the lack of response. What was the delay? The scenario was one of déjà vu. Worse, every time Geronimo's or Pionsenay's warriors raided, whites blamed Victorio and pressured for the Chihennes to be removed. Rumors of an impending return to San Carlos haunted him. At the same time, he heard predictions that his people would go to live with the Mescaleros. As usual, agent Tiffany had no information either way.

By late summer 1878, the Indian Office finally issued the order to send the Warm Springs Apaches back to San Carlos. Reluctantly, Hatch completed the paperwork and made the arrangements. Victorio made one final appeal to Captain Charles Steelhammer, whose Fifteenth Infantry had been stationed at the Cañada Alamosa during his interlude there. He agreed to go on half-rations and plant more crops next spring than ever before. Anything but San Carlos. To return there was a death sentence, he told Steelhammer. Victorio's pleas fell on sympathetic but powerless ears. In October, thirty-five scouts and the Ninth Cavalry under Captain Frank Bennett showed up to escort the Warm Springs Apaches back to Arizona.

Fortunately for Victorio, he was at Fort Wingate when Bennett arrived at Warm Springs with the final removal orders. The chief was on his way back when he heard the news. He sent word ahead that he was coming in, but instead, bypassed Cañada Alamosa altogether and went south, taking as many people as could manage to join him. They rode at breakneck speed for Old Mexico.

Some 170 Chihennes who could not escape with Victorio made the sad trip back to San Carlos. Even then, a few remained hidden around the Warm Springs. As before, they encountered heavy rain along the way. At higher altitudes the rain turned to a thick slushy snow that iced the passes and made them virtually impassible in places. As the heavy wagons strained over treacherous roads, terrified Apache women and children heard the eerie, mournful cries of their free relatives calling out to them from afar. Many of the 150 or so who eluded Bennett's horse soldiers followed the procession at least part of the way, hoping desperately for some sliver of opportunity to free their loved ones. By late November, the Chihennes reached San Carlos.

Nana Goes to the Mescalero Reservation

Earlier, Nana had led approximately sixty people east of the Rio Grande and into the White Mountains. He pleaded with agent Frederick Godfroy for a place to live. Godfroy initially told Nana that he had orders to arrest any of the Warm Springs Apaches who showed up on the Mescalero Reservation, but he allowed the old warrior to camp in the remote Rinconada and issued ration cards to each family head. Nana's band found fresh water, game, and plenty of brush for shelters in the isolated canyon. There was not much wind, they reported, "just a still, dry cold" during the winter months. By January 1879, approximately sixty-eight Warm Springs Apaches lived at Mescalero.

From Old Mexico, Victorio returned briefly to Warm Springs in January or February 1879—long after the bulk of his people had departed for San Carlos—and agreed to personally surrender if his remaining people might live at Mescalero. Apparently fearing captivity, he bolted before getting an answer and hid in the San Mateo Mountains for the rest of the winter to ponder the situation. Hatch expressed hopes that he might induce Victorio to join Nana at the Mescalero reservation. And in June 1879, Victorio surrendered at Mescalero. He found the region around Fort Stanton chaotic. Since February 1878, a violent war between two merchant factions fighting for economic and political control had raged across Lincoln County, where the Mescalero Reservation was located. The Apaches were drawn into the fray in part because Alexander McSween, head of one faction, wanted Godfroy dismissed in favor of his own candidate and therefore accused the agent of corruption and of dealing with his own rivals in the conflict. In addition, hired gunmen on both sides of the dispute helped themselves at regular intervals to the Indian horses, mules, and cattle.

On April 4, 1878, a group of young men calling themselves Regulators, led by rancher Richard Brewer and the infamous William Antrim or Billy the Kid, encountered McSween's rivals at a place called Blazer's Mill. Dr. Joseph H. Blazer, a former dentist, lived on disputed land, which the federal government claimed as part of the Mescalero Apache Reservation, but which he declared belonged to him. He operated a sawmill and leased his two-story adobe house to agent Godfroy and his family. The ensuing gunfight at Blazer's Mill left Brewer and one of the rivals dead and several more wounded. Then, on August 5, 1878, twenty Regulators showed up at the agency, allegedly to visit Brewer's grave. Godfroy and his clerk, Morris Bernstein, were busy doling out rations when gunshots exploded, killing Bernstein. This murder—indeed all such gunplay—further increased tensions on the reservation. Moreover, McSween's allegations that Godfroy was collaborating with the old post trader Lawrence Murphy and his partner James J. Dolan caused the agent to lose his job by fall 1878.

By the time Victorio arrived in spring 1879, Godfroy was gone and Samuel Russell was the new agent. Russell assured Victorio that he could remain if he would be a "good Indian" and even told him that he would try to win release of the families at

San Carlos. Russell assured his superiors, "It will be the end of all the long and serious trouble with the Warm Springs Indians." But Russell was wrong. Although Victorio found Nana settled in, some area whites feared that Victorio's presence would attract more Apaches. Mescaleros, who had already found the Lincoln County War too unsettling for their tastes, also worried that the influx of newcomers might precipitate violence against them. There were, however, some whites in the region who disagreed with the majority consensus. They recognized that "they [the Chihennes] were run outa their own country." Moreover, these whites realized that the Apaches stole cattle because soldiers had killed most of the deer on and around the reservations for sport. With the Warm Springs reservation closed, Victorio's people had no rations. Nor could they hunt their food. No wonder, some whites argued, these Apaches had a reputation for theft and violence.

Victorio pledged peace. He promised the Mescalero chiefs that he would do nothing to bring them trouble. Although the Mescalero chief San Juan accepted his word, he told his bands to avoid Victorio's people. Agent Russell seemed to believe him as well. "I have felt much gratified at my success in getting Victoria [*sic*] and his band of Warm Springs Indians to come in and locate on this reservation," he wrote in his report to the commissioner of August 11, 1879. He added that once the families still at San Carlos arrived at Mescalero, "I feel confident it will end the long contest between them and the Army." Victorio selected a campsite and went into the agency to collect his rations. At that time, he was curtly informed that he needed a ration card to obtain food and blankets. Russell—a very by-the-book agent—refused to issue the necessary cards until he received clearance from Washington.

How long? Victorio asked, well aware of how painfully slow the Indian Office could take to act. Maybe a month, he was told. As Victorio pondered just how long *Russell* would agree to go without eating, Dr. Blazer stepped in and offered to donate some of his personal cattle. He told Victorio to take food and some blankets from the shelves of the store. The agent was new and young, the doctor explained, with Chief San Juan undoubtedly translating. Things would turn out all right. But Victorio's response was indignant. Was this yet another trick? Maybe his people should try to get weapons and hunt for food, he challenged. Or raid. Blazer replied that for him to possess weapons was to invite trouble. Besides, "the cavalry has orders to kill anyone found off the reservation," Blazer reminded him. Victorio knew very well that what the doctor told him was true.

Victorio met with Nana and with the various Mescalero chiefs. "Do as Dr. Blazer suggests," they all cautioned. Fort Stanton was close, so close, in fact, that Victorio could hear the bugle calls at times. In 1879, it was fully staffed with two hundred soldiers, many of them on frequent detail seeking off-reservation Apaches. The lack of rations reminded Victorio that his life still hung in limbo. The families had not yet arrived from San Carlos. Would he soon find himself shackled and on the road to San Carlos? Perhaps they should now consider moving to Juh's stronghold in the Blue Mountains, where they could live as they always had, he told Nana. They might be running out of options.

Victorio's relationship with Russell hit rock bottom soon after, when he tried one more time to explain the situation to the agent and hopefully work out some arrangement. Why he did not simply accept Blazer's offer is not clear, but the answer probably lies with the overall uncertainty of his situation. Still, with Victorio standing before him and waiting to talk, Russell did the unthinkable; he simply ignored the Apache chief. The agent pretended to be busy with papers. "No Indian was ever so ignorant as to misunderstand the insolence of this gesture," said Eve Ball. Furious, Victorio stormed out of the agent's office.

Victorio Bolts the Mescalero Reservation

The final straw occurred in July 1879. According to Russell's version, a grand jury in Grant County, New Mexico, returned three indictments against Victorio in absentia. They indicted him and "unnamed followers" for murder and stealing horses. On August

21, a hunting and fishing party from Grant County rode across Mescalero land to speak with Russell. Victorio was meeting with the agent at the time, and Russell claims that the chief suddenly reached over the desk and yanked his ears. Then Victorio raced from the agency. The next day, Victorio bolted, taking approximately sixty Chihenne warriors and a few Mescaleros with him. Later, unhappy Mescaleros, some Lipans from Texas, and dozens of Comanches joined him and swelled the number to between 250 and 350. The Indian Office would never really know how many Victorio led or where they were hiding out. A November 18, 1880, *New York Times* article would estimate the number at 450 to 1,000.

Russell, however, did not relate this story until his report of October 18, 1879, two months later. In this report, he claimed that Victorio recognized members of the hunting and fishing party and believed they were part of a posse coming to arrest him on the charges of murder and theft. Russell's account, however, raises so many questions that it can almost be dismissed. First, it seems highly unlikely that Victorio would have understood an indictment in absentia against him or demonstrated much concern even if he had. Second, two of the individuals in the so-called hunting party were Judge Warren Bristol and Albert Fountain, both affiliated with the courts of Doña Ana, not Grant County. So, the story remains suspect. It is possible that, by this time, Victorio simply believed all whites were out to get him.

Mescalero Apaches Sam Chino and Percy Big Mouth later recounted their version of the story. They told historian Eve Ball that Victorio had never intended to stay at Mescalero because he wanted to go back to Warm Springs and fight for his land. His plan all along, they said, was to retrieve Nana and recruit Mescalero warriors in his fight. Although Nana and his band were peaceful, Victorio's were not. Russell, whom Victorio easily intimidated, finally summoned the soldiers from Fort Stanton. They arrived with bugles blaring on August 21, 1879, when Victorio was meeting with Russell. Afraid that the soldiers were going to arrest him, Victorio bolted. If this account is true, it might also answer why Victorio refused Blazer's mediation.

Regardless of why he left the Fort Stanton area, Victorio returned to Warm Springs and discovered the crops ready to harvest. Some Warm Springs people were obviously in hiding there and a number of those who had just returned from Mescalero remained, too. Victorio led a raiding expedition into Mexico and, when he returned, he found his newly constructed camp in chaos. Soldiers had attacked and his first wife—Dilth-cleyhen's mother—was among those killed. Most of the dead were women, children, and elders. Desperation now turned to rage. Victorio could not understand white men. They lied, they slaughtered innocents, and they seemed to care more for possessions than for human life. He did not want to assimilate into such a society. Still, his people needed a permanent reservation that was not San Carlos, the place of death. Thus, in October 1879, enmeshed in grief and caught in the jaws of his dilemma, the Chihenne leader acted. The Victorio War began.

CHAPTER 7

Victorio's War

AS he fled the Mescalero agency, Victorio stopped one last time at Blazer's trading post and mill to procure some of the previously offered beef, bran flour, sugar, and coffee that the trader kept on hand. It seems that Victorio trusted the dentist-turned-trader more than most of the white men with whom he had come in contact. Although Victorio entertained no illusions about whose side Blazer ultimately favored, the trader nevertheless possessed a refreshing degree of common sense and honesty. Blazer made it clear that, in his opinion, the Chihennes had received ill treatment from the federal government. Perhaps, too, the man's powerful six-foot, five-inch frame reminded Victorio somewhat of the deceased Mangas Coloradas. Blazer handed over the requested rations, but sensing Victorio's frustration, begged the Chihenne leader to remain patient. Agent Russell was young and afraid to challenge his employers, he informed Victorio, either through a Mescalero interpreter or using a blend of Apache and Spanish. To consider giving up and leaving the reservation now, Blazer cautioned, was to invite trouble and probably death for himself and his people. Victorio nodded, but it was the last time the two saw each other and perhaps the final conversation Victorio ever had with a white man.

As Victorio furtively led his Warm Springs people away from the Mescalero Reservation, they nearly ran headlong into Almer Blazer, the trader's teenage son. Young Blazer and several of his friends had returned from hunting in the remote Rinconada, the region where Nana's bands lived and farmed. Away from the agency for several days, the young men apparently had been thirsty and sought a small spring that they knew contained an abundant quantity of pure drinking water. They headed to the spring in order to fill their canteens. The spring lay off the beaten path, however, and as the boys approached, they spotted a band of Apaches. They realized immediately that these were not Mescaleros. Unsure of what to do next—and undoubtedly fearing detection—the boys beat a hasty retreat. Only later did young Blazer and his companions discover that they had encountered Victorio's people, who were at that very moment in the process of bolting the reservation.

Victorio realized, of course, that once they left Mescalero, danger surrounded them. There was no going back. Victorio undoubtedly held out some hope that he might still somehow negotiate for a Warm Springs reservation site. It is almost certain that his primary reason for going to the Mescalero Reservation in the first place was to persuade Nana to join him. It seems unlikely that Victorio intended to remain there himself for any length of time, but that, of course, is speculation. Significantly, Victorio did not immediately head to Juh's stronghold in the Blue Mountains, a sure sanctuary. Rather, he went right back to the Warm Springs, where he knew the soldiers were searching for him. And he stayed there as long as he could. When soldiers got too close, he moved away. But he always circled back. One might argue that he remained so as not to desert the families at San Carlos. But, conceivably, Victorio could have launched rescue attempts from Mexico.

Hanging around the Black and Mimbres ranges was, for all practical purposes, a ridiculous strategy unless he hoped for more. Capture was always a hazard. He knew soldiers would molest him and his people unceasingly. But neither was this a suicide mission. There is no evidence that Victorio intended his action as a sort of last stand. Clearly, the Chihennes intended to go home. James Kaywaykla told Eve Ball that "Victorio's appeal to agent Russell for admittance to the Mescalero Reservation could not be true, for he determined to fight for his home . . . to the last." Whether Victorio ultimately could have remained at Mescalero is unknown; what seems obvious is that he believed one day the Indian Office would acquiesce to his request. They had done so before.

It is almost entirely from the government records that we obtain information about the final year of Victorio's life, and of course, most of this is secondhand. Previously overlooked and overshadowed by Mangas Coloradas, Cochise, and Geronimo, Victorio and his exploits fill Indian Office memos, military reports, newspaper editorials only after October 1879. Later on, he would figure in the memoirs of soldiers and Texas Rangers, who wrote about their adventures while on his trail. Except for his year-long flight, he might have remained virtually unknown to non-Apaches. Some accounts clearly display empathy towards him. Most are filled with animosity for "Old Vic." Nearly all archives acknowledge, however, his overwhelming desire to live at Warm Springs. Had officials within the Indian Office and the Interior Department relented even a little, it is likely that they could have saved hundreds of lives and millions of dollars.

Historians have praised Victorio's brilliant military strategies. For most of those thirteen months on the run, they argue, Victorio eluded every company of cavalry and infantry thrown at him. His bands dodged or ambushed U.S. and Mexican soldiers, Apache and Navajo scouts, and Texas and Arizona rangers bent upon bringing them in or exterminating them. Victorio drew upon every dihoke lesson he had ever learned; he relied on his intimate knowledge of the land, accumulated since childhood. He stuck to the tried-and-true Apache tactics of keeping to the mountains, holding the high ground, attacking with lightning speed, and using the cover of darkness to shield escape. He covered impossible terrain. He sent word more than once that he wanted to negotiate with whites for a permanent reservation. If one analyzes the Victorio War, it appears a classic case of a people battling a bureaucratic brick wall. Victorio held out some hope for a diplomatic solution; Washington demanded unconditional surrender. Nothing else would suffice. By doing nothing, the Interior Department sat back and hoped that the problem would solve itself. And it eventually did.

The Flight Back to Warm Springs

Ten-year-old James Kaywaykla vividly remembered that mad flight from the Mescalero Reservation. They rode down the western slope of the White Mountains, he recalled, left the Fort Stanton area, and skirted the mysterious, ever-shifting white sands. In the darkness, they tried to avoid the craggy black lava lands that dotted much of the landscape. It was difficult terrain to cross and slowed them considerably. Kaywaykla clung to his grandmother's waist as she gently prodded the horse onward. He also recalled turning his head and looking behind frequently to make sure his mother and infant sister were still following. Once Victorio and his band left the shelter of one mountain range, they moved as quickly as humanly possible across the open, flat dry lands that led to the next. This way, the people gradually worked their way westward. Nana reportedly brought up the rear of the procession while Victorio led. They traveled in silence as every one of them was afraid to speak.

Some of their most fearless fighters traveled with these Chihennes. One of these was Lozen. Another was a promising young warrior named Kaytennae, whom the Mescaleros considered an arrogant troublemaker. But others thought the young warrior modest, courteous, and deferential to his elders. Victorio apparently valued Kaytennae very highly because he frequently appointed him as second-in-command. Although Kaytennae was not descended by birth from chiefs, Victorio was obviously grooming him for a leadership role.

There was also a man named Sánchez traveling with them. Sánchez was Kaywaykla's paternal grandfather. Years earlier—when Sánchez was a young father—Mexicans had captured him and one of his small sons. Although he could have gotten away, Sánchez remained with the Mexicans for the sake of his son. Thus, Sánchez had served his Mexican masters for years and learned the skills of a vaquero or cowboy. He could speak the Spanish language fluently, and he knew Mexican customs as well. Sánchez had finally managed to escape with his son and make his way home, but was always seen as different, a bit odd perhaps, from his years as a slave in Mexico. His son, whose name has been lost to history, married Gouyen, one of Victorio's sisters, and was killed while on a raid during the Victorio War. Gouyen later married Kaytennae. Allegedly, Sánchez was killed by Mescalero witchcraft some time in late 1879 or early 1880. Oral histories convey no details concerning his death. Even so, sudden or untimely deaths seemed to encourage accusations of witchcraft.

Blanco, a medicine man, also traveled with Victorio's band. One of the most important was Lozen, Victorio's youngest sister. In fact, she was called "Little Sister" by her people and "the woman warrior" by Geronimo's. As previously mentioned, Lozen was about twenty years Victorio's junior, or about thirty-five or forty years old in 1879. She could ride, shoot, and fight like a man, and some claimed she had more ability than Victorio in planning military strategy. All this made Lozen one of the most valuable weapons in Victorio's arsenal. Lozen's story often straddles fact and fiction, but the Chihenne people believed that she could locate the enemy. Allegedly, she would stand alone on a hilltop with outstretched arms and palms turned upward. Then she prayed:

> Upon this earth
> On which we live
> Ussen has Power
> For locating the enemy.
> I search for that Enemy,
> Which only Ussen the Great
> Can show to me.

Lozen turned slowly as she spoke to Ussen and her hands would tingle and change color when they pointed toward the foe. The closer the adversary, the more vivid the feelings she received and the brighter the color of her palms. She claimed that she saw as one from a height sees in every direction. Her place within the band was unique. Victorio valued her tremendously and often referred to his youngest sister as his right arm.

Southern Pacific Railroad car carrying Geronimo (bottom row, third
from right) and other Apache prisoners in 1886. Victorio's sister,
Lozen, is thought to be third from right in the top row. Courtesy of
National Anthropological Archives (negative #2517A).

There are other stories of Lozen that the Warm Springs people loved to relate. One of these concerns the flight from
Mescalero. When the band reached the Rio Grande, they found
the river swollen and rushing with rainwater. The people hesitated. There were flashes of turquoise as the people tossed the
magical stones into the raging waters and asked for safe passage.
Prayers rose from the lips of the trapped Chihennes. Still, says
Kaywaykla, nobody dared to move. The river was simply too
wild. Blanco and then Sánchez tried to persuade them, but nobody dared take the plunge into that angry water. Then, Kaywaykla saw

> a magnificent woman on a beautiful black horse—Lozen, sister of
> Victorio. . . . High above her head she held her rifle. There was a

glitter as her right foot lifted and struck the shoulder of her horse. He reared, then plunged into the torrent. She turned his head upstream, and he began swimming.

Lozen led the way, and the rest of the people followed. Her courage inspired the others to take on the Rio Grande and allowed them to eventually make their way home.

A number of Mescaleros bolted with Victorio as well. Among them was a leader named Muchacho Negro, whose grandson, Ralph Shanta, would grant an interview to Eve Ball. Shanta claimed that, according to their oral histories, "many Apaches from Mescalero went with Victorio." In fact, Victorio's force in September 1879 reportedly numbered 350. However, the number of Indians riding with Victorio at any given time fluctuated dramatically. Military reports over the next thirteen months failed to agree on the size of Victorio's following or on the number of warriors available to him. There were always unhappy and bored individuals who left their reservations for short periods and then returned.

Living and Remaining Free

After the flight from Mescalero, one of the first orders of business was finding food. Thus, as the Warm Springs bands neared the Rio Grande, Nana allegedly took about forty of the available warriors and "liberated" a dozen or so horses from some of the small ranches at Three Rivers. Rumors abounded that Victorio had escaped to Mexico. Over the next year, stories of his whereabouts grew more elaborate and, at times, ludicrous. New Mexicans blamed Victorio's warriors for ambushes and raids everywhere across the Southwest. Regardless of the rumors, however, Victorio first took his people back to Warm Springs. There they found caves in which to hide and in which they had previously stored rations.

Because it was home, they knew the area intimately. Here Victorio could intimidate any cavalry unit that dared to come after him. Even better, the natural landscape would impede outsiders long before they could reach the Chihenne camps. Rocky terrain and treacherous switchbacks would slow the cavalry's horses. The occasional flash floods could quickly turn mountain passes into death traps for unsuspecting whites, and the steep arroyos would force soldiers to stick to the old military trails, thereby slowing their progress. The landscape afforded amazing vistas from which Apaches might observe their enemies without detection and strike without warning.

Victorio knew these mountains like a white man knows the inside of his house, and this knowledge offered him advantages and numerous ambush and escape options. Of course, he undoubtedly hoped that whites would soon tire of looking for his people and give up the search. More realistically, though, he realized they would not. But if forced to encounter the horse soldiers, this was the best possible place. Moreover, to take his people somewhere else was to surrender this land forever. Regardless of the risk, they had to stay. Only if they remained was there a chance for peace. One day, he believed, the Americans would understand that his people must remain at the Warm Springs. He merely had to wait for them to see this.

As the Chihennes settled into Warm Springs, soldiers fruitlessly searched the area that lay west of Socorro and east of the Rio Grande to around present-day Truth or Consequences. They scoured the Black, San Mateo, and Mimbres ranges. Naturally, they kept coming back to the Cañada Alamosa and the sacred warm springs. Meanwhile, in early September, Victorio's warriors confiscated forty-six horses from Company E of the Ninth Cavalry of buffalo soldiers, and they allegedly killed five soldiers and three civilians in the process. On September 18, one of Victorio's raiding parties hit the isolated McEvers Ranch, situated a few miles from the tiny village of Hillsboro. Another company of Ninth Cavalry, under Captain Byron Dawson, picked up his trail. The Apaches, burdened with livestock, were moving slowly. Dawson saw his chance. He sent his soldiers along with forty-six Navajo scouts after Victorio's warriors. They dived into the Mimbres Range and found a desolate spot where the Animas River originates in a steep canyon. It was not only a well-protected place but allowed the Chihennes to cover most of the available shelter as well. Indeed, when Dawson later showed Major A. P. Morrow of Arizona the site, Morrow wrote, "It took me one hour and twenty minutes to ascend to the Indian camp.... Under fire it would have been an *absolute impossibility.*" The official record concluded that Dawson was lucky to have survived.

In fact, with Dawson pinned down, a civilian militia from Hillsboro rode out to help the embattled troops. Victorio, who by now had joined his warriors, told them to set a trap. He asked Kaytennae to make the trail so obvious that even white men might follow. In turn, Kaytennae ordered the raiders to butcher a few of the McEvers cattle and litter the trail with blood and entrails. Sure enough, soldiers and civilians followed. Suddenly, Dawson found himself at the bottom of a rocky defile, deluged with Apache gunfire and pinned down. Completely surrounded, Dawson determined that retreat was impossible. The battle between Chihennes and Dawson's men continued off and on all day long. Finally, in a desperate attempt to retreat, the cavalry abandoned fifty-three of their horses and mules and most of their personal belongings. They also left behind a fully equipped hospital wagon. The Americans lost eight men and carried away two more who were severely wounded in the fighting. With mounts and meat, Victorio's raiding party rode back to Warm Springs.

What Victorio could not have known was that on September 17—in response to the initial raid on the ranch—Governor Lew Wallace of New Mexico had sent a telegram to the secretary of war asking permission to recruit volunteer civilians. The secretary refused. But just as a small militia from Hillsboro had assisted Dawson, from time to time impromptu posses and militias would form and assist in the chase. Hence, Victorio frequently found that in addition to cavalry and Indian scouts, there were prospectors, ranchers, and others nipping at his heels.

Victorio warned his people to check and double-check their rations. Keep a food pouch strapped to your belt even when you go to sleep, he commanded. That precaution extended to the children. Nor must the Chihennes forget to carry emergency clothing and moccasins at all times. Hobble the horses so that we can always retrieve them, he told his people. At the same time, Victorio sent Kaytennae, Blanco, and Sánchez on frequent raids to replenish food and Nana to locate ammunition. Survival depended upon a ready supply of both, as well as knowledge of the terrain. Nor was the aging Victorio idle. Now in his mid-fifties, he, too, led many of the raids. He bartered the cattle and horses taken in Monticello, where he still maintained a close friendship with the Mexican farmers. He also planned his people's next moves and tried to determine where they might find safety whenever the whites got too close.

After the battle near the McEvers ranch, the New Mexico soldiers were bolstered by two companies of cavalry from Arizona and their Apache scouts. A. P. Morrow conducted a search of the Black Range, while companies under Lieutenants A. P. Blocksom and Charles B. Gatewood slogged through driving rains to reach the former battle site and hopefully pick up Victorio's trail before it got too cold. It was an especially rainy autumn, and as they traveled, all of the soldiers watched their bread and tobacco rations fall into a pulpy mixture that could not be used. The heavy supply train was forced to stick to the wagon road rather than attempt the more dangerous mountain paths. Because of that, the men had to rely on hard tack and tough mule meat for days at a time. They also endured rainy, cold nights with no fires at all and a terrain that got rockier and more slippery with each mile. When the companies finally converged in the Mimbres Range and began to ride north toward the Black Mountains, they accidentally stumbled upon Victorio.

It was September 29. Having run into a band of warriors at the mouth of Cuchillo Negro Creek in the Black Range, Morrow ordered an attack. Victorio suddenly broke camp, however, and moved farther up Cuchillo Negro Creek. Although Morrow's account makes it sound as if he dislodged Victorio's warriors from their stronghold, Gatewood's clearly describes how the Apaches ran off the troops. Worse, getting away with all their animals was no easy matter for the Arizona soldiers. But, although they found themselves under fire the whole way, they

Lieutenant Charles Gatewood and his Apache scouts having returned from the Victorio Campaign in 1880. Courtesy of the Arizona Historical Society, Tucson (AHS 19763).

continued to follow Victorio at a distance. The next day, fighting continued. Apparently, some of Victorio's men—including his son, Washington—were wounded in the first attack. They retreated slowly up the canyon. In the midst of the fighting, the soldiers managed to capture an Apache woman—possibly she became separated from the rest—and under duress she told them that the chief was now heading toward the Mogollons, which lay west of the Black Range.

Apaches and soldiers camped but a short distance from each other. In the middle of the night, Morrow ordered his scouts to sneak through the rocks, underbrush, and cactus and try to position themselves around Victorio's camp. They moved in under cover of darkness. As one Apache scout approached a small water hole, he accidentally stumbled onto a Warm Springs Apache guarding the spring. Startled, both Chihenne and scout automatically pulled their weapons and fired. They missed each other, but the noise alerted Victorio and the soldiers alike. The rest of the scouts moved in and a handful of buffalo soldiers prepared to attack. Victorio, however, managed to escape and drive away much of the stock. Oral histories describe a sort of rearguard encounter, with Victorio's warriors maintaining gunfire to allow the others to escape. White accounts describe the pandemonium as "enough to set a nervous man wild." Victorio held the water hole, but Gatewood later said he found pools of blood and bloody rags, evidence that a number of the Indians had been struck.

Afterward, New Mexico buzzed with rumors that Victorio himself had died in the battle. However, he was still very much alive and throughout October played a game of cat-and-mouse with the soldiers. Gatewood and Morrow continued their sweeps through the area mountain ranges, thereby keeping Victorio and his people on the move. Colonel Hatch remarked, "Victorio is determined to fight it out," but added, "and so is Morrow."

Constantly on the Move

Terrified New Mexicans poured out tales of Old Vic's bloody massacres to Hatch and Governor Wallace. First, they seemed to report, Victorio was raiding around Warm Springs. According to others, he was wreaking havoc along the east side of the Rio Grande. Hatch received word at one point that Victorio's Apaches had murdered two white men near San José on the Rio Grande, but when the soldiers followed moccasin tracks away from the crime scene, they discovered non-Indian outlaws. On October 5, 1879, Texas Rangers followed up on a report that Chihennes had killed several Mexican men cutting hay over in the Mesilla Valley. The rangers found these farmers alive and well and peacefully harvesting their crop. Fearing attacks, however, ranchers across southeastern New Mexico petitioned for army protection. Ranchers knew that traders were keeping Apaches well stocked with contraband arms. In short, Victorio became the most hated and feared man in New Mexico. Settlers lived in abject terror.

All the while, soldiers relentlessly pursued him. In late October, Victorio ambushed Colonel N. A. M. Dudley of Fort Stanton and a contingent of his Ninth Cavalry, forcing Dudley to abandon a profusion of personal belongings, clothing, ammunition, food, and horses. Victorio wasted no time appropriating the supplies. By the end of that month, Victorio split his people into three bands and headed into Mexico. Nana took one group through Big Bend country, and temporarily at least, Texas went on high alert. Panic ran up and down the border, and a mixed army of Texas Rangers under George W. Baylor and Texas militia responded. Kaytennae probably led the second band and traveled just ahead of Victorio. The chief brought up the rear. He slipped into the Florida Mountains just south of present-day Deming, New Mexico, and then crossed the border into Mexico. Despite the border, Gatewood and Morrow followed right behind him. As Victorio headed straight for the villages in Chihuahua, which had always proven friendly to him and bought his horses in exchange for rifles, the Arizona troops stayed doggedly on his heels.

Victorio knew the Americans were in alien and unfamiliar territory and that the soldiers needed water. Just as the Chichimecas had done four hundred years earlier, Victorio watched from atop one of the many rocky outcroppings that dot the landscape. He saw the Americans making their way to the Corralitos River. But natural obstacles lay between Morrow and that precious water, which made it easier for human barriers to move into place, too. From his higher vantage, Victorio observed Morrow's horses and mules drop one by one in the hot, exposed stretch of desert below. Whenever the Indian scouts approached the hills that separated them from the river, Victorio's warriors were there to fire on them and hinder their progress. When the main contingent of soldiers tried to dislodge the Apaches, the Arizonans encountered a withering roar of Winchesters, which prevented them from proceeding. Unable to cross or to circumvent the ridge, Morrow turned and guided his men towards a well-established spring farther away.

The Apaches reached the water first. They drank their fill and watered their horses. Then the Indians gutted a coyote and threw the carcass into what remained of the spring. Needless to say, Morrow's men found the water contaminated and undrinkable. Farther on, they found other springs similarly depleted or too muddy to consume after Victorio had his men ride their horses through the water. Morrow was ultimately forced to turn tail and order a retreat to the United States. Victorio undoubtedly wondered why whites never learned the telltale signs of underground water sources. There was often plenty of water around if one only knew where to look. Once he returned home, Morrow wrote to headquarters and predicted that Victorio would head back to the states within a month. He requested a pair of mountain howitzers for when that happened.

Morrow was correct in his assessment. Victorio did not remain in Chihuahua for long. With scalp bounties still in effect, he could not count on the friendship of Mexican villagers. In fact, while in Mexico, Victorio cautioned his men against spending too much time socializing and forbade them to drink the tiswin or mescal the Mexicans offered. Because Sánchez had lived with Mexicans for so long and could pass for one of them, he volunteered to ride into Carrizal, a favorite trading area, and get a feel for the attitudes towards the Apaches. Sánchez found a lonely vaquero and killed him. He dressed in the man's clothing and, disguised, visited the town. Sure enough, Sánchez found the villagers talking openly of betraying Victorio. They proposed inviting his people to a fiesta. There they planned to ply the Apaches with great quantities of liquor and then kill as many of the men, women, and children as they could. The villagers looked forward to a huge reward for the scalps.

Sánchez left Carrizal. He rode to the Tiñaja de Victorio waterhole, as the spring came to be called, in the Candelaria Mountains, where Victorio was camped. From this vantage point, the warriors could watch the El Paso-to-Chihuahua City road. It was the site of Victorio's main camp. Sánchez told Victorio everything he had heard. They waited. Sure enough, a few days later a Tarahumara Indian from Carrizal arrived to invite

Victorio to a fiesta, just as Sánchez had said they were planning. Victorio thanked the Indian and sent him on his way. Then, he instructed some of his warriors to run off a herd of horses belonging to the people of Carrizal. Eighteen men almost immediately went after the stolen horses. Victorio sprang the trap and killed every one of them. A rescue party of about thirty men came next, and they, too, fell into Victorio's ambush. Fifteen died, and the rest finally managed to flee. Having demonstrated to Carrizal that to threaten him invited terrible reprisals, Victorio attacked a supply train rumbling down the El Paso-to-Chihuahua City road, replenished his food stores, and made plans to move on.

Nana Versus the Texas Rangers

Meanwhile, Nana kept the soldiers, civilians, and rangers busy in west Texas. Colonel George W. Baylor, commanding officer, transferred a contingent of Texas Rangers to El Paso to assist in the efforts. One of these rangers, a former cowboy named James B. Gillett, readily admitted that Texans—maybe more than other Americans—were pretty ruthless regarding Indians. Their primary goal was seldom to capture the Apaches but to drive them away or exterminate them altogether. Victorio's reputation as probably the best general ever produced by the Apache tribe made extermination the preferred outcome. But it is unclear whether the Texans realized that this was a band of Warm Springs Apaches under Nana and not Victorio.

Like Morrow's soldiers, the Texas Rangers did not hesitate to cross the border after Nana. In fact, Nana was heading straight to Victorio because the rangers stumbled upon the scene of Victorio's revenge on the people of Carrizal shortly after it occurred. It was bitterly cold when they came upon the remnants of the battle and found the still unburied corpses of the second rescue party. There were no Apaches around. Governor Luis Terrazas of Chihuahua had already wired the United States that he thought the hostiles were en route back to New Mexico. After burying the dead, therefore, the Texas Rangers returned to the United States empty-handed, but vowing to patrol the Mexico-Texas border and to return to Mexico if necessary.

It was at this point that Terrazas pledged his assistance in capturing Victorio. On December 20, he sent General Geronimo Trevino into the field with five hundred men. Another officer, the haughty, chain-smoking General Joaquin Terrazas, left Chihuahua City in early January. Thus, by the end of 1879, there were troops from Old Mexico, New Mexico, Arizona, and Texas, all seeking Victorio. Colonel Hatch ordered the entire Ninth Cavalry into the field and personally took charge. The Sixth Cavalry from Arizona combed the Mimbres and Mogollon ranges with their Apache scouts. Texas Rangers watched the border, while Colonel Benjamin Grierson, commander of the Tenth Cavalry of buffalo soldiers in Texas, sent patrols to El Paso and Fort Davis. Louis H. Scott, American consul at Chihuahua City, enthusiastically endorsed a policy of extermination on both sides of the border. The New Mexico legislature, unable to exact funds from the War Department, appropriated $100,000 for committees of public safety. Thus, most of the Southwest went on red alert, as Americans in the twenty-first century would say.

Victorio Alters His Strategy

As his enemies amassed, Victorio welcomed a contingent of Juh's and Geronimo's warriors, temporarily swelling the number of available men. Historian Donald Worcester suggests that by this time there were two distinct changes in the Victorio War. First, the stage got larger. And as Victorio grew more desperate, he was more willing to kill the lone sheepherder or farmer, whom he had previously tended to spare if these individuals shared their food with him. It is still difficult to determine, though, which deaths Victorio was directly responsible for.

In late December or early January, Victorio split his people into small bands and again returned to New Mexico. They forded the Rio Grande and struggled up the Jornada del Muerto until they emerged somewhere in the Mimbres Range. They seem to have made large circles as they traveled. Slowly, the bands filtered back together at Warm Springs, but dared not bathe or drink from the thermal waters right away for fear of detection. Even so, Victorio felt stronger now that they were back home. About January 10, the old trading partner Juan de Zuloaga arrived in Las Cruces with a pack train and told authorities there that Victorio was now north of the border.

Somewhere in the Florida or Black Range, Victorio bid farewell to Juh and Geronimo. They turned their horses toward the Chiricahua Mountains of Arizona. When they got there, they encountered the former Chiricahua agent Tom Jeffords. After negotiations, Jeffords persuaded Juh and Geronimo to surrender. Neither chief, however, offered any information regarding Victorio's whereabouts. This was the last time these bands joined forces until after Victorio's death ten months later. In addition, when Juh and Geronimo left the Warm Springs people, a band of Mescaleros also split off from the Chihennes and went back to their own reservation.

As Victorio swung his people back into the Warm Springs area, he found it peppered with Morrow's soldiers. In fact, on January 17, he ran straight into the Arizona troops in some of the roughest possible terrain in the San Mateo Mountains. Fortunately for him, he escaped. It frustrated him, though, that he could only skim the sacred springs. But it is certainly important to note that at about this time Victorio sent word to anyone still at the Cañada that he wanted to discuss a surrender. He refused, however, to negotiate with the military. He did not trust any of them, he claimed, and perhaps he realized that they had no power to determine his reservation. For weeks, maybe several months, Victorio waited for a response, but received none.

Thus, for most of winter 1879–80, Victorio stayed on the move, circling Warm Springs, moving to the Rio Grande and back, and generally keeping well ahead of the soldiers constantly tracking him. There were occasional clashes, but it was the Apache scouts that most worried Victorio. They were easy to spot. The scouts traveled on foot, fanned out and miles ahead of the regular line of cavalry. These Apaches wore red headbands, their badge of servitude, according to the Warm Springs people.

It was General George Crook who adopted the policy of employing Apache scouts. Using Indians to catch other Indians was not a new idea; in fact, it had been in effect since the late eighteenth century. Crook, however, was the first to apply the policy in the Southwest. Convinced that his troops would never successfully conquer the Apaches, Crook experimented with Navajo scouts and then employed Apaches. Victorio held these scouts in disdain. Once admired warriors, many of the scouts did feel torn between living the dreary, monotonous lives of reservation Indians and serving their former enemy. Others were thrilled to experience freedom again. They even won honors and privileges for their service, and at times, personal satisfaction in hunting down and subduing their rival bands. After they volunteered for duty, their families received better rations. The army labeled any scout who changed his mind and tried to leave the service a deserter and punished him accordingly. Still, Victorio hoped he could persuade scouts to abandon the whites, flock to his cause, and fight by his side. If any of them ever did, the number was minimal, which suggests that the Apache scouts realized the futility of Victorio's position or that the advantages of their situation far outweighed any longing for the old ways.

Once, before they had crossed the border into Mexico and with Morrow's men hot on their tail, Victorio's band sang all night. With drums steady and smoke rising from their fire, Victorio and the others used chants that the scouts overheard and understood. These chants invited them to desert their white masters and rejoin their own people. Although some undoubtedly found the call difficult to resist, there is no evidence that any of the scouts shed their red headbands and bolted. Most of them still had families back at San Carlos. Besides, many were White Mountain Apaches, longtime rivals of the Warm Springs band.

By the end of January 1880, Victorio had played cat and mouse with the military for nearly four months. It appears that he hung around Warm Springs for most of that month, hoping to hear about his surrender proposal. Obviously, he wanted to bring an end to his situation. When he received no invitation to come in, he tried to capture one of Morrow's supply trains on

January 27th, but found the defenders too entrenched. Thus, he gradually moved away from the Black Range. Many of his people lacked horses, so they traveled more slowly than before. Morrow's horse soldiers tried to intercept Victorio by staking out a water hole called Aleman's Well along the Jornada del Muerto, thinking that the Apaches might head in that direction. Morrow sent another contingent of his men to the small village of Las Palomas, hoping to find them there. But Victorio secretly waded his band across the Rio Grande and slipped east into the Caballo, then the San Andres, Range. He was once more making a large circle as he worked his way east across southern New Mexico, trying to shake Morrow's soldiers. In fact, Victorio split his people into groups again to hasten travel and perhaps fool the officer.

On February 3, Kaytennae encountered soldiers on steep bluffs in the San Andres Range. The bluffs overlooked a treacherous canyon, which had been formed by massive layers of black lava rock. Americans and Mexicans often called this the badlands or the *malpais*. Kaytennae held the high ground all day and when night fell led his band across the dangerous white sands, which lay between the San Andres and the Jarilla mountains. The descent from their temporary stronghold was treacherous. The women and children must walk, Kaytennae told them. The men led their few horses one at a time down the narrow cliff trails. "When I have nightmares I still descend that perilous trail. . . . One man stood guard at the gap and another at a sharp point on the trail," Kaywaykla recalled. They were all into the next mountain range by dawn. Morrow wrote that Victorio was "routed," a customary euphemism meaning the soldiers had lost contact.

Then Victorio veered north, and Hatch fumed. The Indians were able to slip back and forth through the army's lines at will. "They even select their own damned battle sites," he undoubtedly swore to himself. "We were miles ahead of the cavalry, as usual," Kaywaykla noted, and for the time being, the people still carried sufficient arms and ammunition. Victorio would have replied to Hatch that of course they were able to elude the soldiers because Lozen rode with him, and they possessed weapons because of Nana's power. Their wounded recovered quickly because Lozen and other women had the power to dress and cure wounds. Once, when Victorio got a bullet through his shoulder, Lozen burned the thorns from a leaf of nopal, split it, and bound the fleshy side to the wound. He later swore that the next day he was healed enough to ride.

Victorio sent emissaries on ahead to the Mescalero Reservation to see if there was any remaining chance for a peaceful negotiation. Again, Victorio reached out, but to no avail. Failing that, he hoped to obtain reinforcements. There were plenty of restless and bored Mescaleros willing to bolt and enjoy a few weeks of freedom. This alerted the agent and area. On March 3, agent Russell gave Mescalero chief Caballero a five-day pass. His job was to contact Victorio and try to persuade him to surrender. Seven days later, Caballero asked his wife to return the pass and tell Russell that he would come back "later." Then Russell sent Chief San Juan to search for and bring back Caballero, but he failed to return as well. Others volunteered to scout, but the moment they left their reservation, most joined the Chihennes. Hatch debated moving in, disarming the Mescaleros, and taking their horses to prevent more from fleeing. He did not. Instead, Hatch streamlined his forces. He created three battalions and placed them under experienced commanders, leading one himself. He also sent for his old friend Colonel Benjamin Grierson in Texas, who arrived at the Mescalero Reservation in early April.

At the same time, Hatch suggested releasing all of the Warm Springs families and allowing them to leave San Carlos. "To leave families at San Carlos is simply to prolong hostilities ... [and] to feed the families of Victorio's band at San Carlos, Arizona, whilst Victorio and the warriors of that band are raiding in New Mexico seems unaccountable. If nothing else, it might lure the renegades back home."

General Sherman similarly tried to persuade the Interior Department that its concentration policy had proven a disaster and that it must alter its previous decisions regarding the Warm Springs Apaches. But agents in the field balked, and the authorities in Washington refused to budge. Victorio would have

Colonel Benjamin H. Grierson, who was commanding officer of the Tenth Cavalry in Texas during the Victorio Campaign. Courtesy of the National Archives and Records Administration.

to surrender to the Interior Department's terms or fight to the death, which is, of course, what he did.

By late March or early April, Victorio was still camped on the eastern side of the San Andres Mountains in a place called Hembrillo Canyon. With no word yet from the Indian Office regarding his request, Hatch decided to attempt to trap the Apache leader. Using his Mescalero reinforcements, Victorio assigned

Captain Henry Carroll, whose unfortunate encounter at a gypsum spring during the Victorio Campaign nearly cost him his life and the lives of his men. Courtesy of the National Archives and Records Administration.

warriors to watch Hatch's Navajo scouts. He knew they were out there searching for him. Suddenly, reports came in to Victorio that the buffalo soldiers were moving in, already beginning to block the route to the northeast. White troops had entered the canyon from the west. Hatch moved troops into the San Andres Mountains to try to flush the Indians out, and fresh soldiers— Grierson's Texas regiment—were cutting off any escape to the southeast. To Victorio's dismay, still more soldiers blocked off Aleman's well to the northwest, his most reliable source of water. The number of soldiers was multiplying. This, he feared, was going to require yet another narrow escape.

Victorio saw his chance to take the offensive on April 5. One group of buffalo soldiers under Captain Henry Carroll—those arriving from the northeast—stopped at a spring long enough to drink and to water their horses, while thirty-one others seemed to be following his trail. At about 5:30 that evening, Victorio attacked the thirty-one soldiers, showering them with a withering fire for almost two hours. When Victorio and Nana finally forced the soldiers to pull back, they watched Carroll and his men, who were suffering from severe nausea and extreme diarrhea. Much to Victorio's amusement, Carroll's regiment had unknowingly drunk from a spring that only hours before he had forbidden his people to touch. It was gypsum water. Men and horses alike were badly affected. The Chihennes observed as a desperate Carroll and his critically ill men stumbled over the sharp rocks seeking fresh water. They found the next spring dry.

Frantic, the buffalo soldiers headed directly into Hembrillo Canyon, where Victorio was determined to prevent them from reaching water. He stationed his warriors at the only remaining water hole in the canyon with orders to shoot any soldier or scout who got through and tried to fill his canteen from the spring. The rest of Victorio's people kept Carroll's main column pinned against the canyon wall with bullets and arrows. The soldiers were violently ill and in a panic, and therefore, fought poorly. During the night, Victorio slowly managed to surround the stricken blue coats. He simply waited for full daylight to pick them off one by one.

Without warning, Victorio heard the familiar bugle call and horses appeared in the distance. Although he could not identify them, these were the Arizona troops under McLellan and Gatewood. They had heard the shots and struggled to reach Captain Carroll and his men. Victorio was still in full control of the water hole as the soldiers crawled behind rock defenses, and he easily kept them back. But as Apache scouts and soldiers moved into position to block all escape routes, Victorio sent Nana away with most of the women and children. Victorio watched Nana and his people slip into the thick mesquite and disappear. He knew that, even as he watched, Nana was ordering the boys to use mesquite to brush out the horses' hoofprints while they mutely circumvented the soldiers. Once safe, Nana took a circuitous route seemingly toward the Black Range, but suddenly dropped into Mexico. With the most vulnerable out of the way, Victorio gathered the warriors and moved over the border as well. By now, Victorio must have sensed that his options were few. His people were tired. Americans apparently wanted to negotiate no deals. Victorio even heard news from the Mescalero Reservation that the soldiers had taken all of the Indians' weapons and horses.

Russell had fought Hatch's action and maintained that the military lacked the authority to interfere. But Hatch had replied that Old Vic was the army's problem now and ordered the agent to summon his Mescaleros. He also commanded his scouts to attack any Mescalero who refused. Reluctantly, Russell followed the order. On April 13, Hatch asked for an official count; there were 309 present. When soldiers began to confiscate guns, however, the warriors started to run away. Hatch sent the scouts to round them up. Small skirmishes between Mescaleros and the mostly Navajo scouts ensued, which simply made the situation more chaotic, and several noncombatants were killed.

One of the Mescalero chiefs interceded and recalled as many of the warriors as he could to the agency. However, the soldiers immediately impounded those who cooperated in a corral at the agency and kept them there for what many admitted was an unreasonably long time. Meanwhile, they seized arms and two hundred horses and mules. Hatch handed over nearly all of the animals to Colonel Grierson with orders to take them back to their original owners, if they could be found, or to keep them.

Agent Russell formally protested Hatch's actions and rough treatment of the Mescalero men. General Sherman's somewhat bewildering reply to the protest was: "Undue sympathy for these savages amounts to aiding and abetting a common enemy." Still, the general turned down Hatch's request for more Indian scouts, citing the additional expense. Historians have argued that the denial came in large part because senior army officers hated to admit that Apaches were more effective fighters than their own soldiers. Russell's complaint launched an Interior Department investigation of the affair, which continued well after Victorio's death in October 1880, but in the end amounted to nothing.

The Warm Springs Apaches Grow Weary

Some Mescaleros made their way to Victorio's camp. He received them warmly. From these newcomers, Victorio found out about Hatch's actions and discovered that the Texas commander Grierson was at that very moment combing the Guadalupe and Sacramento mountains. Thus, Victorio lingered in Mexico for a while longer. At about the same time, Victorio's son, Washington, and fourteen warriors went to San Carlos to visit their families and possibly to persuade Loco to join them. They returned to Victorio with sad stories about how poorly their people were faring in Arizona. The Warm Springs people who remained still suffered from lack of food and shelter. Worse, Victorio's exploits had made their situation more precarious. The government refused to free them, but resented having to feed and house them. Fights broke out frequently with rival White Mountain Apaches and others, especially when their scouts boasted of success against Victorio.

In May—as Victorio was making his way back to New Mexico—Washington led another small party back to San Carlos, presumably to visit or perhaps even free some of their people. The party first raided several Coyotero Apache camps on the outskirts of the reservation in retaliation for their treatment of the

Chihennes and for serving as scouts. In one of these raids, however, the Chihennes got the worst of it and found themselves
pushed all the way back to the Gila River. Washington re-
grouped for a another rescue attempt, but now the Sixth Cavalry was alerted to their presence and, second-guessing their
intentions, sped to the reservation to prevent a break-out. Washington was forced to withdraw, and only with great difficulty did
he escape to rejoin his father.

Unfortunately for Victorio, the failed rescue attempt alerted
Hatch that his prey was heading back to the United States. In
fact, Henry K. Parker, a Texan who was chief of the scouts, located one of Victorio's main camps in an isolated canyon on the
Palomas River not far from the old stomping grounds. Further
surveillance also told the scouts that Victorio's camp was
strangely vulnerable. Perhaps after eight months on the run and
with several defeats behind him, Victorio was tired. Parker divided his scouts and easily surrounded Victorio's camp. At day-
break, Victorio awoke to gunfire. Some of his warriors were so
startled that they left their guns behind as they kicked off their
blankets and ran for cover. They tried to regroup, but the dam-
age was done. During the day-long battle, Victorio probably lost
upwards of thirty or so people, the first major loss for him. In
fact, Victorio himself was among the wounded. As soldiers later
described it, some of the Apache scouts called out for the women
to surrender. Whether the scouts knew Victorio was among the
injured is unclear. However, one of the women reportedly
shouted back, "If Victorio dies, we will eat him so that no white
man ever sees his body." Some Apaches claim that that woman
was none other than Lozen, who at this point was still riding
with her brother. At dusk, Victorio and his band somehow
managed to flee south again. Parker's scouts were dangerously
short of ammunition and could not proceed after them. He had
sent word to Hatch that his scouts were desperate for more
weapons, but for some reason that we may never know, Hatch
ignored Parker's plea. Hence, the scouts withdrew.

However, it was not a victory for Victorio either. In fact, this
defeat set off a series of disasters for him. He fully realized now

that, despite his strategic abilities, superior technology was winning. Whites had unlimited resources. He did not. Even worse, a slow cultural deterioration was beginning to set in. The young Apache men, for instance, were forced into battle without first undergoing their sacred dihoke training and without learning Child of the Water's teachings. Young women received only abbreviated versions of the puberty ceremony and White Painted Woman's instructions. Because the bands were forever on the move, fewer babies were born and many of those that were born did not survive very long. Sadly, when they did live, newborns slowed down the rest, and often the mother had to remain with the Mescaleros or leave the group for a while and hope that she would not be taken captive. There was seldom time enough to craft proper cradleboards or to conduct the ceremonies to guarantee long, productive, and moral lives. Moreover, few di-yins who knew these rituals were among them.

Victorio debated heading to Mexico and joining up with Juh's Nednhis and those Chiricahuas who had managed to escape San Carlos. They were well hidden in the Blue Mountains. Why he did not is a mystery. Victorio appeared unwilling even as late as summer 1880 to make that decision. He continued moving about and apparently hoped that somehow he might still persuade the Americans to negotiate. It is hard to believe that he truly held out much optimism. Therefore, during the last few months of Victorio's War, he must have wrestled almost constantly with the need for an escape plan.

Victorio Heads for Mexico

By summer, New Mexicans heard disturbing rumors that the Apaches and Navajos were about to launch coordinated attacks against settlers. The rumors, of course, proved unfounded, but suggest the tension that gripped the region by this time. In reality, Victorio found few new allies. His situation was perilous. For one thing, Juh and Geronimo still lived at San Carlos in June 1880, and so he could expect no help from them at the moment. Next, some Mescaleros clamored to leave. Chief Caballero and

Victorio argued. The altercation grew bitter. Victorio apparently accused the Mescalero leader of betrayal, and in the heat of the conflict Victorio killed Caballero. Intimidated, the rest of the Mescaleros reluctantly stayed, but no longer as willing allies. Most waited for their chance to escape.

As Victorio headed toward Mexico one more time, Hatch wired the U.S. State Department and asked to negotiate quickly with Mexico for permission for the U.S. Army to cross the border in pursuit of the Apaches. Mexico City ultimately denied the request. Morrow stayed right on Victorio's tail, however, following him to Palomas Lake and killing a few stragglers there. One of those stragglers was Washington, who was probably pulling up the rear of the procession and awaiting some of the slower-moving band members. The death of his eldest son was yet another blow for Victorio.

As Victorio reached Mexico, Joseph C. Tiffany, who took over as San Carlos agent in June 1880, suggested sending some of the Coyotero Apaches after him. Or, he wrote, perhaps they should choose Apaches friendly to Victorio who might persuade him to surrender. Perhaps, Tiffany speculated, Victorio would still listen to reason, and indeed he might have done so. The plan was never carried out, so we cannot know whether Victorio might have negotiated an end to the stalemate in which he found himself.

Grierson was back in Texas, but kept troops stationed around Eagle Pass just in case Victorio or Nana moved in that direction. Sure enough, on July 16, Grierson's lookouts spotted Victorio about one hundred miles north of Eagle Springs. He wired Hatch, who advocated racing cavalry and infantry to the border right away. Grierson suggested another strategy. The Apache route would be determined by the availability of water, he claimed. Grierson posted troops at the most dependable springs. One of these springs was the Tiñaja de Las Palmas. It was not even an especially dependable source of fresh water, but Grierson posted a small contingent of cavalry there anyway. Five days later, Victorio was near Eagle Pass, heading straight for the Tiñaja. He appeared battle worn and exhausted. Above all, his people were thirsty. But Victorio spotted the soldiers and ordered his people to go around the spring. The jog allowed Grierson to reposition his men in such a manner as to prevent Victorio from returning to Texas. It was the first time the soldiers had anticipated the Apache's moves, and Victorio must have realized this, too. Usually, he had preempted the Americans. Now desperate for water, Victorio found all of the water holes and springs blocked.

He retreated. Two weeks later Victorio tried again. His people needed water badly. They had recalled every lesson taught them about where to locate water and failed. This time Victorio took his warriors in the direction of Rattlesnake Springs, for he knew there was a little water at that spot. Again, Grierson anticipated the move. He sent two troops of buffalo soldiers at breakneck speed over sixty-five miles of hot, searing desert terrain in twenty-one hours. They beat Victorio there. Victorio took his only option; he fled deeper into Mexico.

Meanwhile, Nana—in charge of another band—was ushering men, women, and children at a rapid pace down the Jornada del Muerto as quickly as he could. They streamed into the Florida Mountains and managed to get across the border into Old Mexico. Farther west, Kaytennae's group took the Old Smuggler's Trail down from the Warm Springs, met up with Nana, and, according to James Kaywaykla, reached the rendezvous spot before Victorio got there. The New Mexico and Arizona troops quickly sealed the gaps behind them, preventing any return. It was the last time Victorio and the majority of his followers ever set foot in the United States.

CHAPTER 8

Massacre at Tres Castillos

IT was September. The late summer heat was still typically excruciating and largely unceasing except for a few late-afternoon monsoon showers. When Victorio moved out of the Rio Grande Valley, he found mostly sand that, when wet, turned into dangerous quicksandlike mud and rocks that burned so hot during the daytime sun that to touch them was to blister the skin. The miniscule and widely separated water holes were often so alkaline that they caused nausea and abdominal cramps to anyone desperate enough to drink. Horses dropped from sheer exhaustion. Even for Apaches conditioned to brutal temperatures and harsh conditions, an hour's journey seemed to take days to complete. The Indeh, raised from infancy to endure a lack of food and only sips of water for long periods of time, nevertheless screamed inwardly for a few mouthfuls of liquid to loosen their dried lips and soothe their parched throats. Babies lay silent in their misery but wasted no tears.

Victorio felt more exhausted than he ever remembered, and every one of his fifty-five or so years weighed heavily upon his shoulders. Although he had hoped that at the last minute the Americans might send forth an emissary and offer to open negotiations, he now realized that there were no more agents like Steck or Drew who were dedicated enough to intercede. Thus, safety lay only in Juh's stronghold in the Sierra Madres or Blue Mountains, but Victorio still refused to make that decision. As he moved toward the low mountains east of Galeana, contact with the American soldiers seemed broken. Perhaps his people were temporarily out of danger. If so, maybe he could still bargain for time or, at the very least, regain strength. He took no chances, however. Each day he still divided his bands into three groups, and they traveled separately. Victorio led the first group of mostly men. The main body, which included women and children with perhaps thirty warriors to protect them, went with Kaytennae, while Nana brought up the rear. Grierson estimated that Victorio still counted at least one hundred effective warriors.

Each morning the three leaders agreed upon a rendezvous point for that night. For sustenance, they raided. Unlike the earlier days, the raiders ran off whatever stock, especially horses, that they could not use immediately rather than leave the rest to their enemy. Later, Grierson noted the hurried manner in which they tore the flesh from dead animals. He interpreted this as a sign that their rations were nearly gone. They were hungry, and they moved in hurried fashion, killing anyone who dared to resist them.

Wandering in the Desert

The Chihennes and their Mescalero allies camped each night rather than travel under cover of darkness. Some attributed this to a superstitious fear of darkness, but according to James Kaywaykla, Apaches knew that after the sun went down, the rattlesnakes slithered out from their underground tunnels. Traveling in the dark subjected the people and their animals to the unseen reptiles, which could strike at exposed legs. Moreover, stepping in an undetected snake or prairie dog hole could easily break a horse's leg. It was far more sensible to make the journey by day, especially in territory not as familiar to them as their own Black Range and Cañada Alamosa.

During this final flight across Chihuahua, Victorio ordered everyone—children included—to keep their individual food bags with them at all times. Never take the bag off, not even to sleep, he enjoined them. If we are forced to flee in the middle of the night, you must take your blanket with you, too. Otherwise, you may freeze to death when the desert gets cold, he told them. The three bands regularly left trail signs for each other. They arranged stones in such a manner that outsiders would

Tres Castillos and the Victorio Campaign

never notice, but which to them read like headlines in a newspaper. Sometimes men left the party to raid for food. When
danger lurked, the women and children scattered and traveled individually or in groups of only two or three. Then these trail
signs were the only means of finding each other. Unfortunately,
Apache and Navajo scouts could also read trail signs, but as far
as Victorio could tell, he had left them behind. The Americans

and their Indian allies seemed not to have followed his people into Mexico.

Lozen, however, no longer rode with her brother, and her absence was a major loss. On the Mexican side of the Rio Grande, a young Mescalero woman went into labor, and Lozen knew she must try to get the woman home. Lozen left Victorio and rode back to where the woman had isolated herself. She attended the birth and then stole the necessary food and horses to take the new mother back across the river to Fort Stanton. She later informed Nana that they had narrowly escaped soldiers on both the American and Mexican sides of the river. She had detected guards stationed at the water holes and assumed that all such water was now carefully watched. Lozen knew that some American soldiers had indeed crossed the border into Mexico, even if Victorio did not. She had no ability to send such intelligence to her brother, however. To this day, many Apaches believe that because Lozen's power was to locate the enemy, she might have prevented the massacre at Tres Castillos had she been with them. Sadly, she did not return to her people until after Victorio's death.

American Soldiers in Mexico

George Buell, commanding officer at Fort Cummings, which was located in the shadow of the infamous Cooke's Peak, received permission to cross over the U.S. and Mexican border about September 11. His initial company, accompanied by Navajo and some Apache scouts, did just that on September 15. The main regiment, which was weighted down with a supply train that included a four-hundred-gallon water wagon, followed six days later. It is worth noting that prior to Buell's thrust into Mexico, Colonel Hatch had, in fact, made two efforts to negotiate a surrender, but Victorio never knew that. About August 28, Hatch sent a former soldier named Jack Crawford, a scout called Navajo Charlie—who reportedly knew Victorio personally—and a Mexican guide south of the border. Their orders were to locate the Warm Springs people and open talks regarding surrender. This trio allegedly found Victorio and his bands camped in or near the Candelaria Mountains in Chihuahua. Suddenly, they claimed, Navajo Charlie refused to go one step farther. "He would give no explanation," Crawford later reported. "Coaxing and threats alike failed to move him." Not fluent in Apache himself, Crawford gave up the mission, returned to Fort Cummings, and volunteered to travel with Buell's soldiers back into Mexico. Perhaps he still hoped to make contact. In September, Hatch proposed sending 150 Indian police from San Carlos into Mexico to persuade Victorio to return, but this plan was never approved and hence not carried out.

Once in Mexico, Buell's scouts read trail signs and reported that Victorio had quite suddenly changed his course. For some reason, he appeared to be taking his people straight into the rugged Candelaria Mountains. Parker guessed that Victorio had just discovered their border crossing and was reacting to it. In fact, one can well imagine Victorio's shock. American soldiers, who had previously stopped helplessly north of the Rio Grande, now boldly moved south, and again made a point to cut off all water sources. All trails to the United States were blocked.

Colonel Adolpho F. Valle, who had granted permission to Buell to cross the border and whose own cavalry had circled the El Carmen hacienda and the village of Carrizal throughout most of August, suddenly left the field. He reported to Governor Luis Terrazas that his men were exhausted from a summer of searching, and the horses were trail-weary. He refused to go out again despite the governor's pleas. But Joaquin Terrazas was eager. He willingly took Valle's place and was equipped with two hundred or more horse soldiers. Governor Terrazas augmented Joaquin's force with some three hundred or so armed civilians, to whom he promised payment and the possibility of lucrative scalp bounties. Chihuahua citizens had invited the Texas Rangers, too—allegedly to protect them—and they bolstered the general's numbers even further.

As forces amassed against his people, Victorio undoubtedly experienced a sense of sheer desperation. At some point, he must have recalled the Creation story of how Child of the Water had battled monsters from the east, south, west, and north, and wondered if his people were reliving the story. He continued to move ahead of the armies. Terrazas swept through those villages that had the most to fear from the Apaches, sought intelligence, and recruited volunteers. El Carmen, where so many children had been captured over the years, received a visit, as did the old mission and the villages of San Buenaventura, Galeana, Casas Grandes, and Corralitos. Terrazas sent messengers to many of the Rio Grande communities edging Texas as well. In Corralitos, one of Victorio's former trading centers, Terrazas met an old Indian fighter named Juan Mata Ortiz, who quickly volunteered. His skills almost immediately earned Mata Ortiz the position of second-in-command. By the end of September, Terrazas commanded 350 men. Then he began to scout again. His men scoured the area roughly bordered by Chihuahua City and San Andres to the south, Corralitos and Janos in the west, the Candelaria Range to the north, and the Rio Grande to the east. His scouts worked their way deeper into the various mountain ranges, reading trail sign and analyzing the old Apache camps they found.

At the same time—while cutting off every possible water hole between the Candelarias and the U.S. border as they moved south—Buell reached the Candelarias. About September 28, a nervous sentry spotted some of the Apaches. He fired his gun prematurely, thus scattering his own horses and mules and forcing the soldiers to run away on foot. What they did not know was that the Indians were now trapped. The next day, Buell himself approached the Apache stronghold, found no water, and as the sun rose, realized in a moment of panic that his men were easily exposed to ambush. Buell immediately ordered his soldiers back to the supply train. Victorio, momentarily trapped nearby, managed to slip away. It was a close call.

Flight to the Blue Mountains

By October 1, nobody knew exactly where Victorio was hiding. Even the scouts were confused. He was somewhere between the Los Piños Range (or Sierra de los Piños) and the Rio Grande and heading south. Nor could Victorio pinpoint where all of the soldiers were located. He just knew they were not giving up and they seemed perpetually on the move. His people had experienced too many close calls recently. Thus, he called together his warriors to make a major decision. He told Nana and Kaytennae that they were probably safe for a few days, but not for much longer than that. The cavalry would search every mountain until they found them. They needed rest badly. They also needed food and water. As always, they were nearly out of ammunition. Some of the Mescaleros were away raiding and swore they would not return empty-handed. It might take days, even weeks before they returned, if indeed, they had not already fled home.

Victorio suggested that they go west. On the plain east of Tres Castillos, there was a small lake and good grass. Victorio proposed that they camp there and rest up for the long and arduous struggle to the Blue Mountains, where they would join Juh. Given a few days, they could replenish their food stores with the cattle recently raided from a nearby hacienda. The cattle could be butchered the next day and the meat cut for drying in two days of sunshine. What they could not eat they would cut thin and pack. After preparing the meat, the band would move out. Victorio allegedly turned to each leader individually and asked for his opinion. He wanted a consensus.

Nana spoke for them all, but deferred to Victorio. According to Kaywaykla, Nana told Victorio that he had fought with Mangas Coloradas, Cochise, and him. The problems confronting them now superceded what either of the others had ever encountered, he claimed. "Your wisdom has never failed us," he allegedly said to Victorio. The elderly warrior asked permission to take one man on a raid to find ammunition. Victorio nodded, but suggested that Nana choose somebody besides himself to lead the raid, even though Nana's power was to locate weapons and ammunition. Apparently, Victorio wanted Nana to protect the women and children. Nana obediently selected Blanco, who in turn, selected one man to accompany him. That left sufficient warriors in camp.

Then Victorio outlined his plan. After they rested and dried the meat, he would split the people into two groups. He would take half and lead the way. Nana, Kaytennae, and Mangas—Mangas was with them again—would form the rear guard. All would eventually meet at Tres Castillos. It was a lonely place about ninety miles north of Chihuahua City. The Apaches knew it well. In reality, one could hardly consider Tres Castillos a mountain range. But on such a flat and windswept place as the Castillos Plains, even a low outcropping of volcanic plugs qualified as mountains. The remote, battered Tres Castillos—so named because they appeared to the Spanish as three castle turrets—would allow the Apaches a brief respite before they made the final push to Juh's stronghold, Victorio believed. Kaywaykla claimed that Victorio had blankets and other supplies stashed there as well. Perhaps the place was so isolated that Victorio simply knew some Indian people would have placed rations there.

For two days the Warm Springs people stayed where they were. The warriors kept a close eye on the women and children as they butchered, cut strips of meat, and spread the strips across mesquite bushes so that they might dry in the hot sun. Then they pounded the meat thin and compact so that every individual could carry an adequate amount in his leather bag. On the third day, they bound the larger packs of meat, their remaining water, and what was left of the blankets onto their few horses and broke camp. Some of the elders and the very young rode, while the older children and women led the pack animals. The warriors searched for any sign of the troops.

Those who survived the massacre recalled that during the morning hours it was terribly cold, but after the sun rose high in the sky, the temperatures sweltered. As they moved west, the desert vegetation gave way to bristly cactus stumps and then mostly sand and rocks. The sharp sun-baked stones strewn about made travel even more difficult for the poor horses. Of course, of even greater concern were those "queer-looking holes," the daytime tunnels into which the rattlesnakes burrowed during the heat of the day. Although some historians have questioned Victorio and suggested that he led his people out onto the desert toward no fixed goal, this is not entirely true. He always had some plan, albeit not necessarily one clear to historians. He had followed the low mountain chains across Chihuahua throughout August and September, most of which contained unguarded water holes. Keeping to higher elevations was the traditional Apache strategy. Victorio's movements suggest that he wanted to return to the United States, but found the route blocked. The chief seemed to adjust his thinking, and by the time he started across the Castillos Plains, he was traveling the most direct route to the Blue Mountains. As always, his behavior was calculated and deliberate. It is just that Victorio's options had dwindled and his movements, if erratic, perhaps reveal his attempt to reassess his position. When one compares military accounts of this episode against oral histories, they coordinate rather well.

According to James Kaywaykla, the Warm Springs bands stopped only once or twice during the day to sip water, eat a handful of dried meat, and rest the horses. It was late afternoon when they at last approached the long sand dune, which ended at the incline to Tres Castillos. At the foot of those three rock outcroppings were strewn large boulders. As the people drew closer, however, they spotted meager vegetation sprouting up between the rocks and then grass nearer the water. "Grandmother explained that beyond the dune was the lake," Kaywaykla later related to Eve Ball. Between the lake and first mountain was a plain with grass where they could rest and feed the horses. In October the mud flats were usually filled with water, and as a result, attracted birds and small game. Victorio said they could even build a fire and cook their food after they set up camp. General Terrazas noted in his account that a large fire blazed well into the night, indicating that the people obviously had time to collect brush before the Mexican troops arrived on the scene. Historians have since asked whether Victorio's people camped on one of the three hills or in a depression between the two. Oral history suggests the second. Kaywaykla told Eve Ball that he remembered settling down beside the lake and for the first time envisioning the journey's end. He also recalled later climbing to escape the oncoming Mexican soldiers.

The Americans Go Home

Joaquin Terrazas was right behind them. He and Juan Mata Ortiz, along with their Tarahumara and Opata scouts, had followed Victorio's elusive trail for weeks. Then the trail grew
more obvious. Everything suggested that the Warm Springs
people were only a day or two ahead of the troops. "But if you
find them," Terrazas warned, "Huid! Flee!" The officers, he told
them, would plan the attack. By late September, Terrazas realized
Victorio was heading deeper into Chihuahua. The general
stopped in the village of Boracho for supplies, and there he encountered Colonel Buell and a regiment of Ninth Cavalry under
Charles Schaeffer. Buell had the route back to the United States
sealed tight. Now, however, Terrazas decided to finish the pursuit himself.

He thanked the Americans for their efforts, but informed
them brusquely that further intrusion into Chihuahua was not
desired. He bid them a safe journey home. The general also sent
Baylor's Texas Rangers packing, much to their disappointment.
Reluctantly, Buell and Baylor gave up the chase and made an
about-face. Afterward, Terrazas loaded up on supplies and picked
up Victorio's trail again. According to historian Joseph A. Stout,
Terrazas knew approximately where the hostiles were and how
many warriors Victorio had in his arsenal. That he did not intend
to permit the Americans to purloin his glory largely agrees with
Buell's contemporary assessment of the situation. To kill the notorious Victorio would give the middle-aged military officer
considerable popularity in Chihuahua City. Combined with his
already remarkable military reputation, such accolades could
readily translate into political influence and wealth.

Terrazas found evidence of Victorio's deserted camp at Lagu-
nita, and a week later, about October 7, discovered another in the
Los Piños Range. Then he traced the Apaches to Cerro Lagri-
mas and knew his troops were closing in when they spotted the
scraps of recently butchered cows and the mesquite brush where
women had dried the meat in haste. On October 12, Terrazas led
his men onto the plains. He split his troops, sending Juan Mata

Ortiz in one direction and leading a company of men himself in a more westerly trajectory. The soldiers and their civilian allies traveled light. Each man carried no more than one canteen of water and a small pouch of ground, sweetened corn. That way everyone could eat and drink while on the move. The soldiers remained in the saddle all night.

The Initial Encounter

Finally, Terrazas approached Tres Castillos. He had seen clouds of dust before him and realized that he had finally caught up with Victorio's Apaches. He ordered his men to surround all sides of the low mountains. As the soldiers moved into position, Terrazas believed that he finally had Victorio trapped. Still, one could never be quite sure. For a so-called ignorant Indian, Victorio displayed great military genius, second only to the great Lakota warrior Crazy Horse, many claimed. The dust clouds also suggested that Victorio's people had only just arrived. The Tarahumara scouts verified that notion. In fact, according to some accounts, the Chihennes had barely watered the animals, gathered brush, and spread out their blankets when the encounter began. Others, however, suggest that it was well after dark. Regardless, Victorio seemed to have no idea that Terrazas and three hundred or so men were hastily surrounding him and cutting off any escape.

When Victorio heard shots, he turned in the direction from which they had come. Along the lake he saw flashes of metal. He heard the clank of horses' hooves over rock. "Indah!" Victorio shouted. "Indah," which meant "White Man!" "Climb!" The women grabbed their children. A few were still close enough to their horses to mount and ride to higher ground. The rest climbed. They moved from boulder to boulder or slid into the narrow clefts between the rocks. They ran through sharp cholla cactus, dry mesquite, and greasewood. Kaywaykla describes a series of rocky benches over which he climbed. Once most of the Apaches reached the safety of the higher rocks, they saw about a dozen Mexicans below them, galloping at full speed toward the lake. It was nearly dark, though, and those who had squeezed

into the narrow rocky crevices prayed silently to Ussen to keep
the rattlesnakes away for just a few more minutes. They could de-
tect mostly the metal of the guns reflecting in the last of the early
evening light or perhaps in the glow of the moon, and the occasional flash as a gun was fired.

As dusk and a cold white moon hung over the Castillos plain,
the Apaches used the sound of horses and rifle shots to determine where the soldiers were positioned. They had no idea,
however, how many were out there. The Apaches caught an occasional command barked in Spanish. Kaywaykla remembered
that one man halted very near to his hiding place, rolled, and lit
a cigarette. Kaywaykla smelled the smoke as the soldier drew in
and exhaled the fumes, then crushed the spent cigarette with his
boot heel. It could have been the chain-smoking Joaquin Terrazas himself, but was probably one of his enlisted men. Then
they all simply waited.

The Massacre at Tres Castillos

The Mexicans dismounted and prepared for dawn. Terrazas
tried to lull Victorio into a false sense of security. He exposed
only a dozen or so of his men so that the Apaches might believe
there were just a few soldiers and remain confident that they
could defeat such a small force. In reality, the hundreds of
soldiers and civilians camped two miles away planned to ride forward in charge formation once the sun came up and the fighting commenced. In his zeal, Terrazas had circled Tres Castillos
prematurely. That gave Nana and Kaytennae time to observe
what was happening from afar and avoid the trap. Unfortunately,
however, they could not alert Victorio or assist him in any way.

The two sides hunkered down. Victorio ordered his men to fire
at anyone who moved, perhaps convinced that there were only a
few Mexicans out there. But the canopy of darkness overtook
them, and they were nearly out of ammunition. Blanco's raiding
party had not yet returned. The Apaches used the brush they had
collected before Terrazas's arrival to ignite a fire. It probably
served as a means to stay warm and as a signal to Nana and

Kaytennae. Some of the soldiers used the light to creep closer. Judging by the paucity of shots that Victorio's men fired, Terrazas surmised that the Indians were saving their bullets for morning.

About midnight, the soldiers thought they heard Apache death songs. The Tarahumara scouts verified it. Remarkably, even as the Apaches chanted, they were also hastily constructing rock defenses. Furthermore, approximately fifteen women and children used the darkness, the natural vegetation, and the commotion to shield their escape. Kaywaykla was one of those who managed to slip around the Mexicans and get away.

During that long night, Victorio undoubtedly thought many times of his children far away at San Carlos. He missed Dilth-cleyhen and his granddaughter Beshad-e. They were almost certainly still suffering at that terrible place. So, too, was Charlie Istee, if indeed he was still alive. Victorio's three wives were, of course, all dead. He had no idea whether Lozen had made it to Mescalero or lay dead somewhere on the trail. As Victorio prayed to Ussen, he also must have thought about Warm Springs, the place the Creator made specifically for his Apache people. They were strong at that place. If they died here at Tres Castillos, who would take on the sacred responsibility for that land? In fact, had their inability to remain at Warm Springs caused their decline as a people? Why were the whites so blind that they stubbornly refused to recognize that Ussen's people were supposed to live on their chosen land? Even as he asked these questions, Victorio knew he would probably die with them unanswered. Perhaps, the white men were savages. After all, when Killer of Enemies took the gun and left Ussen, he had ceased to be an Apache. When the sun next set, would his people have traveled farther toward the Blue Mountains or find themselves on the trail to the Happy Place? Would it look like Warm Springs? Regardless, at least no white men lived there.

As the first streaks of the sun turned the sky gray, the fighting began. Victorio's warriors held their position, according to reports, for upwards of two hours. Then at about 9 A.M., the Apaches ran out of ammunition. Stories of Victorio's final moments are varied and conflicting. The Texas Ranger Gillett claimed that "Victorio mounted a white horse," and as he prepared to meet the enemy "exposed himself unnecessarily." He was, therefore, the first to die. However, the Texas Rangers were not at Tres Castillos that day, and it was Joaquin Terrazas, not Victorio, who favored white horses. Gillett's is one of several highly romanticized versions that found their way into western folklore over time.

According to one Mexican tale, when Terrazas's men overran Victorio's position, they found the aging chief wounded in several places and writhing in pain. A Tarahumara scout named Mauricio de Coredor walked up and shot the Apache dead. One variation on the story is that Coredor engaged in prolonged hand-to-hand combat with Victorio and eventually won. Another rendition describes Victorio using his last bullet on himself. However, according to Kaytennae, who arrived later and buried the bodies, Victorio committed suicide. A knife, Kaytennae claimed, was embedded in his heart. This is perhaps most accurate. For one thing, Terrazas did not even recognize Victorio and had to ask two Mexican captive boys who were rescued after the battle to identify the body.

When the news and some of the wild stories reached Dilthcleyhen a few weeks later, she concluded, "We will never know the facts." She added that her father was "something big." Many whites considered him a brilliant wartime strategist, and Mexicans sang a song about him long after his death. It went:

> I am the Indian Victorio.
> It is my passion to fight.
> I must attain glory.
> And I will make the world tremble.
> I want to live,
>> I want to die.
>> I want to live, so I can fight.
> To Mexico I'll go,
> I will go to fight,
> And shout War! War!
>> Until I die.

But that, too, was incorrect. Victorio had favored peace when-ever he could. It was only after he grew desperate that he shouted "War!" Even then, had any American authority offered an olive branch, it is almost certain that Victorio would have taken it.

The Aftermath

Terrazas lost three men at Tres Castillos. The Apaches lost sev-enty-eight people, sixty-two of them warriors and the rest women and children. The two recovered Mexican boys—Felix Carrillo and Felipe Padilla, both from New Mexico—were even-tually returned to the United States. The civilian militia mem-bers and soldiers scalped all seventy-eight Apaches for the bounties—Victorio's brought 2,000 pesos—and captured sixty-eight women and children to sell into slavery. They reported recovering 120 horses, 38 mules, and 12 burros. The soldiers di-vided Victorio's personal effects among themselves. Apaches under Nana later ambushed nine Mexican soldiers near the town of Carrizal. In that attack, Mauricio de Coredor, who al-legedly killed Victorio and was said to be using his saddle and wearing several "trinkets," was singled out and hacked to pieces.

In Chihuahua City, Terrazas received a gift of a tricolor flag with gold inscription that read "Triumph over Victorio." Later, Sonorans also applauded the general. The militias rode tri-umphantly through the streets and waved bloody scalps to the accompaniment of bells and music. Mata Ortiz and Coredor were cited for gallantry. Telegrams went to the military command posts in El Paso and Santa Fe. From there, the commanding officers telegrammed the Division of the Missouri headquarters and the secretary of war in Washington. The U.S. State Depart-ment informed Juan N. Navarro, the Mexican consul in New York City, and notified their own personnel in Chihuahua City and Mexico City as well.

On October 21, 1880, the *Santa Fe New Mexican* printed blar-ing headlines that read "Wiped Out!" This edition also titillated readers with graphic reports of an "18-hour fight" and the "al-most utter destruction of [Victorio's] band." When Nana's band ambushed those nine Mexicans in November, the *New Mexican* reconsidered: "It is considered here to be an open question whether or not Victorio is dead." Historian Philip J. Rasch reinforced the notion that it took New Mexicans a long time to recover from the fear that had gripped them for so long. In the end, he aptly concluded, whites defeated Victorio not by tactics or superior intelligence but by technology and sheer numbers.

Some Americans, however, saw Victorio's death as senseless, and many blamed the federal government. General George Crook admitted that San Carlos was a terrible place and the Interior Department's concentration policy had proven a tremendous failure. The Apaches had nothing to do there. They just lay around and were fed after a fashion, he said. A few still told the old stories in a desperate attempt to keep Apache ways alive.

The unconventional Crook's views eventually became almost indistinguishable from those of the civilian reformers, whom he had so detested in the years following the Civil War. In 1890, four years after the last Apache surrender, Crook wrote to President Benjamin Harrison recommending that the Apache prisoners—including Geronimo—be moved from Florida and Alabama, where they were being held, to Fort Sill, Oklahoma. In 1895, the transfer finally took place. Unfortunately, the reformers, who had originally instigated for missionary agents and favored concentration, had already declared the Indian wars over by the time Victorio met his death at Tres Castillos and had turned their attention to devising new reforms. One of these was the outrageous policy of allotment passed in 1887, which over the next half-century would break up many of the existing reservations.

General William T. Sherman also placed much of the blame on the Interior Department. In his 1881 report, he pondered why the Indian Office had so willingly allowed the expenditure of millions of dollars and numerous American lives to capture Victorio when less than a decade earlier, $11,000 would have made Warm Springs a satisfactory reservation site. Officials must have had an exceptionally good reason to insist that the Apaches live at San Carlos rather than Warm Springs, he concluded. Historians have called the government's decision arrogant and evidence of a refusal to acknowledge their error of judgment. During the Victorio Campaign, Hatch said much the same thing.

Still other critics pointed to a political spoils system that kept agents such as Tiffany in the field. On October 24, 1882, the grand jury of the first federal district in Arizona censured the agent for fraud, speculation, conspiracy, larceny, plots, and "counterplots" at San Carlos. Jury foreman James H. Toole wrote: "For several years the people of this territory have been gradually arriving at the conclusion that the management of the Indian reservations in Arizona was a fraud." He added that the recurring outbreaks were undoubtedly the result of apathy or criminal neglect. By 1886, the *Atlantic Monthly* reported that the San Carlos camps of the Warm Springs Apaches still suffered from long and extreme heat, bad water, and fever. They were hungry, bored, and lacked farming implements or instruction towards some useful, self-supporting occupation. These assessments, of course, came too late for Victorio and his people.

The Survivors Regroup

When news of the killing at Tres Castillos reached Nana and Kaytennae, the latter went to examine the scene and bury the bodies. Nana took his small band to Casas Grandes, where Lozen eventually caught up with him and joined in locating survivors and others. Lozen, it is suggested, had grown tired of her dual roles of fighting and safeguarding the women and children, but apparently "she gave no sign of discontent." Sadly, her story is largely lost to documentary history, and so there is almost no written evidence to support claims about her. Oral histories say, however, that Lozen rode with Nana until he surrendered at San Carlos in 1883. She later accompanied Geronimo's band when he bolted from the reservation, and she surrendered with him in 1886. Although we will probably never be entirely certain, she is allegedly in the famous photo of Geronimo's surrendered band. As a prisoner of war, Lozen was shipped to the Mount Vernon barracks in Mobile, Alabama. She died of the "coughing sickness," or tuberculosis, at about the age of fifty.

Kaytennae, his wife Gouyen, and according to some accounts, James Kaywaykla. Photo by Ben Wittick. Courtesy of Palace of the Governors (MNM/DCA) (negative #14221).

Other women continued to straggle back. Kaywaykla's grand-mother, for instance, did not return to her people for approximately six years. She and her granddaughter, Siki, were taken captive after running away from Tres Castillos, imprisoned in Chihuahua City, and then shipped to Mexico City as slaves. They bided their time and eventually managed to escape. It took them months to walk the nearly one thousand miles back to the Cañada Alamosa in search of their relatives. The cavalry picked the women up in the village of Monticello, where they had stopped for supplies and information, and took them to San Carlos.

Nana took over the leadership upon Victorio's death. He immediately realized that Mexicans and Americans expected him to stay in Casas Grandes or head into the Sierra Madres. Therefore, according to oral stories, he fooled them all and headed straight for the Florida Mountains and right back to Warm Springs to continue seeking survivors and, hopefully, gain reinforcements. Blanco and Mangas joined him there, as did some of the long-absent Mescalero raiding party. It was in the shadow of the Black Range that Nana told the children stories of Child of the Waters, who had been required to overcome difficulties. His life had been a series of them. He also emboldened the demoralized band with tales of their peoples' glorious past.

Fearing detection, however, the Warm Springs bands kept quiet. Cavalry still scoured the mountain ranges between Mescalero and the Arizona border. Blanco, in fact, was killed that fall in a skirmish near Cooke's Peak. The people lived by raiding small wagon trains and isolated ranches, but Nana soon realized that they could not remain hidden in New Mexico forever. By November, Nana acquired horses and went to Mexico, taking the time to attack the soldiers at Carrizal as he traveled. In the Blue Mountains, Juh rode out to welcome the survivors.

Nana did not remain in the Blue Mountains. In summer 1881, he took his revenge for the Tres Castillos massacre. He suddenly attacked the presidio of Galeana, where Juan Mata Ortiz was in command. His warriors stole horses and waited for the soldiers to follow. When the cavalry rode out and into Nana's trap, his men killed twenty-two of them, some in hand-to-hand combat.

One of those who died in the attack was the hated Mata Ortiz, whom Nana's warriors mutilated. Historians do not know if Nana realized before the attack that this was Ortiz's presidio. Then, by mid-July 1881, Nana crossed the U.S.-Mexican border near Fort Quitman, Texas. For the next five or six weeks, he led Kaytennae, Mangas, and an unknown number of others in a series of ambushes across southern New Mexico. This was dubbed "Nana's Raid" or "Nana's Campaign of 1881." He and his warriors vented their rage over more than one thousand miles, killing between thirty and fifty men, capturing hundreds of horses, and eluding eight companies of cavalry and infantry and two companies of Indian scouts. Some Chiricahuas may have joined them. According to New Mexico historian Lynda Sanchez, only a strong leader could have executed such a plan. He certainly left the army red-faced. They had proven utterly unable to stop an aging and partly crippled warrior. As General Pope wrote, "There is no great trouble in dealing with Nana's men when found. . . . The difficulty is to find them."

Nana returned to the Blue Mountains. His days of freedom were numbered, and he knew it. Still, he had outwitted the opponent one more time. Ironically, Nana's band grew larger after September 1881. A prophet named Noch-ay-det-klinne, who claimed he could speak to the dead, had attracted a great number of despondent San Carlos men and women that summer. Similar in some ways to Wovoka, the Nevada Pauite whose visions created the Ghost Dance, the Apache prophet introduced a new circle dance. Dancers stood like spokes on a wheel with Noch-ay-det-klinne sprinkling hádndín on them. Believers danced with a religious ecstasy that frightened whites living in nearby villages and on isolated farms. Nana's raid may have added further tensions. Some of the believers insisted that during prayer sessions they saw specters of Victorio, Cochise, and Mangas Coloradas. It is even possible that Nana attended one of the prayer meetings, but if he did so, it was under a shroud of secrecy and at great risk to himself.

On August 30, 1881, two cavalry troops from Fort Apache plus a company of Apache scouts arrived at Cibecue Creek, northwest of the fort, to arrest the prophet. Followers attacked the forces, and in the imbroglio that followed—referred to as the Battle of Cibecue Creek—Apache scouts deserted. It was the only whole-sale mutiny of Indian scouts in U.S. military history. Noch-ay-det-klinne was killed, and in the aftermath, Geronimo and oth-ers bolted. The following spring, Geronimo and possibly Nana returned to San Carlos to "liberate" as many friends and relatives as they could reasonably persuade to leave, including a middle-aged and hesitant Loco.

Nana surrendered to General Crook on May 23, 1883. In 1882, the War Department had reassigned Crook to Arizona. When Nana arrived at San Carlos, he found Dilth-cleyhen and Beshad-e, but not Charlie Istee, who was probably still riding with Juh. In fact, for a while, Juh was the only major Apache leader still living free. Then, one day after Nana's surrender, Juh went into Casas Grandes to trade. According to rumors, he got drunk on the way home and slipped from his horse. It was said that he fell headlong into a swollen river and drowned. Witnesses, however, claimed he was not drunk when he left Casas Grandes. Thus, his death was more likely the result of a stroke or heart attack.

Nana and Geronimo bolted from San Carlos again in autumn 1885, when they supposedly heard rumors that some of the chiefs would be executed. They took forty-two unhappy warriors and ninety-two women with them. Nana was recaptured with Geronimo in 1886, and according to historian Dan L. Thrapp, General Crook always considered Nana the brains of the hostile group. Kaytennae would have accompanied them except for an intervening event. Undoubted bored, Kaytennae had by 1884 earned a reputation as a surly troublemaker. Fearing that he might incite an uprising, agent Crawford and Britton Davis, now in charge of the scouts, used Kaytennae's reputation and rumors to arrest him on June 21, 1884. Eve Ball maintains that Chato and Mickey Free, the young man whose disappearance as Felix Ward had caused the notorious Bascom affair, started the rumors that Kaytennae was planning to lead other malcontents in a rebellion. Tried on June 27 before a San Carlos Indian court consisting mostly of White Mountain Apaches, Kaytennae was convicted of attempting to incite an uprising and sentenced to three years' confinement at Alcatraz Island. Released in 1886, he not only was absent when Nana and Geronimo bolted but helped Crook ferret them out in 1886. Nevertheless, for his efforts, Kaytennae was sent as a prisoner of war to Florida along with the others. Kaywaykla, his adopted son, reported that when Kaytennae was sent off to Alcatraz in 1884, his wife—Kaywaykla's mother—gave birth to a girl. Settled now at San Carlos, Gouyen found a special di-yin, a cradlemaker, to carve the precious tsoch. Grandmother was not yet returned from her captivity in Mexico, so another elderly woman strapped the girl into the cradleboard, and Gouyen buried the umbilical cord. Thus, a new generation began, and this one was defined by reservation life.

Nana, "still unreconstructed," died in 1896. Loco remained on the San Carlos reservation and died there in 1905. Charles Istee, Kaywaykla, and Mangas later moved with their families to Mescalero. In August 1912, Victorio's grandson, a child named Evan Istee, was born. Angie Debo, met with the Istee family on July 24, 1971, and among them was a young male child who was Victorio's great-grandson. He would be in his mid- to late thirties today. So life for Victorio's Warm Springs people entered a new cycle.

Taking a Closer Look

In 1930 a leading scholar of the Western Apaches, Grenville Goodwin, investigated sightings of "wild Apaches" in the Sierra Madres. He encountered none, but found evidence of their camps and concluded that these Apaches were probably the remnants of Juh's, Geronimo's, and maybe Nana's bands, who eluded soldiers and refused to surrender in 1886. They had led a precarious, hand-to-mouth existence ever since, raiding tiny Mexican villages for food and supplies just as they always had, but mostly remaining isolated in the still-forbidding Blue Mountains. There were no further sightings of them after 1934. Goodwin estimated that at the time there were maybe thirty left.

MASSACRE AT TRES CASTILLOS   215

The massacre at Tres Castillos did not, of course, occur in a vacuum. The battles between the Apaches and the federal government lasted longer than those with any other tribal group. The Apaches held out the longest of any Indians partly because their exceptionally fluid political structure and because their rugged environment worked to their advantage. Without the need to move or hide large communities, the Apaches could flee at a moment's notice and scatter with amazing speed. Unencumbered by horse herds, they could disappear far more easily than, say, the Plains people. Their raid-and-trade networks were difficult to eradicate. They were brilliant guerilla warriors, who frustrated even the nontraditional military. In addition, the inability of their land to support large numbers of people meant that few whites sought to move onto Apache land. Mining strikes and hardscrabble farms aside, southwestern New Mexico attracted comparatively few settlers, and this also helped the Apaches.

Government bureaucracy came slowly to the Southwest, but when it did, it failed to syncretize well with Apache culture. Nor did it try very hard to do so. Unfortunately, Americans have often proven unwilling to understand or respect other cultures. Moreover, because of the Hispanic majority in New Mexico, the federal government failed to demonstrate much concern. A wide-open border and general lack of economic opportunities in the Southwest encouraged illegal trade, which continues to this day. Back in 1849, Governor Calhoun found that he had little influence over traders in the region. Nor did President Hayes in 1877, when his order forbidding arms sale to Indians had no effect whatsoever. The off-reservation Apaches maintained these networks for as long as they could and even kept their reservation relatives fed, mounted, and armed. Into the twenty-first century, the U.S.-Mexican border remains a no-man's land of illegal immigration, drugs, sex trade, and other illicit operations.

For these reasons, and because the Apaches were so tenacious, Americans seemed to hate them more than any other indigenous Indians. Nowhere except in California was the cry for all-out extermination louder. Arizona openly advocated a policy of genocide in 1862, and an article in the *Arizona Citizen* called for the murder of every Apache man, woman, and child in order to "send to high heaven the grateful incense of festering and rotting Chiricahuas." Thus, many residents turned a blind eye to such killers as King Woolsey and to Mexico's scalp bounties even in the 1880s.

Hollywood also carried on the Apaches-as-villains theme. Although Victorio has appeared as a character in surprisingly few films and then as peripheral, Geronimo and Cochise have often taken center stage. The bloodthirsty Apache tradition established itself early, but perhaps reached a peak in John Ford's 1939 *Stagecoach*, where not only is Geronimo the author of all sorts of atrocities, including the murder of a white women, but the conviction that Apaches always scalped their enemy is also firmly reinforced. Fortunately, as Americans rethought their view of American Indians, Hollywood depicted kinder, gentler versions of Geronimo and Apaches overall. For example, although Geronimo remains surly, he is not savage in *Broken Arrow* (1950) and Cochise is downright introspective and conciliatory. In the 1986 remake of *Stagecoach*, the Apaches are misunderstood, while the 1993 film *Geronimo* depicts the chief—albeit not most of the other Apaches—as complex. Sadly, however, *The Missing* (2003) returns to the earlier theme. There are the obligatory noble Apaches who sacrifice themselves to save the white woman and child, but the focus is on a brutal and inaccurate depiction of Apache witchcraft, and the overall image is one of savagery.

One is reminded that, even during the nineteenth century, there were, of course, other voices. Unfortunately, these were too frequently ignored in Washington or brushed aside, especially when many settlers found it profitable to supply food, hay, lumber and freighting to the military fighting in the continuing Apache wars. Certainly many ranchers and farmers were victims, but even these individuals realized that federal dollars kept the economy of the Southwest going. Historian Howard Zinn has argued that one does not have to have a capitalistic society in order to sustain frequent wars, but capitalism feeds upon war, and war feeds upon capitalism. A military occupation meant economic stability and, for some, untold opportunities to line their pockets legally or otherwise. When, for example, agents dared to suggest that the San Carlos Apaches supply hay to area forts and become more self-sufficient, locals censured them. When Charles Drew challenged business practices of contractors, the Indian Office threatened to remove him. Furthermore, the *Mesilla Valley Independent* correctly pointed out that corruption reached all the way to Washington.

The anthropologist Richard Perry also places some responsibility on large corporations such as Phelps Dodge, which sought access to the Southwest in order to open up large-scale silver and copper mining. The Apaches were obstacles, and once defeated, corporate interests bought up the newly available land. With the help of the Indian Office, they sometimes managed to usurp the minerals located on Indian reservations. This sale of Indian resources perpetuated Apache poverty and dependency into the twenty-first century.

The so-called Indian reformers played a role in the drama. As Francis Prucha has noted, after such monumental events as the capture of Chief Joseph and the surrender of Crazy Horse in 1877, reformers considered the Indian wars over. Their new approach to Indian policy unabashedly combined religion and a nationalistic patriotism. The historian Robert Utley says that these crusaders carried the concept of concentration beyond any previous lengths and operated with a deadly combination of wealth, influence, and the belief that God was on their side. Their vision of the Americanized Indian was virtually a fusion of nationalism and Protestantism. Their ardor created magnificent rhetoric, but clashed head on with reality. In addition, they seemed to resent the pesky tenacity of the Warm Springs Apaches, who apparently did not appreciate the so-called advantages of assimilation into the dominant culture—or, failing that, getting out of the way of it.

Does that make Victorio an innocent victim? Of course not. Although he preferred peace, he killed whites and Mexicans in unprovoked attacks, sometimes out of rage and occasionally because they got in his way. He probably should have stayed at Mescalero longer and demonstrated more patience towards the young and inexperienced agent Russell. On the other hand, Victorio was perfectly willing to live on a reservation, as the Indian Office demanded. He simply wanted to remain at Warm Springs. In fact, he believed that it was his sacred responsibility to live at Warm Springs. The land was as revered to him as, for example, Jerusalem is to adherents of several religions. Recent events in the Middle East have made clear that one piece of land does not always equal another. The Indian Office dictated San Carlos, which Victorio despised. Victorio offered to negotiate. Authorities demanded unconditional surrender. It was primarily the American government that chose to obliterate any functional middle ground between. The Tres Castillos massacre reveals, then, a perfect storm of clashing ideologies and few compromises. So the United States ended up sacrificing thousands of soldiers and spending millions dollars to end the Victorio War, making it a profound example of arrogance, stupidity, and Indian policy at its most callous. It also makes the story of the Warm Springs Apaches all the more tragic. On the other hand, Victorio had the audacity to believe that he controlled his own fate. And in the end he did. He died a free man.

Victorio's Legacy

Why study Victorio? What can his life tell people living 126 years later? So many mysteries still surround Victorio's life, and he left no documents and made no speeches that might answer our questions. Thus, we find none of the closure that is so frequently called for today. That ambiguity alone adds intrigue and complexity to his story. We will undoubtedly never know exactly why he refused until the last minute to seek refuge with Juh in the Blue Mountains. We can not truly understand why he bolted the Mescalero reservation in 1979.

We might ask why Victorio never achieved the renown of a Geronimo or Chief Joseph. After all, the Victorio War of 1879–80 terrorized a significant portion of the Southwest. Travelers avoided the entire region whenever possible. Certainly, they refused to journey alone. Some businesses temporarily halted.

Ironically, Victorio's son, Charles Istee, feared for his life long after his father's death, further evidence of the impact of this year-long event. Moreover, Victorio's desperate search for a place to live, his flight, and the Tres Castillos massacre contain all the drama that Hollywood could ever hope for. Yet a film of it is yet to appear.

There are several possible explanations. First, he was aloof, perhaps even shy, and certainly wary around whites. Anglos at the time overlooked him in favor of the more gregarious Cochise, Geronimo, and to a degree Nana. Americans have always seemed to favor the outgoing personalities. Second, Billy and Kid and the Lincoln County War—which occurred at the same time and and in the same region—has enthralled writers ever since and largely overshadowed the Victorio War. Finally, Victorio died not in the United States but in Chihuahua at the hands of Mexicans. There are no tales of gallant cavalry charges or harried Texas Rangers overcoming almost insurmountable odds here. The Americans drove Victorio's people into Mexico, and Mexican soldiers massacred him and his followers. End of story.

But Victorio deserves a prominent place in the history of the American Southwest because his story is more than that. For one thing, his life reminds us that Indian policy was often cruel, racist, and indifferent toward the Native peoples. The concentration policy as it pertained to Apaches was certainly callous, but decisions today can be more enlightened. Significantly, at present, the Cañada Alamosa region is still rather sparsely populated. There was no reason why the Warm Springs people could not have lived there, and yet men like Crook, Hatch, and Steck who argued for just such an outcome were ignored. Always, voices that challenge the mainstream must grow louder. That there is no closure or tidy ending to Victorio's story forces students of history to discuss uncomfortable and ambiguous realities.

Finally, Victorio's life reveals clearly the tenacity and adaptability of the Apache people. Faced with a repressive federal government, farmers seeking land and water, miners exploring for silver and gold, and corporations eager to move in, Victorio negotiated, avoided whites whenever possible, gave in and attempted to live at San Carlos, tried to find a reservation at Fort Wingate or Fort Stanton, fled, and fought. He maintained trade relationships with whites and Mexicans alike, and he tried at the same time to perpetuate his own culture and style of living. This was not the face of an unyielding savage. Moreover, when we examine Victorio's story, we see men and women such as Loco and Dilth-cleyhen, who surrendered and made the best of San Carlos. Some Apaches became army scouts. Others lived part of the time on a reservation and then slipped away for part of the year. Officials generally called these Indians "renegades," but we have discovered that they contributed significantly to feeding, clothing, mounting, and arming reservation Indians. In addition, off-reservation Apaches brought news of family and friends. In short, when we examine Victorio's life, we see a people in flux. Desperately trying to carve out a new existence, the Apaches neither vanished nor totally lost their spirituality and culture. They adapated as rapidly and as best they could.

In the end, Victorio chose his own option. Rather than face dependency within the reservation system, he fled. Instead of returning to San Carlos, he and his followers decided that they wanted to control where they lived out their lives. When Warm Springs was ultimately denied them, Victorio must have finally concluded that, as predicted in the Creation stories, Killer of Enemies had returned with his white men. For now, the white man had won. But the Creation story also told the Apache people that life was cyclical, not linear. One day, Child of the Water would again rise up to slay the monsters.

Bibliographic Essay

NEARLY everything written about Victorio has its origin in a few government archives and oral histories, and one must comb out the information, which is scattered throughout. The most important of the government documents are those in Record Group 94, records of the Adjutant General's Office. Three microfilm reels in this series focus solely on the Victorio campaign and are subtitled "Papers relating to military operations against Chief Victorio's band." RG 94 also contains detailed documents pertaining to the Ninth and Tenth cavalry units of buffalo soldiers in New Mexico and Texas, the reports of the Vincent Colyer and General O. O. Howard missions to the Warm Springs Apaches, and documents relating to border crossings, including letters to Chihuahuan and Mexican authorities.

Record Group 75 contains the records of the Bureau of Indian Affairs, including the correspondence of its various superintendents, and Record Group 48 is the collection of letters received and sent by the secretary of the interior. The annual reports of individual Indian agents to the Bureau of Indian Affairs were printed separately and provide details concerning the Southern Apache, Ojo Caliente, San Carlos, and Mescalero reservations and their agents. Few of these reports include much information on Victorio himself until his departure from San Carlos, but one can certainly use them to reconstruct reservation conditions and to assess the attitudes and understand the abilities of the personnel involved. Agent John Clum's reports are especially informative. Generally, the Indian Office reports go back to 1849, and most federal repositories can often obtain a nearly complete run of these, especially those published after 1865.

Territorial archives of New Mexico are more difficult to obtain, but provide basic information on the Warm Springs

Apaches with some details on the Mexican captives taken over the years and accounts of the Mesilla militia, which was organized in 1850. Most are housed at the New Mexico State Records and Archives in Santa Fe and are also on microfilm. Five boxes in the A. Schroeder Collection, also at the Records and Archives, contain territorial papers, including a copy of the 1853 provisional compact that Victorio signed. The Lucien A. File Collection—in particular boxes 4, 11, and 26—is worth examining. The Center for Southwest Research at the University of New Mexico houses agent Michael Steck's papers, which are not well organized but are nicely detailed. He was one of the most important Indian agents of the Southern Apache Reservation and superintendent of Indian Affairs during the James Carleton years. In addition, the Pioneers Foundation Oral History Collection, also at the Center, carries some lively accounts from settlers regarding Apaches in general and Victorio in particular, and Eve Ball supplies a few surprisingly sympathetic tidbits in *Ma'am Jones of the Pecos* (Tucson: University of Arizona Press, 1972).

One can read accounts of the Victorio campaign in the *Santa Fe New Mexican, Mesilla Independent,* and *Silver City Enterprise.* The *Arizona Miner* and *Arizonian*, both published in Prescott, contain some of the best examples of vitriolic rhetoric towards Chiricahuas following the Civil War. At the same time, these newspapers often raged against Hatch and his efforts—the editors called these efforts feeble—to capture the Chihennes. Also, most of these newspapers include published accounts from the San Carlos reservation about the various Peace Policy missions to the Apaches, John Clum, Victorio's flight, the Woolsey and Camp Grant massacres, and agent Tiffany's legal battle. Some articles are reprinted in Jay J. Wagoner, *Arizona Territory, 1863–1912: A Political History* (Tucson: University of Arizona Press, 1970, 1980), which is probably the best political history of Arizona's territorial days. There is plenty of information about the so-called Tucson Ring, which operated during the frontier period, as well. Because the Victorio Campaign received such broad coverage throughout the country, the 1879–80 *New York Times* editions often carried articles.

Military officers, traders, and adventurers loved to tell stories of their encounters with the Apaches. Although their insights are usually well wrapped in nineteenth-century bravado, they are nevertheless worth reading. It is from some of these works that stories such as the flogging of Mangas Coloradas were born. Some of the best accounts are James O. Pattie, *Personal Narrative of James O. Pattie*, edited by Timothy Flint (Chicago: Donnelley, 1930); John C. Cremony, *Life among the Apaches* (1868; reprint, Tucson: Arizona Silhouettes, 1954), and Daniel Ellis Conner, *Joseph Reddeford Walker and the Arizona Adventure*, edited by Donald J. Berthrong and Odessa Davenport (Norman: University of Oklahoma Press, 1956). Unfortunately, these focus more on Mangas Coloradas and Cochise than on Victorio. Firsthand accounts of the Indian missions under Grant's Peace Policy and directly related to any study of Victorio are W. F. M. Arny, *Indian Agent in New Mexico: The Journal of Special Agent W. F. M. Arny, 1870*, edited by Lawrence R. Murphy (Reprint: Santa Fe: Stagecoach, 1967), Vincent Colyer, *Peace with the Apaches of New Mexico and Arizona: Report of Vincent Colyer, Member of the Board of Indian Commissioners, 1871*, (Reprint: Freeport, N.Y.:Books for Libraries, 1971), and Oliver O. Howard, *My Life Experiences among Our Hostile Indians* (Hartford, Conn.: Worthington, 1907). On the other hand, John P. Clum's much-touted "Victorio, Chief of the Warm Springs Apaches," *Arizona Historical Review* 2, no. 4 (January 1930): 74–90, is fictive at best. His son, Woodworth Clum, wrote *Apache Agent: The Story of John P. Clum* in 1936 (Reprint: Boston: Houghton, Mifflin, 1963), which is based on his father's accounts and is likewise biased. John Russell Bartlett, in charge of the border commission that surveyed the U.S.-Mexico boundary following the Mexican War, maintained significant relations with Mangas Coloradas and with his Chihenne Apaches, sometimes dubbed the Coppermine Apaches. Bartlett's 1854 *Personal Narrative of Explorations and Incidents in Texas, New Mexico, California, Sonora, and Chihuahua . . .* (Reprint: Chicago: Rio Grande, 1965) is significant.

Military memoirs abound and are remarkably similar. Some standouts, however, are George Crook's *General George Crook:*

His Autobiography, edited by Martin F. Schmitt (Norman: University of Oklahoma, 1960), James B. Gillett, *Six Years with the Texas Rangers, 1875–1881*, edited by Milo Milton Quaife (Chicago: R. R. Donnelley, 1943)—especially worth reading because the author participated in the Victorio campaign—and Thomas Cruse, *Apache Days and After*, edited by Eugene Cunningham (Caldwell, Idaho: Caxton, 1941). Peter Cozzens has compiled myriad military reports and newspaper and journal accounts in *Eyewitnesses to the Indian Wars, 1865–1890: The Struggle for Apacheria*, Vol. 1 (Mechanicsburg: Penn.: Stackpole Books, 2002). It includes Charles B. Gatewood, "Campaigning against Victorio in 1879," which also appeared in a periodical *The Great Divide* (April 1894): 102–104, and Indian inspector E. C. Kemble's "Victorio and His Young Men," originally published in the *New York Times*, November 28, 1880. *Eyewitnesses* is a weighty volume packed with important primary-source material. John G. Bourke, *On the Border with Crook* (New York: Scribners, 1891) is worth mentioning, and for the Spanish version of the Victorio War, D. Joaquin Terrazas, *Memorias, Imprenta de "El Agricultor Mexicana"* (Juarez: Escobar, 1905) is of value, although it has not been translated.

Of course, some of the most important sources are oral histories. Most involve interviews recorded years later, and although vital to a study of Victorio, are surprisingly few in number and often as deficient in specific information relating to Victorio as are the documentary sources. The best by far is Eve Ball, *In the Days of Victorio: Recollections of a Warm Springs Apache* (Tucson: University of Arizona Press, 1970). This is James Kaywaykla's story as told to Eve Ball. Kaywaykla was Nana's young grandson and Kaytennae's stepson, and his family rode with Victorio until just before Tres Castillos, when they managed to escape under cover of darkness. At the time of the massacre, Kaywaykla was only ten years old, and the reader can tell that either he did not know Victorio well or stood in tremendous awe of him. For one thing, the language grows formal and rather stilted when he recreates conversations with Victorio. Furthermore, the major players are his grandmother, mother, sister, and to some degree Nana, rather than Victorio. Still, it was Victorio who allegedly gave Kaywaykla his name, and it is the best oral source covering the major events of 1879–80 and beyond, even if Victorio himself is frequently absent. One learns a great deal about Apache customs, taboos, and relations.

Ball's book *Indeh, an Apache Odyssey*, edited by Nora Henn and Lynda Sanchez, is based on interviews with Ace Daklugie, son of Nednhi chief Juh, and with Eugene Chihuahua, who rode with the Apache scouts. Again, Victorio is a shadow, but Chiricahua culture—including the Chihennes, who some claim were not Chiricahuas, although the two are frequently lumped together—comes across clearly. In addition, there is "The Apache Scouts; A Chiricahua Appraisal," *Arizona and the West* 7, no. 4 (Winter 1965): 315–28. *Apache Voices: Their Stories of Survival as Told to Eve Ball* (University of New Mexico Press, 2000) was drawn straight from the Ball manuscripts housed at Brigham Young University. Much of this was previously published, but editor Sherry Robinson successfully pulled the material together and reorganized it. The interviews are worth reading. *Apache Mothers and Daughters* by Ruth M. Boyer and Narcissus D. Gayton (Norman: University of Oklahoma, 1992) focuses primarily on the women in Victorio's life, including his daughter Dilth-cleyhen and granddaughter Beshad-e. It is history passed down from Victorio's generation to his great-great-granddaughter. Some have expressed doubts regarding its accuracy, but the book offers a wealth of detail on domestic life found nowhere else. Oral histories of marginal importance are Jason Betzinez, *I Fought with Geronimo* (Harrisburg, Penn.: Stackpole, 1959) and *Geronimo: His Own Story*, as told to S. M. Barrett (New York: Penguin, 1906).

Additional published primary works include John G. Bourke, *The Medicine Men of the Apache* (Washington: Smithsonian, 1892), which provides observations of Apache culture along with sketches of such items as the Chihenne medicine hats; J. Ross Browne, *Adventures in the Apache Country* (New York: Promontory, 1871, 1974), and Britton Davis's 1929 *The Truth about Geronimo*, edited by Milo Milton Quaife (reprint: Chicago: Donnelley, 1951). Also see Jack Crawford, "The Pursuit of Victorio," *Socorro County Historical Society: Publications in History* 1 (February 1965): 1–8; Edwin R. Sweeney, ed., *Making Peace with Cochise: The 1872 Journal of Captain Joseph Alton Sladen* (Norman: University of Oklahoma Press, 1997); John S. Watts, *Indian Depredations in New Mexico* (1958; reprint: Tucson: Territorial Press, 1964), and Martin L. Crimmins, ed., "Colonel Buell's Expedition into Mexico in 1880," *New Mexico Historical Review* 10 (1935): 133–42. Primary sources dealing with Mexico are Donald E. Worcester, ed.,"Advice on Governing New Mexico, 1794," *New Mexico Historical Review* 24 (July 1949): 236–54; José Cortes, *Views from the Apache Frontier: Report on the Northern Provinces of New Spain*, edited by Elizabeth A. H. John (Norman: University of Oklahoma Press, 1989), and José Carlos Chavez, "El Indio 'Victorio,'" *Boletin de la Sociedad Chihuahuense de Estudios Historicos* 5 (April 1944): 509–13.

The best secondary account of Victorio's life is Dan L. Thrapp's 1974 biography *Victorio and the Mimbres Apaches* (reprint, Norman: University of Oklahoma Press, 1980). It relies heavily on the military accounts, and therefore, its primary focus is on the events surrounding Victorio's life rather than Victorio's life per se. An exceptionally thorough account of military operations and the role of the Indian Office, it is an outstanding source. Two of Thrapps's earlier books also deserve attention. These are *The Conquest of Apacheria* (Norman: University of Oklahoma Press,1967), which is generally acknowledged as a superior account of the Apache wars, and *Al Sieber, Chief of Apache Scouts* (1964). A chapter titled "Apache Chief Victorio: Seeker of Peace and Master Strategist," by Glenda Riley appears in a collection of biographical essays titled *Chiefs and Generals: Nine Men Who Shaped the American West*, edited by Richard W. Etulain and Glenda Riley (Golden, Colo.: Fulcrum, 2004). The same collection contains "Geronimo: the 'Last Renegade,'" by L. G. Moses and chapters on General O. O. Howard and George Crook. Edwin R. Sweeney, *Mangas Coloradas, Chief of the Chiricahua Apaches* (Norman: University of Oklahoma Press, 1998) provides painstaking research into the life of Victorio's mentor and predecessor and discusses a vast array of secondary chiefs. It is a highly readable volume. Angie Debo, *Geronimo: The Man, His Time, His Place* (Norman: University of Oklahoma Press, 1976) goes well beyond the life of Geronimo and is one of the first examples of an ethnohistorical biography.

Books on Apaches and the Apache wars include James L. Haley, *Apaches, A History and Culture Portrait* (Garden City, N.Y.: Doubleday, 1981); Ralph Hedrick Ogle, *Federal Control of the Western Apaches, 1848–1886* (Albuquerque: University of New Mexico Press, 1940); Richard J. Perry, *Apache Reservation: Indigenous Peoples and the American State* (Austin: University of Texas Press, 1993); David Roberts, *Once They Moved Like the Wind: Cochise, Geronimo, and the Apache Wars* (New York: Simon & Schuster, 1993, 1994), a somewhat popular account; C. L. Sonnichsen, *The Mescalero Apaches* (Norman: University of Oklahoma Press, 1958); William B. Griffen, *Apaches at War and Peace: The Janos Presidio, 1750–1858* (Norman: University of Oklahoma Press, 1988, 1998); Joseph A. Stout, Jr., *Apache Lightning: The Last Great Battles of the Ojo Calientes* (New York: Oxford University Press, 1974); John Upton Terrell, *Apache Chronicle: The Story of the People* (New York: Thomas Y. Crowell, 1974), and Donald E. Worcester, *The Apaches: Eagles of the Southwest* (University of Oklahoma Press, 1979). Those dealing specifically with Apache women are H. Henrietta Stockel, *Chiricahua Apache Women and Children: Safekeepers of the Heritage* (College Station: Texas A & M University Press, 2000), *Women of the Apache Nation: Voices of Truth* (Reno: University of Nevada Press, 1991); "Lozen: Apache Warrior Queen," *Real West Yearbook* (Fall 1983): 36–39; and, again, Eve Ball, *Apache Voices: Their Stories of Survival as Told to Eve Ball*, edited by Sherry Robinson.

Works that deal generally with Apaches within the larger context of the Southwest or western history include W. Eugene Hollon, *The Southwest, Old and New* (Lincoln: University of Nebraska Press, 1968); Erna Fergusson, *New Mexico: A Pageant of Three Peoples* (New York: Alfred A. Knopf, 1951); Trudy Griffin-Pierce, *Native Peoples of the Southwest* (Albuquerque: University of New Mexico Press, 2000); Lee Myers, "Fort Webster on the Mimbres River," *New Mexico Historical Review* 41, no. 1 (January

1966): 47–57; Ralph A. Smith, "Apache Plunder Trails Southward, 1831–1840," *New Mexico Historical Review* 37, no. 1 (January 1962): 20–42; and Donald E. Worcester, "The Beginnings of the Apache Menace, *New Mexico Historical Review* 16, no. 1 (January 1941): 1–14. Several articles from popular or nonscholarly journals are still worthy of notice. These are A. N. Blazer, "Beginnings of an Indian War," *New Mexico Magazine* 16 (February 1938); Sherry Robinson, "Lozen: Apache Woman Warrior," *Wild West*, 10, no. 1 (June 1997): 52–56, 81–82; H. Henrietta Stockel, "A Good Day to Die": Historical Burial Customs of Western American Natives," *Old West* 35, no. 4 ((Summer 1999): 36–41 and "Lozen: Apache Warrior Queen," as previously noted, Walter Prescott Webb, "Last War Trail of Victorio," *Old West* 1, no. 1 (Fall 1964): 30–31, 50–51; and Donald Worcester, "Apache Scouts and Pack Trains," *True West* 43, no. 2 (February 1996): 14–21.

In an attempt to place Victorio's life within the context of post–Civil War Indian reform, it was necessary to examine sources that focused on the policies of Abraham Lincoln's administration and on Grant's Peace Policy. These explain the policy of concentration in great depth, as well as the jurisdictional battle between the Departments of the Interior and War over the Indian Office and Indian affairs in general. Only by understanding some of the individuals involved and events taking place in Washington, D.C., can one place Victorio's situation within the larger context. Perhaps the best of these is Francis Paul Prucha, *American Indian Policy in Crisis: Christian Reformers and the Indian, 1865–1900* (Norman: University of Oklahoma Press, 1976). Prucha was one of the first to investigate this topic, and remains one of its most exhaustive researchers. Richard J. Perry, *Apache Reservation: Indigenous Peoples and the American State*, which was previously cited, directly applies these reforms and tensions to the San Carlos Apaches. Also full of valuable information are Richard N. Ellis, *General Pope and the U.S. Indian Policy* (Albuquerque: University of New Mexico Press, 1970), William T. Hagan, *The Indian Rights Association: The Herbert Welsh Years, 1882–1904* (Tucson: University of Arizona Press, 1985), Frederick E. Hoxie, *The Campaign to Assimilate the Indi-*

ans, 1880–1920 (Lincoln: University of Nebraska Press, 1984, 2001), and Charles Lewis Slattery, *Felix Reville Brunot, 1820–1898* (New York: Longmans, Green, 1901). David A. Nichols, *Lincoln and the Indians: Civil War Policy and Politics* (Urbana: University of Illinois Press, 1978, 2000) is perhaps the best treatment of the Lincoln years.

No bibliography could be complete without an assessment of sources dealing with the Spanish and Mexican periods in Apache history. Although Victorio was born following Mexican independence and does not appear in historical documents until 1853, well after the American take-over, it is impossible to understand the Apache situation without a thorough look at what came before. It was during the Spanish period that officials alternately warred, wrote treaties, and used food and weapons to purchase peace. Prior to 1821, the Spanish constructed their presidios, attempted to protect settlers and converted Indians, and developed a deep-seated hatred towards the nomadic Apaches. It was during the Mexican period that scalp bounties came fully into effect. Among the most useful works dealing with the Spanish and Mexican eras are William B. Griffen, *Utmost Good Faith: Patterns of Apache-Mexican Hostilities in Northern Chihuahua Border Warfare, 1821–1848* (Albuquerque: University of New Mexico Press, 1988) and *Apaches at War and Peace: The Janos Presidio, 1750–1858*; Ana Maria Alonso, *Thread of Blood: Colonialism, Revolution, and Gender on Mexico's Northern Frontier* (Tucson: University of Arizona Press, 1995); and Florence C. Lister and Robert H. Lister, *Chihuahua: Storehouse of Storms* (Albuquerque: University of New Mexico Press, 1966). One can find an outstanding overview of these periods—and before—in Colin G. Calloway, *One Vast Winter Count: The Native American West before Lewis and Clark* (Lincoln: University of Nebraska Press, 2003). Gary Clayton Anderson, *The Indian Southwest, 1580–1830: Ethnogenesis and Reinvention* (Norman: University of Oklahoma Press, 1999) offers an excellent look at the beginnings of the Apache raid-and-trade pattern from the El Paso region and into Texas and the Great Plains. James F. Brooks, *Captives and Cousins: Slavery, Kinship, and Community in the Southwest Bor-*

derlands (Chapel Hill: University of North Carolina Press, 2002) also provides an in-depth look at this trade, particularly the trade in human beings. An older, but extremely insightful book on slavery in the Southwest is Lynn R. Bailey, *Indian Slave Trade in the Southwest: A Study of Slave-Taking and the Traffic in Indian Captives* (Los Angeles: Westernlore, 1966). All of these books blur what would later become the U.S. and Mexican border. Similarly, Ralph Adam Smith, *Borderlander: The Life of James Kirker, 1793–1852* (Norman: University of Oklahoma Press, 1999) and "The Scalp Hunt in Chihuahua—1849," *New Mexico Historical Review* 60, no. 2 (1965): 117–40 analyze the politics, economics, and social implications of scalp-bounty hunting, which gripped Chihuahua, Sonora, New Mexico, and at times even Durango.

Other more general accounts include Elizabeth A. H. John, *Storms Brewed in Other Men's Worlds: The Confrontation of Indians, Spanish, and French in the Southwest, 1540–1795* (College Station: Texas A & M Press, 1975), Max L. Moorhead, *The Apache Frontier: Jacobo Ugarte and the Spanish-Indian Relations in Northern New Spain, 1769–1791* (Norman: University of Oklahoma Press, 1968) and *The Presidio: Bastion of the Spanish Borderlands* (Norman: University of Oklahoma Press, 1975), H. Henrietta Stockel, *On the Bloody Road to Jesus: Christianity and the Chiricahua Apaches* (Albuquerque: University of New Mexico Press, 2004), Nona Barrick and Mary Taylor, *The Mesilla Guard, 1851–61* (El Paso: Texas Western, 1976), Odie B. Faulk, "The Presidio: Fortress or Farce," in Oakah L. Jones, Jr., ed., *The Spanish Borderlands: A First Reader* (Los Angeles: Lorrin L. Morrison, 1974): 70–77; John Q. Ressler, "Indian and Spanish Water—Control on New Spain's Northwest Frontier," also in Jones, *The Spanish Borderlands*, 233–41, and Joseph F. Park, "Spanish Indian Policy in Northern Mexico, 1765–1810," *Arizona and the West* 4, no. 4 (Winter 1962): 325–44.

In addition, some studies of post-1848 Mexico and the Apaches are Clarence C. Clendenen, *Blood on the Border: The United States Army and the Mexican Irregulars* (New York: Macmillan, 1969), Shelley B. Hatfield, *Chasing Shadows: Indians along the United States–Mexican Border, 1876–1911* (Albuquerque: University of New Mexico Press, 1998), and Lister and Lister, *Chihuahua: Storehouse of Storms*, previously mentioned. Some general, but still useful, references are John L. Kessell, *Spain in the Southwest: A Narrative History of Colonial New Mexico, Arizona, and California* (Norman: University of Oklahoma Press, 2002); Ralph E. Twitchell, *Old Santa Fe: The Story of New Mexico's Ancient Capital* (Santa Fe: New Mexican, 1925); and David J. Weber, *The Spanish Frontier in North America* (New Haven: Yale University Press, 1992). General works, which include details on New Mexico, are W. Eugene Hollon, *The Southwest, Old and New*, previously noted; William H. Leckie, *The Buffalo Soldiers: A Narrative of Negro Cavalry in the West* (Norman: University of Oklahoma Press, 1967, 2004); and Robert M. Utley, *Frontiersmen in Blue: The United States Army and the Indian, 1848–1865* (New York, Macmillan, 1967) and *The Indian Frontier of the American West, 1846–1890* (Albuquerque: University of New Mexico Press, 1984, 2004). I obtained some picturesque descriptions of Apachería from Erna Fergusson, *New Mexico: A Pageant of Three Peoples,* previously cited, and from John A. Murray, *The Gila Wilderness Area: A Hiking Guide* (Albuquerque: University of New Mexico Press, 1988), which also included some of the best maps of little-known wilderness trails.

It is impossible to imagine piecing together pre-Apache days and stories of the first Apaches in the Southwest without numerous anthropological accounts. Richard Perry, *Apache Reservation*, previously cited, was perhaps the most useful of these, as well as his *Western Apache Heritage: People of the Mountain Corridor* (Austin: University of Texas Press, 1991). At the same time, Perry's "The Apachean Transition from the Subarctic to the Southwest," *Plains Anthropologist* 25 (1980): 279–96, was one of the best sources regarding Canadian origins of the Apaches. The works of Keith H. Basso and Morris E. Opler proved invaluable. Basso's *Western Apache Raiding and Warfare: From the Notes of Grenville Goodwin* (Tucson: University of Arizona Press, 1971) and *Western Apache Witchcraft* (1969) provided tremendous insights into Apache culture, attitudes, and material culture. *Apachean*

Culture, History, and Ethnology, co-edited with Morris E. Opler, was a wonderful source of stories, as was Opler's *Myths and Tales of the Chiricahua Apache Indians* (Menasha, Wisc.: George Banta, 1942). There are many versions of these stories, especially the Creation story, but this particular work captures perhaps the best of these. Also extremely valuable were Opler's *An Apache Life-Way: the Economic, Social, and Religious Institutions of the Chiricahua Indians* (New York: Cooper Square, 1965), *Apache Odyssey: A Journey between Two Worlds* (New York: Holt, Rinehart, & Winston, 1969), and his edited work *Grenville Goodwin among the Western Apache: Letters from the Field* (Tucson: University of Arizona Press, 1973). Alan Ferg, ed., *Western Apache Material Culture: The Goodwin and Guenther Collections* (Tucson: University of Arizona Press, 1987, 1996) offers stunning photographs of Apache material culture along with an in-depth comparison between the cultures of the Western, Chiricahua, and Plains Apaches.

Anthropologist Grenville Goodwin is himself a fascinating study. In a sense, he "went native" during his exhaustive research on the Apaches in the 1930s and died an early death. He still managed to write a painstakingly researched work titled *The Social Organization of the Western Apache* (Tucson: University of Arizona Press, 1946; 1969), which documents his years with the Apaches. As one can see in the titles of other books, Goodwin also left myriad field notes, which have since served as the basis of additional studies. Goodwin's son, Neil, used his father's notes to document the search for so-called wild Apaches in the Sierra Madres in the 1930s and to embark upon his own journey. The book is *Apache Diaries: A Father-Son Journey* (Lincoln: University of Nebraska Press, 2000).

Additionally, the following works are notable. In fact, I could not have reconstructed the Canada-to-New Mexico migration of the proto-Apaches without them. They include Alan D. Macmillan, *Native Peoples and Cultures of Canada: An Anthropological Overview*, (Vancouver: Douglas & McIntyre, 1995, 1999), Patrick Moore, "Na-Dene," in *Aboriginal Peoples of Canada, A Short Introduction*, edited by Paul Robert Magocs (Toronto: University of Toronto Press, 1999: 214–236); and Edward H. Spicer, *Cycles of Conquest: The Impact of Spain, Mexico, and the United States on the Indians of the Southwest, 1533–1960* (Tucson: University of Arizona Press, 1962). Morris E. Opler and Harry Hoijer, "The Raid and Warpath Language of the Chiricahua Apache," *American Anthropologist* 42 (1940): 617–34, was vital in understanding the dihoke or novice training of the young Chiricahua male. Also see David French, "Comparative Notes on Chiricahua Apache Mythology," *Memoirs of the American Folklore Society* 37 (1942): 103–111; Morris E. Opler, "An Interpretation of Ambivalence of Two American Indian Tribes," *Journal of Social Psychology* 7 (1936): 82–116; and "An Outline of Chiricahua Apache Social Organization," in *Social Anthropology of North American Tribes: Essays in Social Organization, Law, and Religion,* edited by Fred Eggan (Chicago: University of Chicago Press, 1937), all of which offered additional insights.

For those who wish to do additional research, I have placed an endnoted copy of this manuscript in the Center for Southwest Research, University of New Mexico, in Albuquerque. A second manuscript, along with those microfilmed government archives that I was able to purchase, and any of my original notes will be housed at the Halle Library, Special Collections, Eastern Michigan University in Ypsilanti, Michigan, and labeled the Victorio (Apache) Collection. I sincerely hope that research into Victorio's life, and the lives of many other Apache leaders, will continue.

Index

References to illustrations are in italics.

African Americans. *See* Buffalo Soldiers
Apache Canyon and Pass, Ariz., 89, 94, 102; battle in, 97–99
Apaches, 53–56, 59, 71, 73, 92, 111, 129, 162, 214–15, 221; Aravaipa, 121; Coyotero, 188, 191; Gilas (*Gileños*), 20, 60, 104; Hollywood depictions of, 55, 216; Jicarillas, 10; language of, 25; Plains Apaches, 21, 23; scouts, 141, 143, 150, 166, *174*, 180–81, 187, 195–97, 220; Western Apaches, 10, 140–41, 214; White Mountain, 122, 141, 151, 154, 181, 188, 213. *See also* Bedonkohe Apaches; Chihenne Apaches; Chiricahua (Chokonen) Apaches; Copper Mine Apaches; Mescalero Apaches; Nednhi Apaches
Arizona, state of: Confederate control of, 97, 106; legislature, 106–108; rangers, 166, 173
Arizonian (Prescott), 32
Arny, William, 119–20
Athapascans, migration of, 9–10
Ayres, John, 113, 131–32

Baca, Luis M., 111–12
Ball, Eve, 28–29, 161, 162, 165, 170, 201
Bartlett, John Russell, 73–76. *See also* International Border Commission

Bascom, George N. (Lieutenant), 92–93. *See also* Cochise
Baylor, George W., 176, 178, 202
Baylor, John R. (Colonel), 106
Becknell, William, 25–26
Bedonkohe Apaches, 13, 14, 71, 82, 148
Bent's Fort, Colo., 49, 63
Bernstein, Morris, 159
Beshad-e (Victorio's granddaughter), 69, 108, 110, 115, 125–26, 148, 150, 205, 213
Betzinez, Jason, 101, 137
Bi-duye. *See* Victorio
Billy the Kid (also called William Antrim), 159, 219
Black Mountains, N. Mex., 13, 27, 63, 125, 134, 155, 165, 194; campaigns in, 171, 173–74, 180–82, 187; Nana returns to, 211
Blanco (Chihenne), 168–69, 173, 199, 204, 211
Blazer, Dr. Joseph H., 159, 160–61, 164
Blocksom, A. P. (Lieutenant), 173
Blue Mountains. *See* Sierra Madre Mountains
Bonneville, Benjamin L. E., 83
Bosque Redondo, N. Mex., 103–106, 108
Bourbon Reforms, 22–24
Buell, George (Colonel), 196–98, 202